THE ROMANTIC POETS

GROVER CRONIN, JR.
PROFESSOR OF ENGLISH
FORDHAM UNIVERSITY

Revised and edited by

FRANCES K. BARASCH
ASSISTANT PROFESSOR OF ENGLISH
STATE UNIVERSITY OF NEW YORK

MONARCH PRESS

Published by
MONARCH PRESS
a division of Simon & Schuster, Inc.
1 West 39th Street
New York, N.Y. 10018

Standard Book Number: 671-00518-9

Library of Congress Catalog Card Number: 66-29029

Printed in the United States of America

CONTENTS

one ✗ THE ROMANTIC PERIOD   **7**

The historical period and literary and philosophical characteristics of Romanticism

two ✗ WILLIAM BLAKE   **13**

His beliefs and their relation to his poetry; his life and works

Analysis of his poetry:

POETICAL SKETCHES *19*

THE BOOK OF THEL *22*

SONGS OF INNOCENCE AND SONGS OF EXPERIENCE *24*

THE FRENCH REVOLUTION *34*

THE EARLY PROPHETIC BOOKS *36*

THE LATER PROPHETIC BOOKS *44*

An historical survey of criticism on Blake's poetry *44*

three ROBERT BURNS   **47**

The Romantic characteristics of his poetry; the Scottish literary tradition; his life and works

Analysis of his poetry:

POEMS, CHIEFLY IN THE SCOTTISH DIALECT *52*

An historical survey of criticism on Burns's poetry *65*

four ✗ WILLIAM WORDSWORTH   **70**

His influence on Romanticism and philosophy; his life and works

CONTENTS

Analysis of his poetry:

LYRICAL BALLADS WITH A FEW OTHER POEMS   *75*

THE PRELUDE, OR, GROWTH OF A POET'S MIND   *89*

POEMS, 1807 *94*

An historical survey of criticism on Wordsworths poetry *102*

five   SIR WALTER SCOTT   **105**

His contribution to Romanticism; his life and works

Analysis of his poetry:

THE LAY OF THE LAST MINSTREL *108*

MARMION *110*

THE LADY OF THE LAKE *111*

LAST POEMS *113*

An historical survey of criticism on Scott's poetry *113*

six   SAMUEL TAYLOR COLERIDGE   **115**

His influence on Romanticism; his life and works

Analysis of his poetry:

THE RIME OF THE ANCIENT MARINER *119*

CHRISTABEL *121*

KUBLA KHAN; OR, A VISION IN A DREAM *127*

DEJECTION: AN ODE *132*

BIOGRAPHIA LITERARIA *134*

An historical survey of criticism on Coleridge's poetry *135*

seven   GEORGE NOEL GORDON, LORD BYRON   **141**

Byron as Romantic hero; his life and works

Analysis of his poetry:

ENGLISH BARDS AND SCOTCH REVIEWERS *143*

CHILDE HAROLD'S PILGRIMAGE *144*

CONTENTS

TURKISH TALES *145*

MANFRED *146*

DON JUAN *147*

An historical survey of criticism on Byron's poetry *150*

eight PERCY BYSSHE SHELLEY **157**

His beliefs and their relation to his poetry;
his life and works

Analysis of his poetry:

ALASTOR *160*

THE REVOLT OF ISLAM *161*

PROMETHEUS UNBOUND *161*

ODE TO THE WEST WIND *164*

THE CLOUD *169*

TO A SKYLARK *171*

ADONAIS *173*

An historical survey of criticism on Shelley's poetry *175*

nine JOHN KEATS **182**

His life and works

Analysis of his poetry:

ON FIRST LOOKING INTO CHAPMAN'S HOMER *184*

ENDYMION *184*

THE EVE OF ST. AGNES *186*

ODE TO PSYCHE *187*

ODE TO A NIGHTINGALE *188*

ODE TO MELANCHOLY *190*

ODE ON A GRECIAN URN *191*

An historical survey of criticism on Keats's poetry *193*

ten THE MINOR ROMANTIC POETS **199**

A summary discussion of their lives and works

GEORGE CRABBE *199*

CONTENTS

ROBERT SOUTHEY *199*

WALTER SAVAGE LANDOR *201*

THOMAS MOORE *203*

LEIGH HUNT *204*

JOHN CLARE *205*

THOMAS HOOD *205*

THOMAS LOVELL BEDDOES *206*

eleven   TEST QUESTIONS   **208**
Essay questions and detailed answers

twelve   FURTHER READING   **221**
Suggested topics for research papers *221*
Bibliography *224*

INDEX   **237**

INTRODUCTION

The so-called *Romantic Period* in the history of English literature extends from the late eighteenth century to the third decade of the nineteenth century. The dates are necessarily imprecise. History cannot be as tidy as some historians would like it to be.

Some landmarks useful in the description of the period can be listed:

1. The outbreak of the American Revolution in 1775 with its emphasis on individual rights and the principle of self-determination.

2. The publication in 1783 of William Blake's *Poetical Sketches*.

3. The French Revolution, which began in 1789.

4. *Lyrical Ballads,* a collection of poems by William Wordsworth and Samuel Taylor Coleridge, published anonymously in 1798. The Preface to this famous volume, written by Wordsworth and published with the second edition in 1800, is one of the most important accounts of what the new, "Romantic," poets were trying to do.

5. Sir Walter Scott's collection of old ballads entitled *Minstrelsy of the Scottish Border,* 1802.

6. The passage of the Reform Bill of 1832 in England, which gave voting powers to members of the lower middle-class who had not before this enjoyed these rights.

7. The accession of Queen Victoria in 1837.

The label "Romantic" that has been attached to this period (roughly 1783–1837) is not altogether satisfactory. It directs attention to a notable interest in the Middle Ages (Scott's collection of ballads and novels like *Ivanhoe,* Keats's *The Eve of St. Agnes*), but it fails to suggest that the poets of this generation were very much involved in the political and social issues of their day.

It is not easy to give a definition of Romanticism. It is, perhaps, best understood as a kind of revolutionary philosophy, a violent reaction against convictions and habits of mind that had prevailed in England and Europe from the middle years of the seventeenth century.

NEOCLASSICISM: In 1642 growing dissatisfaction with the policies of the Stuart monarch, Charles I, erupted into civil war and led to the establishment of what was called the Commonwealth, under the leadership of Oliver Cromwell. On Cromwell's death in 1658, England found itself without effective leadership and in 1660 invited the exiled son of Charles I to return to the throne of England as Charles II. The Restoration was felt to mark the beginning of a new era. Deliberately setting out to rival the accomplishments in arts and letters that graced the reign of Augustus Caesar when the Roman Empire was established, men of the Restoration spoke of being part of a new Augustan Age.

Although this new classical movement (neoclassicism) was ambitious, progressive, and forward-looking, it was also characterized by a sense of tradition. Poets, for example, felt obliged to imitate great poems of the past. It was believed that in the course of centuries men had come to agree on certain fixed ways of doing things. Thus there were rules for pastoral poetry, for satire, for the epic. The first outstanding characteristic of neoclassical poetry, therefore, is its imitativeness.

It should be stressed that this imitativeness does not derive from intellectual timidity. Rather it is the result of a belief that we cannot effectively communicate with one another and thus make progress in the understanding of the world about us unless we agree on certain conventions. This concern for effective communication can be described as the neoclassical emphasis on clarity. Clarity can be listed as a second characteristic of neoclassicism.

Related to the ideal of clarity is that of objectivity. It is painfully clear to all of us that we are not only rational animals but are also, at the same time, victims of our individual quirks and oddities. An admirable part of the neoclassical effort was the attempt to look beyond surface eccentricities into a central human nature. Put in other words, an important characteristic of neoclassicism is objectivity.

Existing side by side with a deep reverence for the artistic accomplishments of classical antiquity was a general consciousness, already mentioned, that a new day had dawned. The discovery of the New World had widened the horizons of European man, and the astonishing growth of scientific knowledge in the seventeenth century gave man a fresh confidence in his powers, particularly in his reason. Rationalism, accordingly, must be included in any list of characteristics of the neoclassical period. Indeed, sometimes the period from 1660 to the end of the eighteenth century is called The Age of Reason. Sometimes, too, it is called The Enlightenment.

This sketch of English neoclassicism is, of necessity, brief and incomplete. The period, like virtually all periods of human history, is bewildering in its complexity. Its great writers, like all great writers, defy easy classification.

ROMANTICISM: Enough has been said, however, to make possible a few introductory notes on the nature of English Romanticism. It is perhaps best understood not so much as a movement back toward the spirit of the Middle Ages as manifested in Arthurian romances, in tales of high adventure, of encounters with giants and dragons, of wild and passionate love, but rather as a protest against almost all that was most typical of neoclassicism.

SUBJECTIVISM: It has been noticed that the neoclassical writer, typically, believed in an intelligible world. He believed that he possessed faculties, notably a mind, that enabled him to make some kind of sense out of the universe. He also believed that what was dark and obscure was probably not worth man's attention. And he believed that all men (at least all educated men) shared his convictions and attitudes. The Romantic writer, on the other hand, typically was interested in the uniqueness of his response to the world, to historic events, to external nature. The Romantic writer typically looked inward and examined the peculiarity, the particularity, of his own private emotional history.

This does not mean, of course, that the Romantic could not be at times, indeed often, objective. What it does mean is that the classical or neoclassical view of reality is fundamentally matter-of-fact, down-to-earth, and objective, and that the specifically Romantic point of view is subjective.

EMOTIONALISM: Subjectivism, of course, implies an interest in one's emotions. Romantic poetry, accordingly, tends to be more self-consciously emotional than neoclassical poetry. The distinction cannot be pressed too far, but neoclassicism tends to be a religion of the head, Romanticism a religion of the heart. Neoclassical writers strove for common sense, Romantic for heroic madness. The difference can best be sensed by reading a typical neoclassical poem, for example, Pope's *An Essay on Man,* and then a typical Romantic poem, say Keats's *The Eve of St. Agnes.*

It must be emphasized that neoclassical poets were not cold. They were intensely interested in emotions and they knew that poetry had to have intensity and fire. At all times, however, they acknowledged their responsibilities as thinking human beings. The Romantics remind us that there are times when we had better trust our feelings rather than our sober judgments.

LAWLESSNESS: It must be borne in mind that the Romantic age was one of high aspiration and of noble endeavor. In 1660, as has been remarked, England felt that it was entering a new golden age. There had been the golden age of the first Queen Elizabeth. It was followed by the disillusioning reign of King

James. When Charles I came to the throne, civil war broke out and through the succeeding tumultuous years the arts of peace were, on the whole, neglected. In 1660 there was a new burst of creative energy. English poetry is permanently richer for the superb achievements of Dryden and Pope. There is some evidence, however, that the creative impulse that had made itself unmistakably felt at the Restoration was beginning to show signs of exhaustion by the time of Pope's death in 1744. The true Augustan Age ends with Pope. Men still went on believing in the "classical" values that shaped the Augustan Age, and some, such as Samuel Johnson, working within this set of values made an abiding place for themselves in the history of English literature. But it was time for a change. In 1775 Americans asserted their independence. Not too many years later the French were to storm the Bastille and to challenge the elaborate system of privileges and prerogatives that we now call the *ancien régime*, the old established order of things.

One should distinguish between revolution and lawlessness, but revolution cannot take place until men are willing to re-examine the validity and the structure of their laws. Romanticism is, in a sense, one manifestation of this willingness.

A neoclassical faith in a body of "rules" that can guide all writers of all times and of all places is unquestionably the invention of systemizing historians. But it must be conceded that neoclassical writers were, generally speaking, more docile than their aggressive successors, the Romantic writers. In the eighteenth century there was a proper way to enter a drawing room, a proper way to drop a curtsy, a proper way to manage a fan; as the new revolutionary spirit more and more asserted itself, men came to feel that these niceties were of little importance. This skeptical and critical attitude, naturally, soon left the drawing room and exhibited itself in every area of human activity. Poets, for example, stopped being willing to be told how they should write an ode or an elegy.

There is no question that Romanticism can be seen as a protest against a neoclassical docility toward "rules." It should be noticed, however, that the best Romantic poetry shows a concern for form, a sense of voluntary self-discipline that is every bit as scrupulous as that found in earlier poetry. There is a Romantic "lawlessness," perhaps best seen in the career of Byron, but, even when one studies Byron's art, the lawlessness is a highly qualified lawlessness. Some of the Romantic poets were what we today would call "radical." One thinks of Blake and his defiance of traditional religions, of Shelley and his proud atheism. The "lawlessness" of the Romantics, however, is a quality of mind rather than a consciously espoused principle. It shows itself in different ways in different poets. It is not a constant through the entire career of any major Romantic poet with the possible exception of Byron. Insofar as it points up, however, a contrast between Romantic and neoclassical basic attitudes toward life, it is an ingredient of Romanticism that retains some value.

THE CHIEF ENGLISH ROMANTIC POETS: It is generally agreed that the following are the major English Romantic poets: William Blake (1757–1827); Robert Burns (1759–1796); William Wordsworth (1770–1850); Sir Walter Scott (1771–1832); Samuel Taylor Coleridge (1772–1834); George Noel Gordon, Lord Byron (1788–1824); Percy Bysshe Shelley (1792–1822); John Keats (1795–1821).

WILLIAM BLAKE

His rejection of literary tradition, his development of a new and energetic mythology, his imaginative exploration of the human psyche, his visionary accounts of man's physical and spiritual life, and his literary war against restraint and moderation in all forms of human experience mark William Blake as one of the first Romantic poets in English literature.

RELIGION: Any religion which preached damnation, taught humility, forbade the free enjoyment of the body, and worked hand in hand with an oppressive government was Blake's chief victim. To Blake, the priests were the first oppressors, for in the name of Reason, they had stultified Art and systematized into "Religion" the imaginative dreams of ancient poets. It was the priests who first forged the chains which bound men to their five senses and prevented them from penetrating the mysteries of God through their imaginations; the ancient poets had had no chains. Blake saw as his life's mission the dissolution of these fetters through the explication of his singular view of history and through his poetic exhortations to all men to overcome the repressive forces of Church and Reason. Single-handed, he would restore imagination to its own dominion.

THE STATE: Because the priests had for centuries dictated the terms by which all men must think and act, those who founded governments and held kingdoms thought their right to do so was moral and divine. Priests gave this sanction to these monarchical notions, and kings willingly defended the rights of the Church. Even when the State became stronger than the Church, their interdependence remained, except that the balance of power shifted from one side of the scale to the other. The State which still claimed its divine and moral origins, nevertheless trafficked

in slavery, allowed children to be worked to death, and suffered
the poor to die of starvation or be hanged for hunger crimes.
The State was, by its emphasis on poverty, inhumane, malicious, un-Christian. Fed superstitions by the Church, deprived
of a State education, the people became ignorant and passive.
But, as Blake saw it, the time for the resurgence of human
energies which had so long been repressed was at hand. The
spirit of revolution had already emerged, and in fire, smoke, and
terror, the State would fall.

REASON AND IMAGINATION: Blake despised the tidy "scientific" system of Bacon, the legal equalitarianism of Locke, and
the rationalist conceptions of Newton which stressed knowledge
of the material world and produced what Blake called "Newton's sleep," a blindness to the realms of the imagination. An
oculist could never account for Blake's vision of the world.
Blake had physical eyes, and very good ones at that, but he also
believed that man is a creature with faculties that go beyond the
physical, the material, beyond what can be described by "science." Blake demanded that, in addition to physical vision, we
acknowledge the vision of the imagination, the vision of the
emotions, the vision of the spirit. He himself had a fourfold
vision of the world which was really "One Vision," a cosmic
and holy perception of God, and man, and all nature as one. To
Blake, man and every object in the universe had a special kind
of holiness. He repudiated conventional distinctions between
matter and spirit, good and evil, God and man, time and space,
and he advocated a kind of morality that was beyond the
natural and completely free of natural laws. He protested
against the cold and repressive nature of traditional religious
doctrines which divorced God from man and good from evil,
and which classified ideas, feelings, instincts, and acts according
to hidebound conceptions of right and wrong. He asserted that
man cannot be fragmented, cannot be made to withhold one
part of himself from another. He sensed the mystery of man's
totality, but, although he recognized Reason as part of man, he
placed a higher value on the imaginative mind and gave more
importance to the emotions and the body than to Reason. He
described Reason as "the bound or outward circumference of
Energy" and the body as the source of Energy, "the only life."
All the energies of life were valuable: sexual energy, the energy

to work, and the energy to rebel. In Blake's mind, the free use of bodily energy led to action and experience, both of which provided fuel for the imagination first, the act of creation second.

SYMBOLISM: In order to express his unique perceptions, his view of history and his concept of Oneness, Blake used old Christian symbols, often enriching their meaning for his own purposes. For example, Jesus is God, the Redeemer, the Lamb, but he is also imagination. Hell, in the traditional sense, is the abode of the lost. In Blake, the lost are those without imagination. To Blake, Hell is also the home of energy, sex, passion, all the impulses which conventional religions suppressed, but which Blake saw as the life forces of mankind. Old symbols, however, had only a limited use for Blake. He created new symbols and myths in order to project his highly individual visions. Old Greek fables had been overworked in Western poetry and had become cliches. Blake's original mind required original forms of expression. "I must create a System or be enslav'd to another man's," Blake declared. "I will not Reason and Compare, my business is to create." Blake's symbols were gods no one had ever heard of before; his myth of Creation was entirely new. The verbal and pictorial symbols and images which Blake created for his system were personal and highly ambiguous and are the subjects of much controversy among Blake's interpreters. There are for Blake's poems and pictures almost as many meanings as there are readers, and the student would do well to become familiar with the critical works listed in the bibliography at the end of this book as well as with the interpretations offered in this chapter.

LIFE: Born on November 28, 1757, at 28 Broadstreet, Carnaby Market, London, William Blake was the son of a hosier who could afford him only a modest education. In 1767, Blake was enrolled in Parr's Drawing School where he learned to copy Gothic designs; he produced his earliest known poems in 1769, and was apprenticed in 1771 to the engraver James Basire with whom he remained for seven years. At the end of the apprenticeship in 1778, Blake studied painting briefly at the Royal Academy, but he left after a disagreement with his teacher, the famous artist George Michael Möser, over Blake's preference for Renaissance rather than Rococo art. In 1782, against his father's objections, Blake married an illiterate but intelligent girl named Catherine Boucher. Although barren, Catherine was "the perfect wife." She learned to read after her marriage and became Blake's uncomplaining assistant, colorist, and companion in poverty until the end of his life. In 1783, under the auspices of Rev. Henry Matthew, whose wife conducted a literary salon which Blake attended, his first volume of verse was published. He opened a print shop in 1784 where he was assisted by his brother Robert, five years his junior. When Robert died of consumption in 1787, he became the subject of several of Blake's later visions, the first having occurred when Blake was four. In one of these visions, Blake claimed, he saw the deceased Robert ascend through the ceiling in a great show of mirth. In another, Robert taught him the secret of his new copper engraving technique. Blake discovered his new method of printing soon after Robert's death, and for the next dozen years, he worked on his engravings and poems with little financial success. During this period, he moved into the circle of publisher Joseph Johnson, met Tom Paine, Mary Wollstonecraft, and Henry Fuseli, all leading liberals of their day. In 1800, he and his wife moved to Felpham as guests of his friend and patron William Hayley. The association proved a failure, and to escape Hayley's domination, Blake returned to London in 1804. In the same year he stood trial for sedition, but it was shown that he had been falsely accused. The falling out with Hayley, the trial, advancing age, and poverty took their toll of Blake. He became more and more covert in his expression, and in his declining years shaped the mystic, often obscure, allegorical works known as the Prophetic Books. He died on August 27, 1827, and was buried at Bunhill Fields in a pauper's grave which was soon forgotten. (See Mona Wilson, *The Life of William Blake,* London, 1948; and Ruthven Todd, ed., *Life of William Blake,* Alexander Gilchrist, New York, 1942.)

THE ARTIST: Blake's meager livelihood came not from his poetry but from his engravings of other men's designs. He also did original designs as illustrations for other men's books. Of special interest are his original bookplates for Young's *Night Thoughts* (which sold poorly) and Robert Blair's *The Grave.* Blake's rejection of traditional art forms and symbols can be seen in these early engravings. For example, in one of the *The Grave* drawings, the soul is a female figure which defies Newton's law of gravity and in full flesh hovers over the body of a dead male, reluctant to part from it. Blake expressed spiritual not scientific truth, and this picture signifies Blake's belief that the body and soul were in love with, not at war with, each other. (See Max Plowman, *Introduction to the Study of Blake,* London, 1927, p. 25.)

Blake's illustrations for his own work, many of which are available in facsimile editions, are of special value to the reader of this magnificent and puzzling poet. These designs, like his poetry, require at least a general explanation. Because Blake's mission in life was evangelical and his vision was apocalyptic, he had to communicate his special vision in a special way and created a new composite art form, consisting of language and design, with which to do it. In his early works, the designs served mainly as borders surrounding the words, or as half-page illustrations beneath which his words were printed. The illustrations punctuated and emphasized ideas expressed in the words on the same page and were sometimes naively obvious and unnecessary. But as his art progressed and as he evolved a mythology of his own, the words and designs became more and more inextricable, representing graphically what Blake was trying to achieve imaginatively—the unity of all creation in the union of the arts.

An example of Blake's early work can be found in the title page of *Songs of Innocence.* A tree of life is represented in the right foreground of the plate, spreading up and moving left across the page in an intricate arabesque of branchwork, some of which forms the title of the poem. Within the branches, minute figures, humans and birds, perch or fly about. In the left foreground are a boy and a girl, holding the hands of a seated woman who is apparently their mother. These are the innocent, protected by their mother in a garden of joy and life.

Blake's pictures and scenes often bear a close relationship to the words and ideas they illustrate. At other times the symbolic intention of Blake's pictures is entirely obscure. His illustration of "The Tyger" in *Songs of Experience,* for example, has provoked considerable disagreement among the experts who claim on the one hand that Blake's tiger is a fierce one; on the other, that the tiger is actually smiling. The temper of the pictured tiger very naturally affects the reader's interpretation of the poem, which is itself a cryptic one. If, as Joseph Wicksteed and David V. Erdman believe, the tiger is smiling as gently as a lamb (which is also God), then Blake is expressing in this poem a vision of Eden, where all things become their contraries. Or, if the tiger is really fierce, his burning brightness suggests "clarity and energy" emerging from the dark forests of the night, "which are to be thought of in a derogatory way," as a symbol of the fall of man into the material world. (See Hazard Adams, *William Blake: A Reading of His Shorter Poems,* Seattle, 1963, pp. 58–59.)

Blake's composite art is complex and controversial, but he leaves no doubt in his readers that "he molded the sister arts, as they have never been before or since, into a single body and breathed into it the breath of life." (See Jean H. Hagstrum, *William Blake, Poet and Painter,* Chicago, 1964, p. 140.)

WORKS: Only one of Blake's poems was published professionally during his lifetime: *Poetical Sketches,* 1783. *The French Revolution,* 1791, was prepared for the press by Joseph Johnson but was never printed. Other poems issued from his own engraving shop, made by his special process of etching called "Illuminated Printing." The remainder of his poetry was left for posterity to disseminate. The following are Blake's most representative works with their dates of composition and publication (based on Geoffrey Keynes, *Poetry and Prose of William Blake,* third edition, 1939; and J. Bronowski, *A Man without a Mask,* third edition, 1944). *Poetical Sketches* (1769–78; 1783); *An Island in the Moon* (1787, —); *There Is No Natural Religion* I and II (1788; 1788); *The Book of Thel* (1789; 1789); *Tiriel* (c.1789; —); *Songs of Innocence* (1787–89; 1789); *Songs of Experience* (1789–94; 1794); *The Marriage of Heaven and Hell* (1790–93; 1793); *The French Revolution* (1790–91?; 1791); *The Visions of the Daughters of Albion* (1793; 1793); *America* (1793; 1793); *Europe* (1794; 1794); *The First Book of Urizen* (1794; 1794); *The Book of Los* (1795; 1795); *Vala, or The Four Zoas* (1795–1804;

—); *Auguries of Innocence* (1801–3; —); *The Mental Traveller* (1803?); *Milton* (1804–8; 1804–8); *Jerusalem* 1804–20; 1804–20); *A Descriptive Catalogue* (1809; 1809); *The Everlasting Gospel* (c.1818; —); *The Ghost of Abel* (1822; 1822).

POETICAL SKETCHES

A series of poems written by Blake between the ages of 12 and 20, the *Poetical Sketches* (1783) are of two kinds, those written in imitation of earlier English poets, particularly the Elizabethans, and those written in imitation of his contemporaries. Experimental as well as derivative, the poems betray the faults and reveal the virtues of Blake's unschooled early style. Although metrically irregular, the lyrics nevertheless speak with rhythmic clarity and hint at the visionary poetics which were yet to come from Blake's graver. The first four poems celebrate the four seasons in mood and technique which are reminiscent of pre-Romantics like Thomson and Collins.

"TO SPRING": For example, Blake here employs Thomson's nature theme and an unrhymed stanza of the sort Collins used. Personifications, popular throughout the eighteenth century, are used for both spring, the season of rebirth and love, "O thou with dewy locks," and for England, "the love-sick land." Blake addresses the goddess Spring as neoclassicists did, to invoke her blessings of lush gifts, her "perfumèd garments" and "pearls," upon the bewintered land of the "languished head." But the techniques of the ancient pagan poets and their neoclassical imitators are overlaid in this poem with Christian connotation. The skies are "bright pavilions," a Biblical metaphor; Spring has "angel-eyes" and "holy feet." She suggests, in fact, a visionary holy image of nature, of the kind which becomes more prominent in Blake's later symbolic books.

"HOW SWEET I ROAMED": This poem of four quatrains, rhyming abab, cdcd, etc., also belongs in its form and imagery to the neoclassical age, but it looks forward in its symbolism to Blake's mature work. On the surface, the lyric describes the torment of a fey creature who has been captured by the Prince of Love. If we allow Blake's later works to instruct us, we find a significant layer of meaning beneath the deceptively simple surface of the poem. The winged creature (something like a fly) who wanders joyfully from field to field is one of Blake's innocents. Attracted, however, to the garden of experience, the world of the senses, he allows himself to be guided by the Prince of Love (a priest of the religion of love, Christianity). Trapped in the silken net of religious restriction, caught by the beautiful trappings of the church, the creature is placed in a cage; his body and bodily senses are imprisoned. The image of the mocking god who toys with the wings of the creature is reminiscent of Gloucester's famous lines in *King Lear,* a play which had impressed Blake deeply: "As flies to wanton boys are we to the gods; / They kill us for their sport." Thus, the innocent is encaged in a mineral-gold hell where he is made powerless and is mocked for his inability to break the restraints of religion.

"MY SILKS AND FINE ARRAY":   This poem provides a fine example of the rich musical quality of Blake's early lyrics. Here can be seen Blake's metrical irregularities, his remarkable sense of rhythm, and his feeling for the importance of subtle variation within the rhythmical pattern. In this lovely complaint, a young maiden in despair mourns the loss of love. The three stanzas contain six lines each. The first four lines of each stanza are in iambic trimeters (lines of three iambic feet, in which a stressed syllable follows an unstressed syllable). In the fifth line only, the meter changes to trochaic tetrameter (four trochees, in which the stressed syllable precedes the unstressed syllable). The last foot of this longer line, however, is an incomplete trochee, lacking the final unstressed syllable. The result is that the rhyme word ("grave" in stanza one) receives the final stress of the line. "Grave" in line five and "have" in line six, unexpectedly, do not sound alike; these two words comprise an eye-rhyme rather than a rhyme which satisfies the ear. Nevertheless, the ear is better pleased with this imperfect rhyme because the very imperfection provides relief from the monotony of too many like sounds. Furthermore, the long fifth lines of each stanza produce a rhythmic emphasis of the poem's meaning. When the stress falls on the final monosyllable of each fifth line, the mournful words "grave," "tomb," and "clay" receive special emphasis and thus stress the misery of the maiden and the nature and degree of her despair.

"TO THE EVENING STAR": This unorthodox sonnet of fourteen pentameter (five-foot) lines in blank verse echoes the somber night thoughts of the pre-Romantic poets. But there the similarity ends. The imagery and evangelical spirit of this lyric anticipate the mature poetry which sets Blake apart from all other poets. Blake's distinctive imagery—the howl breaking through the silence, the awesome light piercing the dark—emerges in lines 11 and 12. The imagery in this poem helps us share Blake's individualistic view of the multiplicity of life. When the star fades, "the wolf rages wide, / And the lion glares thro' the dun forest." The brightness, fire, and light of the star, which is a "bright torch of love," represent a pure and holy "innocence" for mankind. When the star departs, as it must, wolves and lions, representing the untamed forces of men and nature, appear in the night. But even in the night in the dun forest (which may well represent the world of human suffering man must experience in the dark journey through life), "the lion glares." The lion, like the star, projects light and, in this sense, he is pure and holy too.

"TO THE MUSES": This effortless neoclassical poem of four quatrains, rhyming abab, cdcd, etc., is both a parody of and a complaint against the poetry of Blake's time. The complaint is made in a series of speculations about the present abode of the missing Nine Muses (whom ancient poets acknowledged as their sources of inspiration). Whether they now live on earth (Mount Ida, the famous abode of Paris of Troy), or in heaven (where, early Christians believed, the spheres made music which poets heard), or whether under the sea, they are surely not with us now, Blake states.

"FAIR ELENOR": This narrative poem reminds us of the popularity of the ballad, which began in Blake's time, and also of the new Gothic vogue for the strange and the terrible. The first stanza is sufficient to illustrate both the metrical pattern and the horrific atmosphere which this type of poem employed:

> The bell struck one, and shook the silent tower;
> The graves gave up their dead: fair Elenor
> Walk'd by the castle gate, and looked in.
> A hollow groan ran through the dreary vaults.

"KING EDWARD THE THIRD":   This fragment, or one act of a verse drama, deals with a historical figure in the manner of Shakespeare. The play, an attempt to reproduce the verse and thought of the Elizabethan history play, shows us the range of Blake's literary interests, his readiness to experiment with many forms, and the profit with which he read earlier poets.

THE BOOK OF THEL

When Blake wrote *The Book of Thel* (1789), he had probably already composed most of the *Songs of Innocence* (to be discussed later) and also a poem called *Tiriel* (c.1789), in which he explored the religious and social tyranny over the senses and posed questions which became part of the opening Motto of *Thel*:

> Does the eagle know what is in the pit?
> Or wilt thou go ask the mole?
> Can wisdom be put in a silver rod?
> Or love in a golden bowl?

In *Tiriel*, the answer to the questions seems to be that wisdom cannot be put in silver or gold, but must be found in experience which is earthen. (See J. Bronowski, *A Man without a Mask,* p. 41.) In *The Book of Thel*, however, the questions have remained an enigma; some of the answers proposed to solve the riddle will be offered presently. Meanwhile the student may enjoy compiling a list of possible meanings for this brief but extremely challenging epigraph.

A single long poem, rather than a collection of short ones, *Thel* is divided into four parts, opening with the cryptic Motto. **Part I.** In the first art, Thel, the youngest daughter of Seraphim, separates herself from her sisters who are tending "sunny flocks" and mournfully makes a tour of her valley. She is sad because life is short and all things must pass away. The lily of the valley answers Thel's complaint. The lily is content with her brief period of usefulness and rejoices in God while awaiting eternity. Thel sees no analogy between herself and . the lily. **Part II.** Next Thel learns that the Cloud is content because it contemplates its eventual passage into unity, into a "tenfold life, to love, to peace, and raptures holy." Still Thel claims that she is worthless and when she fades away, "all shall say, 'Without a use this shining woman lived; / Or did she only live to be at death the food for worms?' " But the Cloud insists the feeding of worms is a worthy function, for " 'Everything that lives / Lives not alone nor for itself.' " **Part III.** A worm appears, and Thel's closed heart suddenly opens. She pities the worm who seems to her like a motherless child. But Earth, "The Clod of Clay," rises to mother and protect the helpless worm and teaches Thel that even a Clod is holy. Having made the remarkable discovery that God is concerned with all of nature, even the lowliest creature, Thel accepts the Clod's invitation to enter her house. **Part IV.** Thel enters earth through "the eternal gates," and sees "a land of sorrows and of tears." She finds her own grave, "a hollow pit," from which a sorrowful voice, presumably Thel's, emanates. The voice questions the functions of the bodily senses through which evil is experienced: the ear listens to the voice of its destroyer, the eye witnesses "the poison of a smile," bodily flesh curtains "the bed of desire." "The Virgin" Thel shrieks and flees from the bosom of earth back to the "vales of Har," her childhood home.

Among the numerous interpretations offered for *The Book of Thel,* two of the more interesting ones are Robert F. Gleckner's and George McL. Harper's. Gleckner sees Thel as a tragic figure who believes she can substitute inquiry for experience. She tries to learn about life by merely asking. Then, satisfied, she turns "her back upon experience without ever really having seen it" and accepts "in its stead the shadows of eternal delight, in a mundane paradise," that is, a world of hypocrisy. (See *The Piper and the Bard,* Detroit, 1959, pp. 161–62.) Harper claims that Blake, well-read in Thomas Taylor's *Eleusinian and Bacchic Mysteries,* was reinterpreting the pagan myth of Persephone, signifying the descent of the soul into earthly existence. Harper explains that in Thel's Motto, "the silver rod is a symbol of the phallus, and the golden bowl represents the vulva." Wisdom can be found in the rod and bowl, for intellectual strength, according to Blake, is derived from energy, represented in part by the sex act which involves "rod" and "bowl" sexual organs. However, Harper explains, Thel fled from this sexual desire. (See *The Neoplatonism of William Blake,* Chapel Hill, 1961, pp. 246–47, 253.)

An older view of the rod and bowl of the Motto explains the former as a symbol of authority, the latter as "a restrictive ethic that would mete out the immeasurable spirit of love." In this view, Thel escapes into freedom to "the wisdom and joy of eternity" from the imprisoning world of the physical senses and "the tyranny of abstract moral law . . . upon natural and, therefore, innocent desires." In other words, in this view, the poem ends happily. (See J. P. R. Wallis, *Cambridge History of English Literature,* 1914, XI, pp. 186–87.)

In the explanation offered by J. Bronowski, *The Book of Thel* is based on the belief "that knowledge is not bounded by the senses, but it must be made actual through the senses." Thel, a virgin, "who has held back from experience finds knowledge only in death," the symbol of death meaning the experience of sex. Bronowski's answer to the questions of Thel's Motto is the one he gave for the same questions in *Tiriel,* "that experience is neither gold nor silver, but earthen" (p. 41).

SONGS OF INNOCENCE AND SONGS OF EXPERIENCE

Although *Songs of Innocence* was first engraved in 1789, it was reproduced along with *Songs of Experience* in 1794, when a number of poems in each collection was shifted to the other. The fact that Blake was able to make these changes and the titles of the companion collections call our attention to Blake's view of the human situation. He saw that there were contrary states in the human soul and recognized that there was a close relationship between them. Both collections celebrate the simple joys of childhood and touch upon the limits of these joys in the world of experience; the first series, however, emphasizes innocence, while the second deals more noticeably with experience.

"INTRODUCTION" OR "PIPING DOWN THE VALLEYS WILD": This first poem of five quatrains sets the tone of holy innocence which pervades the *Songs of Innocence.* The piper (a traditional symbol of the untrained poet of rustic airs because his poetry and music are still in shapeless form) roams the "wild" valleys. Upon a cloud, he sees not the graceful Muse of distant times, but a child. The heavenly innocent may be a symbol of pure imagination, spiritual vision, Jesus, mercy, or pity. He inspires or commands a theme of innocence and holiness: "Pipe a song about a Lamb" (also an innocent, a child, and Jesus). The poet or piper, having experienced this vision, finds his pipe (melody) and obeys the child's command to sing (write). This poem on its simplest level is as innocent and fresh as the "rural pen" made from the "hollow reed" and dipped in the ink made from "the water clear." But, as R. F. Gleckner points out, deeper meaning is found in the sequence of words which expresses Blake's ideas about spiritual progression from infant joy to higher innocence. "Wild," "pleasant," "merry," "happy," and "full of joy" suggest two kinds of innocence which man is capable of knowing, the "wild" untutored joy of the child and the "full" joy of the man who has suffered and conquered the world of experience. (See *The Piper and the Bard,* p. 85.)

"THE LITTLE GIRL LOST" AND "THE LITTLE GIRL FOUND": These are two apocalyptic songs in which Blake describes the two states of innocence man can enjoy. One is symbolized by the child Lyca, the other by her parents who, in following the child, are led back to innocence. In the first poem, Lyca innocently "loses" her parents and roams the world. She goes into the "desarts wild," where she fearlessly confronts the beasts of energy and passion. The beasts are tamed by Lyca's purity and innocence. When the lion sees Lyca, "From his eyes of flame / Ruby tears there came." In other words, because Lyca is not afraid of animal energy, she dwells in harmony with herself and the passions within her. In the second poem, the parents sorrowfully travel through the world of experience, searching for Lyca. They come face to face with the beast they fear most. But to their amazement, the lion is a friendly creature and leads them to the cave where Lyca lies among the wild beasts of passion and energy. Led by the child, the parents overcome fear and rediscover innocence. It is clear that the road to higher innocence is through experience, and that the guide is a child. (See *The Everlasting Gospel,* c.1818, which is quoted below. In this poem Jesus "loses" his parents in order that they may "find" him again.)

"A LITTLE GIRL LOST":   This poem in *Songs of Experience* deals antithetically with the same theme. Ona, the daughter in this poem, has experienced a pure and innocent love through the body, but cannot lead her father to innocence. She is crushed by the jealous love and fears of her father, whose symbol is "the holy book," the selfish, tyrannical love of traditional religion.

"THE LAMB":   This poem (contrasted by "The Tyger" in *Songs of Experience,* to be discussed below) expresses a child's wonderment at God's creation in the visible lamb. The lamb's holy symbolism (Jesus, innocence) is implicit. A jewel-like lyric, this song is structured like a catechism: ten lines of questions, followed by ten of answers. Blake makes use of frequent repetition, and paraphrases are employed with studied simplicity. The effect is Biblical, childlike, and beautiful.

"THE ECCHOING GREEN":   The key to this poem is in the identification of the speaker. He is neither child nor "old folk," but a poet "who Present, Past, and Future, Sees" (see "Introduction" to *Songs of Experience,* below). He describes the merry, bell-like melodies of spring and speaks of the future when *"our* sports shall be seen / On the Ecchoing Green"; that is, he perceives the Green from an objective position in the present and at the same time anticipates joining the children in their play. Later, when the children tire, they gather "Round the laps of *their* mothers."

The speaker is not among those who return to "their mothers." He remains, presumably after the children have gone to rest, to watch "joy" depart from the "darkening Green." By the same token, although the speaker is not a child, neither is he one of the "old folk" who "laugh at *our* play." But he can see the "old folk" recapture the past in the spirit of youth and innocence they are watching. The speaker, a true poet or "bard," can partake of life in many ways and at different times all at once.

"THE GARDEN OF LOVE":   From *Songs of Experience,* this is a companion piece to "The Ecchoing Green." In this poem, an aging speaker who "used to play on the green" in the Garden of unrestricted love returns to his former haunt. He finds, however, that a chapel inscribed "Thou shalt not" has been built on his playfield, and the Green has been turned into a graveyard of dead joys and desires, tended by "Priests in black gowns." Blake's view of traditional religion, a part of the world of experience, as a repressive force is explicit here.

"THE DIVINE IMAGE":   An often repeated idea in Blake's work is that God can only be found in man; therefore, brotherhood is true religion. An early and very clear expression of this idea is found in "The Divine Image." The first stanza states that all men "in their distress" pray "To Mercy, Pity, Peace, and Love." The second stanza identifies these so-called "virtues of delight" with God and also with man.

> For Mercy has a human heart,
> Pity a human face,
> And Love, the human form divine,
> And Peace, the human dress.

It follows from this, as the next-to-last stanza affirms, that we pray not so much to God as to God in man, to the "human form divine." Therefore, the poem concludes, "all must love the human form, / In heathen, Turk, or Jew."

"THE HUMAN ABSTRACT":   Contrasting with "The Divine Image" in *Songs of Experience* is a poem entitled "The Human Abstract," which Blake originally called "The Human Image." In it, Blake describes the same abstract virtues of "The Divine Image," but they are shown perverted by conventional religion into selfishness and cruelty. Blake employs the metaphor of the tree to describe the history of religion as he views it. First there was fear of natural events, then humility before a God who caused the events. These feelings of fear and humility took root and grew into dark branches which concealed God in mystery. None of the mystery is necessary, however, Blake believes, for the concepts of fear and humility are false. They were created by stunted imaginations, which stopped functioning as soon as the "roots" (doctrines and regulations of formal religion, based on fear and humility) took hold. Natural spirits may seek where they will and never find such a tree in nature. For a tree created in fear can only grow "in the Human Brain."

"THE CHIMNEY SWEEPER":   This poem, from *Songs of Innocence,* reveals Blake's deep awareness of the plight of children in his inhuman society where babes who could barely speak were sold by impoverished parents or drafted from orphanages into employment as chimney cleaners. Despite the protests of humanitarians like Blake, begun as early as 1767, child sweepers were not freed until 1834, seven years after Blake's death. The mortality rate was high for these overworked, underfed waifs who inhaled soot for long hours day after day. But the children were given the comfort of religion in Sunday schools where they learned about angels and heaven. In the innocent acceptance of this hypocritical instruction by little Tom Dacre, Blake expresses both pathos and irony, which he combines superbly. The poem is remorseless in its explicit and terrifying description of the chimney sweeper's lot. Nonetheless, it belongs to the *Songs of Innocence* because Blake is emphasizing the fact that the essential innocence of childhood can triumph over all odds.

The companion poem to "The Chimney Sweeper" in *Songs of Experience* has the same title. The later poem, however, employs a different tone. It is not ironic but direct in its attack upon the hypocrisy of the parents, the indifference of the church, and the cruelty of the state toward children. The child tells an inquirer that his parents have gone to church "to praise God and his Priest and King" because they assume that the natural joy they see in the child means he is happy: "And because I am happy and dance and sing, / They think they have done me no injury."

"INFANT JOY":   This is a brief dialogue between the speaker and a two-day-old child, in which the child identifies himself as "joy." The poem is frequently cited as the key to Blake's symbol of the child. Its companion poem in *Songs of Experience* is "Infant Sorrow," in which the child tells how his joy and innocence were repressed by the father (a symbol of religious, social, and political repression) and how he sought comfort by withdrawing into his mother's bosom (unrestrictive love, pure spirit).

"HOLY THURSDAY":   Blake's awareness of the hard realities of life in eighteenth-century England is made clear in two other companion poems of the same name. Holy Thursday is the fortieth day after Easter when Christians celebrate the feast of the Ascension of Christ into Heaven.

The first poem presents a joyous view of the procession of schoolchildren to the great church of St. Paul's in London. Blake recaptures the color of the scene and stresses the radiance and innocence of the children who are contrasted with the "Grey-headed beadles [who] walk'd before, with wands as white as snow." (The white wand, it may be noticed, is very much like the "silver rod" of "wisdom," which has been seen as a symbol of repression in connection with *The Book of Thel,* above.) The children are being misled by the priests, but they rise above the false principles of their leader with the energetic "harmonious thunderings" of innocence.

The second "Holy Thursday" has a markedly different mood. Direct statement replaces the subtle irony of the earlier poem. The second poem focuses on the inhumanity of the grave economic abuses then prevalent in England, on the exploitation of labor in general, and of child labor in particular. Blake directs our attention not to childhood itself but to the abuses of childhood:

> Is this a holy thing to see
> In a rich and fruitful land,
> Babes reduc'd to misery,
> Fed with cold and usurous hand?

"THE LITTLE BLACK BOY": Perhaps the most famous of the *Songs of Innocence* is "The Little Black Boy." Compassionate, tender, and fundamentally hopeful that all men can come to an understanding of one another, the poem, nevertheless, reminds us that here and now, we often fail to understand our common humanity. Blake's interest in Negroes belongs to the pre-Romantic literary tradition of the "noble savage," but as Hoxie Fairchild points out in *The Romantic Quest,* the poem is superior to its predecessors because it is the first in which the poet speaks of a black boy as a human being, not as an idealized primitive. The poem, of course, is a protest against slavery and a clear expression of Blake's humanitarian impulses.

"INTRODUCTION" TO *SONGS OF EXPERIENCE*:   Like its counterpart in *Songs of Innocence,* this poem establishes the tone and the context of the poems which follow. The speaker in this case is neither Piper (as in "Introduction" to *Songs of Innocence*) nor Bard; he is an omniscient voice who introduces the Bard of multiple vision "Who Present, Past, and Future, Sees." Having thus been introduced, the Bard himself addresses Earth, Blake's symbol for the world of experience and the flesh, and tells her to leave her fears and to rise and achieve a higher state of unity and love. " 'The starry floor, / The wat'ry shore, / Is giv'n thee till break of day!' "

"EARTH'S ANSWER":   In the poem which follows the "Introduction," Earth replies that she is a prisoner within her own realm, held back from unity with the waters and stars by a jealous God, "Father of ancient men." She bewails the restrictions which have been imposed on Earth, that is, imposed on humans, for these religious restrictions have divided man within himself and have caused him to fear his own desires, so "That free Love [is] with bondage bound."

"THE CLOD AND THE PEBBLE":   The conflict between free love and restrictive love which is found in the world of experience continues to be developed in the third poem. The Clod of Clay (Earth) would like to love freely and unselfishly, for free love "builds a Heaven in Hell's despair," but the polished "Pebble of the brook" insists upon restrictive love, the selfish kind which "builds a Hell in Heaven's despite."

"THE FLY":   A metaphysical poem, reminiscent of "How Sweet I Roamed" in *Poetical Sketches* where the "winged creature" is a kind of human fly, "The Fly" is susceptible of many interpretations. Only one can be offered here. In short childlike verses, "The Fly" deals with the doctrine of love in an unusual way. As Blake had indicated in *Thel,* even the smallest of God's creatures is holy. Here it is a fly who demonstrates that principle to the speaker who has inadvertently brushed one off his sleeve. At the same time, Blake makes fun of seventeenth- and eighteenth-century rational thought. He has the speaker identify himself with the fly because both creatures can cease to be at the brush of a "thoughtless" or "blind" hand. Despite his seemingly simple manner, the speaker employs a sophisticated pun on the word "thoughtless," which can mean "careless" or "nonthinking." He also toys with the philosophic notion of *cogito ergo sum* (I think therefore I am), Descartes' rationalist principle which accepts "thought" as proof of human existence. If to think is to exist, the speaker reasons, that is "If thought is life," and not to think is death, then either way the speaker is "happy." For if he has thought, he will live. If he is "thoughtless," he will not live and thereby will be one with the "blind" hand which, by implication, belongs to an indifferent or nonthinking God. The idea amused Blake, who regarded all rationalist approaches to life or death as ridiculous.

"THE TYGER": In the *Songs of Innocence,* Blake had included the poem called "The Lamb," which reminded us that the little woolly creature, tender, meek, and mild, who "became a little child," was created by God. In its companion poem "The Tyger," we are reminded that this fearful beast was also made by God. In *Songs of Innocence,* the very fact of creation delights the speaker; in *Songs of Experience* the speaker is compelled to explore the deeper mystery of creation and the extraordinary complexity of life. A detailed examination of "The Tyger" can tell us much about Blake's art and about the nature of poetry in general. The well-known contemporary critic John Ciardi prefers not to discuss "what" a poem means but "how" it does. Let us follow his example in determining "how" Blake's "Tyger" conveys meaning.

The poet begins by addressing his imagined tiger:

> Tyger! Tyger! burning bright
> In the forests of the night,
> What immortal hand or eye
> Could frame thy fearful symmetry?

Clearly the tiger has become a symbol of all that is most terrifying. The terror that the poet is talking about, however, does not exist in isolation from other qualities, here, notably brightness and beauty of form. In reading a poem, of course, the skillful reader does not turn from the symbol to what is symbolized. He continues to look at and to relish the symbol in itself. We admire the effectiveness of Blake's description of a tiger "burning bright," all the more startling because of the chosen setting, "the forests of the night." The reader also notices the structure of a poem. This poem significantly begins with a question. It heightens our curiosity and subtly introduces the theme of mystery.

The second stanza parallels the first and continues to work with similar images.

> In what distant deeps or skies
> Burnt the fire of thine eyes?
> On what wings dare he aspire?
> What the hand dare seize the fire?

Although in a sense the question of the first stanza is asked anew, there is progression. The first stanza suggests that the creator of anything so terrifying as the tiger must be a creator whose power goes beyond our human understanding. In this second stanza he emphasizes the distance that separates this creator from ourselves. The questions convey a feeling of awe. The tiger with his tawny coat and flashing eyes is like fire in the jungle. But what must be the eyes of the creator? The reference to the creator's wings and to his working, like Vulcan or any of the gods of pagan mythology, should not, needless to say, suggest that Blake subscribed to a creation-myth. It is simply a vivid way of making us realize the immensity of the creative act.

The third stanza continues the image of the forge and stresses the role of intelligence, of mind, in creation. It reminds us again of the frightful strength of the tiger and suggests that if a tiger terrifies us by his strength and savagery we should be no less terrified of divine strength.

> What the hammer? what the chain?
> In what furnace was thy brain?
> What the anvil? what dread grasp
> Dare its deadly terrors clasp?

The reader notices that this is much more vivid than any statement in prose such as "God is awe-inspiring."

In the next stanza we encounter again Blake's fondness for contrasts, for playing off one thing against its opposite.

> When the stars threw down their spears,
> And water'd heaven with their tears,
> Did he smile his work to see?
> Did he who made the Lamb make thee?

Following on the suggestions of amazing strength and intelligence and majesty, here we are reminded that there may be other divine attributes. The stars are personified as a kind of heavenly army (as warriors wielding spears, fierce and formidable and expressive of divine might) capable of pity and compassion. The poet's question makes us reflect on the possibility that at times heaven throws aside the weapons of war and weeps. Why would the stars weep? Although Blake does not say so, they weep for poor suffering humanity, for the very existence of sorrow and misery here or in any universe. And, to turn as the poet does in his climactic fourth line from the heavenly army to the dread creator himself, how wonderful it is that he (Blake prefers in this poem not to capitalize references to God) who made the terrifying tiger also made the gentle lamb. The question forcefully reminds us that we cannot comprehend the many-sidedness of God. God, and all reality, in Blake's view is made up of contraries.

The final stanza repeats the first with a single change of word. In the fourth line of the first stanza we read "Could frame thy fearful symmetry." Having been through the experience of imagining the magnificence and the fear-inspiring mysteriousness of the creative act, we enjoy having our fresh awareness of creation expressed in this variation of the line: "Dare frame thy fearful symmetry."

Blake's ideas are always stimulating and important, but the artistry with which he expresses them is a sign of his genius too: his metrical patterns have a rich variety, his sense of structure is musical and harmonious, and his images, such as the stars which throw down their spears in "The Tyger," are powerful and evocative. On the surface, Blake's early poems are clear and simple, but they are also profound utterances on all the major concerns of men, and they are skillfully crafted works in language and in picture which reveal a deeply challenging mind and original talent.

THE FRENCH REVOLUTION

Concerned as he was with religious tyranny over the mind and body of man, eager as he was to explore the complexities of life, Blake was perhaps even more concerned with the political and social freedom of mankind through which he believed man would also achieve psychological freedom. He saw in the spirit of revolution, which pervaded his time, the means to an end of all repressive authority—an end to the church and an end to the state which cosponsored the enslavement of the citizens of the world.

The title page of *The French Revolution* promised there would be seven books of poetry, but only one book was ever finished, or if any others were written, they have long since been lost. Blake intended this poem to be seen by the public, and he enlisted the aid of his friend, the publisher Joseph Johnson, to see that the poem was printed professionally. But in 1791, their friend Tom Paine was in trouble for publishing *The Rights of Man,* and the Proclamation against Divers Wicked and Seditious Writings, issued the following year, was already being threatened in 1791. Blake himself helped Paine escape an arrest warrant in September 1792, so there is every reason to believe that because the time was not right to make public a book which glorified revolution and the rights of man, this book was suppressed. (See Geoffrey Keynes, ed., *The Complete Writings of William Blake,* New York, 1957, p. 887.)

The poem deals with events leading up to the French Revolution beginning with the Council of State held on June 19 to 21, 1789, and ending with the removal of the troops from Paris on July 15. (See David V. Erdman, *Blake: Prophet Against Empire,* Princeton, 1954, p. 149.) Blake treats the history of the events freely and invents a few noble characters to symbolize his hopes for peaceful revolution, for in reality he knew none. At the beginning of the poem, the sick king, symbolizing the decadence of monarchy, calls his aide Necker to help him to his Council. There he listens to the war-mongering of the Duke of Burgundy, an archenemy of the people, and of the Archbishop of Paris, who fears the church will fall if the state is overthrown. The Abbé de Sièyes, representative of the people, arrives and is given audience, although noblemen like Burgundy resent having to deal with commoners. But because Sièyes is accompanied by the ghost of Henry IV, the good king of legend, they agree to listen. The Duke of Orleans, hitherto quiet, is encouraged by the presence of Henry IV to speak for peace. Sièyes asks the king to withdraw his troops from Paris, but the king is adamant: " 'Go command yonder tower, saying: "Bastille depart! and take thy shadowy course . . . / . . . then the king will disband / This war-breathing army.' " Sièyes returns to the people with the king's answer. In Blake's "history," (La) Fayette withdraws the army when the Assembly votes for peace. But the king's "frozen blood" still flows and there is promise of trouble to come as the poem ends. (See D. V. Erdman, pp. 151–59, for a detailed analysis of the historical allegory in *The French Revolution*.)

The images of the poem are strong and horrifying. The cruelty of tyranny, for example, is painfully concrete: "In a tower named Bloody, a skeleton yellow remained in its chains on its couch / Of stone, once a man who refus'd to sign papers of abhorrence; the eternal worm / Crept in the skeleton" (ll. 33–35). The king's position is stated with heat, although the heat is "with'ring" and dying out: "The nerves of five thousand years' ancestry tremble, shaking the heavens of France; / Throbs of anguish beat on barren war foreheads, they descend and look into their graves" (ll. 70–71). Blake could well imagine the pride and fear of kings, reluctant to give over their centuries-old dominion to their erstwhile slaves.

Blake's antipathy for the church is reflected in the person of the Archbishop who condones war on the grounds that the church must be protected at all costs. The Archbishop's vision is typical of Blake's feelings about organized religion which is more concerned with its laws than with the spirit of love. In Blake's view, the Archbishop blasphemes when he dares to suggest that God would disappear if the church disappeared: "My groaning is heard in the abbeys, and God, so long worshipp'd, departs as a lamp / Without oil; for a curse is heard hoarse thro' the land from a godless race / Descending to beasts; they look downward and labour and forget my holy law" (ll. 137–39).

True love, on the other hand, is practiced by the Abbé de Sièyes who speaks for Blake when he says that the people have long been "enslav'd; black, deprest in dark ignorance, kept in awe with the whip / To worship terrors, bred from the blood of revenge and breath of desire / In bestial forms, or more terrible men; till the dawn of our peaceful morning, / Till dawn, till morning, till the breaking of clouds, and swelling of winds, and the universal voice / Till man raise his darken'd limbs out of the caves of night" (ll. 214–18). When the church and the state shall have been destroyed by the new men of the revolution, then shall Eden return. And again Sièyes speaks for Blake in his vision of the New Eden: "The mild / peaceable nations [will] be opened to heav'n, and men [will] walk with their father in bliss" (l. 237).

THE EARLY PROPHETIC BOOKS

The French Revolution is generally not regarded as one of Blake's visionary or prophetic books, yet most of the characters in it have visions or dreams of the past or future, and the poem, although written "after the fact," presents its history as a vision or forecast of it. Such a procedure was useful in an era of repression, when free speech was still a hope and not a right. Yet *The French Revolution* was suppressed by his publisher or by Blake himself. It spoke too openly, and a thicker veil had to be woven over the truths of Blake's messages if he hoped to continue free from persecution.

THE VISIONS OF THE DAUGHTERS OF ALBION: This work speaks out against slavery, sexual repression, moral and economic bondage. But an obscure mythology is created here from which Blake borrowed, sometimes altering his symbols, for his later prophetic works. The story is of the female Oothoon, whose spirit is free but whose body is owned by Bromion. Theotormon loves her, but he is possessed by false ideas of love and can only be a jealous, impotent, and destructive lover. The story of Oothoon is not only about sex but about slavery as well. Bromion is not only Oothoon's rapist, he is her owner. (See D. V. Erdman, p. 212.) The daughters of Albion are women of England. Slaves of a different kind, they are bound to their social positions (see *The Rights of Women* by Blake's friend Mary Wollstonecraft) and to the factories and mills of the land. They sigh "toward America," which is symbolic of the freedom they desire. (D. V. Erdman, p. 212.)

AMERICA: A "prophecy" of the same period as *The Visions of the Daughters of Albion,* this poem (1793) tells the veiled history of the American Revolution, whose spirit is embodied by the mythical figure of Orc. His enemy, the Prince of Albion, is George III. (G. Keynes, p. 893.) The poem is meant to be a warning to England that its war against France which began February 1793 might turn out to be as disastrous as was its war against America. (See David V. Erdman, in *Discussions of William Blake,* ed. J. E. Grant, Boston, 1962, p. 20.)

EUROPE: Another early prophecy, *Europe* (1794), deals with England's war against France. The prologue, to some extent, clarifies Blake's system of fourfold vision:

> Five windows light the cavern'd Man: thro' one
>   he breathes the air;
> Thro' one hears music of the spheres, thro' one
>   the eternal vine
> Flourishes, that he may recieve [sic] the grapes;
>   thro' one can look
> And see small portions of the eternal world that
>   ever groweth;
> Thro' one himself pass out what time he please;
>   but he will not,
> For stolen joys are sweet and bread eaten in
>   secret pleasant.

Blake meant that visions perceived *through* the senses are eternal; impressions felt *with* the senses are not. The fifth "window" is sexual; man who is repressed will not use this sense freely. Blake omitted this prologue from several of the original printings of the poem, possibly because he felt his association of the sensual with ideas of revolution would be misunderstood.

The history of Christianity from its beginning to the eve of the English-French war is told in terms of Enitharmon, the female principal of inspiration, who has been asleep for 1800 years. At the end of that time, she is awakened for a single night by Newton's trumpet blast (science's challenge to religion). She calls her enslaved children to sport under the moon. When morning comes, however, everyone flees—except for "terrible Orc" (the spirit of revolution). When Orc sees morning, he plunges down into France and enflames the people, giving them the energy to revolt. Then Los (the father of man and poetry, and eternal husband of Enitharmon) awakens, "And with a cry that shook all nature to the utmost pole, / Call'd all his sons to the strife of blood." The revolution of men against 1800 years of oppression is about to begin as the poem concludes.

THE MARRIAGE OF HEAVEN AND HELL: Especially useful in helping us to understand Blake's unique mind is this poem, begun about a year after the completion of *Songs of Innocence*. Like *Songs of Innocence*, the poem was etched and illustrated by the author. It took shape as a critique of conventional morality and marks Blake's turning away from the mystic philosophy of Swedenborg, whom Blake had regarded as the savior of the modern world. In addition, the poem states Blake's theory of human perception and also his political views on the French Revolution.

The title of the book alerts us to Blake's interest in the reconciliation of contraries. Traditionally, Heaven and Hell are involved in an eternal feud. Blake's father had rejected the Church of England and had turned to Swedenborgian mysticism; for a while, Blake too leaned in this direction. But he found in this religion many of the same worthless principles which, in his opinion, had caused other organized religions to stagnate. Swedenborg had acknowledged Hell, a place in which the human passions warred among themselves. Blake came to realize that Heaven was a sterile place from which no evil emanated only because no desire existed there. Hell, on the other hand, was the source of evil because it was the home of desire and passion, which created the energy for action and ultimately for evil. He discovered that the spirit and hope of Heaven and the instinctive energies of Hell were both necessary for human existence. And he believed the two great contraries could be combined or "married" in the poetic or imaginative vision.

The central theme of this poem is the nature of human existence, and its key words are "Reason" and "Energy," by which Blake meant the human desire for order and the human desire for creation, desires which are represented by two kinds of men, whom he called angels and devils. Both were necessary for the achievement of total "Human existence," according to Blake. (See Max Plowman, *Introduction,* p. 116; Martin K. Nurmi, in *Discussions,* ed. J. E. Grant, pp. 98–99; H. Bloom, *PMLA,* December 1958, p. 501.) Blake also associated the spirit of revolution (America's in 1776 and France's at the time the poem was conceived) with energy, with what the "religious" called "evil." Counter-revolutionary forces were associated with oppression, passivity, tyranny, with what the "religious" called "good." Thus, underlying its religious concerns, the poem urges psychological freedom and deals with the politics of revolution. The position from which Blake argues each case is that of total freedom for the total man.

The poem proper begins with "The Argument," is followed by six expository sections (3, 5–6, 14, 21–22), "The Voice of the Devil" (4), five playful visionary sections, each called "A Memorable Fancy" (6–7, 12–13, 15–17, 17–20, 22–24), and the famous "Proverbs of Hell" (7–11). In other words, the progress of Blake's poem is achieved through five different literary techniques, which are alternated throughout the poem in a pattern not unlike a symphony. (For a description of the musical scheme, see Martin K. Nurmi, *Blake's Marriage of Heaven and Hell,* Kent, Ohio, 1957.) "The Argument" is poetry; the expository sections are prose-poetry (that is, prose which obeys the rules of poetry and does not attempt the usual orderly exposition of prose forms); "The Voice of the Devil" is like a bill of particulars used in formal legal argument; and the "Fancies" are dialogues, narratives, or both. The proverbs, of course, are just that, sententious statements, succinctly phrased.

"The Argument," a poem in irregular lines and stanzas, projects an image of the angry god Rintrah (identified in later poems as

the hysterical William Pitt the Younger). Rintrah is hungry for
the blood of just men. "The Argument" provides a narrative
account of the revolution of 1789 which brought peace and new
hope to the French peasant, the "meek" man, until aristocrats
and priests, the "villains" and "serpents" of the piece, began to
conspire against them. And so (in 1792), the clouds of war
hang low over France once again. (See D. V. Erdman, *Blake:
Prophet Against Empire,* pp. 174–76.)

In the first expository section, Blake damns Swedenborg, an
"Angel sitting at the tomb" of religion, which is death. Here
Blake issues the manifesto of his own revolutionary philosophy:
"Without contraries is no progression. / Attraction and Repul-
sion, Reason and Energy, Love and Hate are necessary to
Human existence." Here also is the clear presentation of
Blake's definitions of Good and Evil: what the religious call
"Good is the passive state that obeys Reason." What they call
"Evil is the active [state] springing from Energy."

"The Voice of the Devil" next defines the errors of traditional
religions: their separation of the body and soul, their proscrip-
tion of the energies and functions of the body, and their threats
of Hell to those who follow the laws of the body. None of these
doctrines are true, Blake's devil states. The body is part of the
soul and houses the five senses through which the rest of the
soul (the larger part which belongs to all the natural and
supernatural world) may ultimately be perceived. The body
provides the energy for this total perception, and "Energy is
Eternal Delight."

In the second expository section, Blake speaks out against
traditional religious repression of desire over centuries of Judaic-
Christian indoctrination. Milton's God in *Paradise Lost* is
offered as an example of the finite God, sterilized by misconcep-
tions handed down through the ages. But, Blake points out,
despite the repressive forces working against it, Milton's poetic
genius—unconsciously—expressed itself with passion and energy in the passages on Satan.

The first "Memorable Fancy" restates the principles uttered in
the preceding exposition in a whimsical fiction of Blake in Hell

among the poet-geniuses of the nether-world. Blake sees on the wall, which divides the visionary and corporeal worlds, lines written by a Devil (a genius), which say there is more to be perceived by man than his five senses will allow.

The "Proverbs of Hell" which follow are brought back from Blake's visit to the underworld. The proverbs invalidate the ideas of old religions and teach that "the bones of the dead" should be plowed under. Another proverb, which says "Excess leads to the palace of wisdom," overthrows the classical doctrine of restraint. Other proverbs invalidate the deadly sins of Christianity. Pride, lust, wrath are the glory, bounty, and wisdom of God; they are God's gifts of desire, energy, and action. The energies of beasts and other untamed forces in nature are also eternal though man cannot comprehend them. "The tygers of wrath are wiser than the horses of instruction"; even excess energy is better than passivity, the proverbs teach. And, rejecting Christian shame over the body, Blake's proverbs teach that the body itself is aesthetic, a testament to God's gift: "The head sublime, the heart Pathos, the genitals Beauty, the hands and feet Proportion."

The next expository passage elaborates on the themes of human perception and false religion; pagan poets of ancient times saw God everywhere, for their unrepressed imaginations were highly developed. They created a great new mythology to convey their visions. Unfortunately, their mythology became systematized by unimaginative priests, who soon began to attribute to the gods, their own oppressive and restrictive ideas. The priests made rules for other men to follow. "Thus men forgot that All deities reside in the human breast," that the idea of God is a human idea, a wonderful imaginative conception, but not a "solid" form. The priests corrupted the religious spirit by taking God away from the poets.

The second "Memorable Fancy," another whimisical vision, dramatizes the preceding exposition. In conversation over dinner with Isaiah and Ezekiel, Blake hears the Old Testament prophets affirm imagination and "the Poetic Genius" as "the first principle" of human perception. It was their conviction that their imaginative conceptions were the true ones that made the

Jewish prophets predict the domination of the Jews over all other nations, Ezekiel explains. And this has come to pass, "for all nations believe the jews' code and worship the jews' god," Blake is convinced.

The next expository section describes the millennium, man's return to Eden after man has learned to perceive the world imaginatively. Using images of the engraving shop, Blake explains how his own work with corrosive acids helps him to perceive the infinite beneath the surface of metals.

The following "Memorable Fancy" again takes place out of this world. This time printing images are employed to depict the Printing House in Hell where the actions and forces involved in transmitting knowledge through the printed book are symbolized by dragons, vipers, lions, and other unnamed forms. In Blake's imagery, the transmitters of knowledge are all disagreeable creatures. The men who build the cities and mills, however, are "Giants who form this world into its sensual existence." Nevertheless, having done the work, they are placed in chains, oppressed by those who depend upon them, for "the weak in courage is strong in cunning." (Religion and feudalism, for example, are cunning means of enslaving Giants by teaching them to restrain their fearful energies and accept bondage.) Thus, the world is divided into Producers and Devourers, and the two must be enemies forever. For certain contraries, Blake maintains, "are essential."

The "Memorable Fancy" of plates 17–20 of Blake's illustrations is a visionary scene in which an Angel, presumably Swedenborg, and the fearless revolutionist poet debate over the future each envisions for the other. The Angel shows the poet the Abyss, a flaming Christian Hell, to which the poet will surely be sent if he continues his radical ways. But the poet sees only the fires and fumes of energy, the forces of "spiritual existence," which he embraces. Blake's treatment of the Angel who is frightened by his own imagined Hell is ludicrous. As the Angel flees, the dauntless poet can be found "sitting on a pleasant bank beside a river by moonlight," where he hears another poet sing of the psychological torment of the passive and conservative man who "breeds reptiles of the mind." The Angel who has conjured this vision is frightened by an image of his own stagnant imagination. He is also afraid to see the fate the poet has dreamt up for him. But forcing him along, the Angel is conveyed through space by the poet. They pass the planets and come to a void in which an altar and Bible form an entry to the Hell the poet has invented for the Angel. It is a Dantesque pit in which chained apes and baboons claw at each other and sometimes destroy the weak among them. Some hypocritically kiss the bodies they devour. In effect, Blake has shown the Angel (conservative churchman, politician, and king's man) the spirit of English society, a spirit as cannibalistic as the apes in his Hell. The Angel is annoyed because the poet has imposed this vision upon him. But this is precisely what the poet has intended to do: "We impose on one another," the poet replies.

The Fancy ends with a motto that is completely appropriate: "Opposition is true friendship." And one does feel that the Angel and the poet, despite their differences and because of their differences, are true friends. Blake did admire Swedenborg (the Angel), although he thought him misguided.

The friendship motto acts as a transition to the final "Memorable Fancy" of plates 22–24. Here a Devil (poet) tells an Angel (conservative) that the love of God is the love of man. There is humor in the description of the Angel's change of color when he hears this blasphemy. Then as he is able to think of a rebuttal, the Angel's color returns; he becomes "white, pink, and smiling." Did not Christ himself sanction the ten commandments? No, the Devil replies, for he directly or indirectly broke every one of them: "No virtue can exist without breaking these ten commandments," and "Jesus was all virtue."

At this shocking truth, the Angel at once converts to the Party of the Devils, embraces energy and passion, and becomes one with the prophet Elijah. The fancy ends on an even lighter note, as the poet and his new friend the Angel-turned-Devil read the Bible together, in its "diabolical sense," of course, and the poet playfully promises that "the world shall have it if they behave well."

The closing aphorism restates the theme of contraries which are necessary for human existence. At the same time, it reflects

Blake's opposition to the notion of equality before the law. Spirits of energy must not be regulated by laws which are made by and for passive Angels. "One law for the Lion and the Ox is Oppression."

THE LATER PROPHETIC BOOKS

Blake's later prophecies are not so easily scanned as are the early ones, and the study of *Vala, or The Four Zoas, Milton,* and *Jerusalem* is usually reserved for the advanced student. These later books elaborate the mythology which Blake had begun to develop in his earlier writings.

THE EVERLASTING GOSPEL: This book, however, does not employ Blake's mythological system. For this reason, it is well worth the study of beginning students who will find in its version of the Gospels, many familiar ideas, which, however, are reinterpreted in Blake's inimitable fashion. The poem provides clear clues to the meanings of some of Blake's earliest poems. Compare the following with some of the *Songs of Innocence* and *Songs of Experience,* or with *The Book of Thel* and *The Marriage of Heaven and Hell:*

> Was Jesus Humble? or did he
> Give any proofs of Humility?
> When but a Child he ran away
> And left his Parents in dismay.
> When they had wander'd three days long
> There were the words upon his Tongue:
> . . . .
> He wrote, "Ye must be born again."

CRITICISM: Except for a small circle of friends and acquaintances, Blake had no reading public during his lifetime. Only three years before Blake's death, Charles Lamb indicated that he had only recently and vaguely heard of him. In a letter to a friend, Lamb wrote: "His poems have been sold hitherto only in Manuscript. I never read them; but a friend at my desire procured the 'Sweep Song.' There is one to a tiger, which I have heard recited . . . which is glorious, but alas! I have not the book; for the man is flown, whither I know not—to Hades or a Mad House." (*The Letters of Charles Lamb and Mary Lamb,* ed. E. V. Lucas, 1935, II, p. 425.)

Such was the general impression of Blake in his own time. Those who heard his poetry thought him a genius, but also perhaps a madman. After his death, he was all but forgotten for thirty years, when his biography was begun by Alexander Gilchrist who died before its completion. The work was finished by other Blake devotees, Mrs. Gilchrist and the brothers Dante and William Rossetti, in 1863. The biography brought Blake into the public eye. A critical study of Blake by the admiring poet Algernon Swinburne also helped his reputation along, but it was not until the Oxford Press issued an edition of his works in 1905 that a wide audience could begin to read and evaluate Blake. The following year, from the pen of Paul Elmer More, came this evaluation: "On the whole, it must be said that Blake is greater, at least more complete, as an artist than as a poet; and this, I think, is due mainly to his superior discipline as a draftsman. In verse he never produced anything more exquisite than some of his juvenile songs; in drawing he grew in power to the end. . . ." (*Shelburne Essays.* Fourth Series, 1907, p. 225.)

In 1916, when scholarly studies still had provided few clues to the meaning of Blake, he was found difficult and even crude: "It is his elaborate new symbolism for which we have not a satisfactory key that makes him so difficult to follow and his prophetic books so crude to the taste . . . ," Charles Gardner wrote in *Vision and Vesture* (p. 46). In 1924, S. Foster Damon assumed the burden of explicating Blake. Stymied, however, by his limited but extremely significant successes, Damon reached the conclusion that "Blake did not believe in unveiling the Truth completely. . . . There never was a greater intellectual snob. He elaborated a marvellously woven veil for his Sanctuary, so heavy that none has moved it very effectually, so beautiful that none has refused some genuflection." (*William Blake: His Philosophy and Symbols,* p. x.)

Indeed, Blake remained obscure to most of his readers for a long time, but he continued to fascinate them. In one of the most influential appreciations of its time, Max Plowman wrote: "Blake cannot be classed. He was the most independent artist that ever lived. He had his own sources of inspiration (so peculiar and strange that no one else has dared to drink from them). . . ." (*Introduction to the Study of William Blake,* 1927.) The difficulties in reading Blake have been considerably diminished by the numerous studies of his symbolic system and visionary worlds made by Northrop Frye (see Bibliography). David V. Erdman added immensely to our understanding of the poems in his major treatise on Blake's thought in relation to the political events and social movements of his own time. Present-day critics are still fascinated by Blake and still pose the same questions about him: "Why did Blake establish his own set of symbols?" But they are beginning to find answers, realizing "that a careful study of his work often serves to explain even the most incomprehensible of them." (Karl Kiralis, in *Criticism,* I, No. 3, Summer 1959, p. 209.)

ROBERT BURNS

The poetic and personal qualities of Robert Burns were unlike those of any other Romantic poet. He had no quarrel with neoclassical literary principles as Blake had; he lacked the egocentricity which Wordsworth had; he avoided the melodramatic posing which the cynical Lord Byron assumed; and he did not attempt the prophetic profundity which Shelley sought after nor the sensual explicitness which Keats achieved. But Burns does not have to be like anyone else in order to be a Romantic poet. He is a Romantic for other reasons. He was interested in the past, particularly in the old songs of his native land, and did more than any other man to rescue and preserve his literary heritage. In his original work, he showed the continuing vitality of the literary tradition he had rediscovered and studied. He shared the Romantic belief in the importance of the common man. Interested in America and sympathetic to the French Revolution, he thought of himself as one of those working for a new and better world. His poetry was predominantly lyrical, another Romantic characteristic, and his use of dialect was a way of revolutionizing poetic diction. There is an extravagance in his imagination which is also Romantic and totally alien to the neoclassical spirit of restraint. He was able to unite nature and man into a single vision. For these reasons, among others, he is truly a Romantic spirit.

LIFE: Unquestionably the best known and best liked of Scottish poets, Robert Burns has commanded the attention of the entire world, in spite of the difficulties posed by the dialect of his poems. Born in Alloway, Ayrshire, Scotland, in 1759, the son of a tenant farmer, Burns received a good, although limited, formal education. He studied French and Latin as a boy and read English literature—Milton, Pope, Gray, and Goldsmith—as an adult. But he learned more from personal experience and popular tradition than from books. After his father's death in 1784, Burns managed his family's tenant farm, and felt a new freedom he had not known before. He had already turned to poetry in his spare time, recording his first pieces in a "Commonplace Book" begun in 1783. Now he became involved in anti-Calvinist activities in his defense of Gavin Hamilton, a Sabbath-breaker. He had fathered an illegitimate child by Elizabeth Paton; now he became the father of a set of twins by Jean Armour whom he married in 1788. His first volume of verse, called *Poems, Chiefly in the Scottish Dialect,* published at Kilmarnock in July 1786, was immediately successful, and a second edition was published the following year. While in Edinburgh seeing to the details of the new edition, Burns met the leading literary figures of the city and began to move in their circle. At the same time he struggled to maintain his family and farm at Ellisland. In 1789, he succeeded in obtaining a government position, which improved his finances considerably. Two years later, he moved to Dumfries where he remained until his death of heart disease in 1796.

In the thirty-seven years of his life, Burns rose from the humble condition of tenant farmer to that of unofficial Scottish national poet. He had received his inspiration from his own soil, had made use of the songs and tales of old Scotland, and had chosen, for the most part, the locale, idiom, and dialect of his own people. Although his idiom was Scottish, he wrote with a deep understanding of all humanity, and some of his best songs—"A Red, Red Rose" and "John Anderson My Jo"— reveal with beauty and depth the emotional and lyrical side of man. Burns wrote from experience which taught him religious skepticism, and some of his finest works—"The Holy Fair" and "Holy Willie's Prayer"—are in the satirical mode. His farmer's life gave him a strong sense of social injustice, which he expressed in protest poems such as "The Twa Dogs" and "The Jolly Beggars." And his love of gaiety, the life of the tavern, and of bonnie lasses gave him the verve and flair for some of our finest convivial songs—"Green Grow the Rashes, O" and "For A' That, An' A' That." The spirit of his nation which had almost lost its identity under English rule surged in his breast and flowed into his poetry. Poems like "Scots Wha Hae" and "My Heart's in the Highlands" endeared Burns to his fellow Scotsmen who recognized in his patriotic outbursts their own voices.

SCOTTISH LITERARY TRADITION: The national tradition in which Burns did his best work can be traced back to the Middle

Ages when Scotland was an independent country with cultural ties in France as well as England. In France, Scots such as William Dunbar, Gavin Douglas, and John Major acquired a taste for courtly verse, polished meters, rhythmic variety, and the aureate style (a way of embellishing their own crude tongue with elegant words). In England, the Scottish King James I, the poet Robert Henryson, and William Dunbar, again, found inspiration in London's master poet Geoffrey Chaucer. But there was also a continuous production of native Scots poetry, free from foreign influence, full of witchery, elfin humor, anti-clerical satire, antifeminist attitudes, and enormously tall tales and high fantasy, which taught Burns his heritage and gave him material for many of his poems.

From poets like William Dunbar, Burns received the gift of elvish humor, the boisterous satiric style, and the convivial spirit. His "Address to the Deil" and "The Death and Dying Words of Poor Maillie" may be profitably compared to Dunbar's "Ballad of Kynd Kittock," the tale of a thirsty alewife who enters heaven on a snail, searching for a drink, and rides right out again. Refused readmittance, she returns to the alehouse where you may find her to this day. Although Burns's sentimental quality is totally lacking in Dunbar, it takes little effort to recognize the spirit of the older poet in Burns's drinking songs. Compare with Burns, Dunbar's lines: "A barell bung ay at my bosum, / Of varldis gud I had na mair; / Et corpus meum ebriosum / I leif onto the toune of Air."

Burns also knew the fifteenth-century fables of Robert Henryson, the lively descriptive poetry of Gavin Douglas written in the sixteenth century, and the collection of native songs and ballads preserved in *Tea-Table Miscellany* (1724–32) by Allan Ramsay. From the anonymous Scottish poets of early popular tradition, Burns took the "Wowing of Jock and Jenny" and reworked it as "Duncan Gray." The old ballad of "Allan-a-Maut" supplied the matter for "John Barleycorn," and the wife in "Lichtounis Dreme" who chides her drunken husband as he wallows in the mire of an overturned chamber pot may well have been the ancestress of the wife of "Tam o'Shanter." Perhaps the most important native influence on Burns's poetry was his near-contemporary Robert Fergusson (1750–1774) who wrote original poems in the native tongue, following the old Scottish style. Burns returned to Fergusson's poems again and again for inspiration and encouragement in carrying on this tradition.

THE DIALECT: Some readers are kept from reading Burns by the fact that almost all his best poetry is written in Scottish dialect. The poetry's effectiveness, however, would have been completely lost if standard English had been used. There are many editions of Burns's work which provide the reader with a glossary and notes, and it does not take long to become reasonably familiar with his language. Consider, for example, this description of the congregation in "The Holy Fair":

> Here some are thinkin' on their sins
> An some upo' their claes;
> Ane curses feet that fyl'd his shins,
> Anither sighs an' prays:
> On this hand sits a chosen swatch,
> Wi' screw'd up, grace-proud faces;
> On that a set o' chaps, at watch,
> Thrang winkin' on the lasses
> To chairs that day.

Even without a glossary, the reader might guess from the context that "Ane" is "one," and that "claes" means "clothes." The occasional omission of final consonants should cause no trouble either. A little thought might suggest the relationship between "fyl'd" and "defiled" (dirtied). "Thrang" is the old past tense form for "thronged," which follows the linguistic pattern still in use for forming the past tense of verbs like "swim" ("swam") and "drink" ("drank"). The desire to practice and an open mind are all that are necessary for an appreciative reading of a poet universally acknowledged as one of the greatest.

WORKS: Three volumes of verse under the title *Poems, Chiefly in the Scottish Dialect* were published under Burns's name in the years 1786, 1787, and 1793. His songs and ballads, many of them unsigned, appeared during Burns's lifetime in *Scots Musical Museum,* ed. James Johnson, 5 vols.,

1787–97; and in *Collection of Original Scottish Airs,* ed. George Thomson, 4 vols., 1793–1805. Among the more famous of the individual poems which appeared in these collections are: "Mary Morison" (1780); "John Barleycorn" (1782); "The Death and Dying Words of Poor Maillie" (1782); "Green Grow the Rashes, O" (1784); "Holy Willie's Prayer" (1785); "The Jolly Beggars" (1785); "The Cotter's Saturday Night" (1785); "Address to the Deil" (1785); "To a Mouse" (1785); "Scotch Drink" (1785); "The Twa Dogs" (1786); "The Rantin' Dog, the Daddie o't" (1786); "To a Louse" (1786); "The Holy Fair" (1786); "Auld Lang Syne" (1788); "John Anderson My Jo" (1788); "Tam o'Shanter" (1790); Sweet Afton" (1790); "Ae Fond Kiss" (1790); "Duncan Gray" (1792); "Highland Mary" (1792); "Scots Wha Hae" (1793); "O,Wert Thou in the Cauld Blast" (1796).

"HOLY WILLIE'S PRAYER": Among the poems in the 1786 collection (often called, from its place of publication, the Kilmarnock poems) were several satirical pieces in which Burns attacked hypocrisy and pious affectation. But "Holy Willie's Prayer," written before the Kilmarnock volume was published, was deliberately omitted from this volume. The poem is a virulent attack on Calvinist doctrine, and Burns, no doubt, did not wish to alienate conservative readers from his first published work. The religion of the Presbyterian Church of Scotland was Calvinism, a harsh, authoritarian, uncompromising form of Christianity, as Burns saw it. His own belief in the natural goodness of man contradicted the stern doctrine of election which taught that man's salvation was a predetermined matter, that some men were destined for Hell, others for Heaven, and that no will on the part of the individual would alter the course his soul would take after death. The sense of freedom Burns enjoyed in rejecting this religion (Calvinism not God) is reflected in "Holy Willie's Prayer," perhaps the best of his satirical poems.

It should be noted at the outset that the poem is a "dramatic monologue," a form popularized by Robert Browning, in which a single character speaks (as in the soliloquy of a play) and reveals his own nature to the reader. In lively and comic verse, Burns composes a mock prayer designed to reveal the mind of a smug, self-centered, narrow-minded pretender of virtue. The humor of the poem was especially delightful to the poet's friends because Holy Willie was sketched from life.

The "prayer" begins with allusions to the doctrine of predestination. This was the theory that salvation comes about only by divine election. God, in other words, arbitrarily decides who will be saved and who will be damned. Since Willie is solemnly and humorlessly convinced that he is one of the chosen, he can express complete approval of a God who "Sends ane to Heaven and ten to Hell," that is, condemns ten souls for every soul saved. Although the touch is light and the poet's jests are meant to entertain, it is clear that beneath the laughter is a feeling of horror at what Burns thought the meaningless savagery of the God worshiped by the Holy Willies of this world.

As he proceeds in his prayer, Willie admits that he is not altogether without sin. He casually says that he is sorry for his sins. It is obvious that he is not very sorry; indeed, the poet persuades us that Willie is not sorry at all. Convinced as Willie is that he is one of God's chosen, he sees even his sins as part of God's plan. He has his little faults only in order that he may avoid the dangerous sin of pride. The poet's irony here is at its best.

POEMS, CHIEFLY IN THE SCOTTISH DIALECT

The volume of verses which made Burns famous contained poems which are still among his best known: "The Twa Dogs," "Scotch Drink," "The Holy Fair," "Address to the Deil," "The Death and Dying Words of Poor Maillie," "To a Mouse," "To a Louse," and "The Cotter's Saturday Night." Burns's work is exceptionally varied and extensive in scope. In a brief survey, only a few illustrations of his remarkable talents can be attempted.

"SCOTCH DRINK": In his favorite tail-rhyme stanza, also called the "Burns Stanza," the poet sings the praises of Scotch whiskey, a subject worthy of a Scottish Bard:

> Let other Poets raise a fracas
> 'Bout vines an' wines, an' drunken Bacchus,

> An' crabbed names an' stories wrackus,
> An' grate our lug!
> I'll sing the jice Scotch bear can mak us
> In glass or jug.

The stanza consists of six lines, four rhymed tetrameters in lines 1, 2, 3, and 5, two rhymed dimeters in lines 4 and 6. A stanza well suited to his lyrical gifts, Scottish brogue, and earthy themes, Burns used it frequently in poems such as "To a Mouse," "To a Louse," "Address to the Deil," and numerous epistles, dedicatory verses, and elegies.

The poem "Scotch Drink" incorporates in its raucous, rollicking stanzas, several of Burns's favorite themes: Scotland, barley crops, the hardship of taxes, good drink, and the service of drink to the inspiration of the poet.

"ADDRESS TO THE DEIL":   A good-natured spoof of the puritan conception of Satan in Milton's *Paradise Lost,* the "Address" treats Old Nick with the traditional irreverence of Burns's native culture. Burns assumes the familiar tone of the Highlander well-schooled in "eldritch tradition" (lore of elves and unearthly creatures), which he learned from William Dunbar and Allan Ramsay, and at first hand from the people of his village. He also inserts, with amusing caution, his own religious skepticism about the existence of Hell. The poem is a brief history of the Devil's mischief since he corrupted the first innocents Adam and Eve, visited Job with boils, and was pierced by the sword of the Angel Michael. Local superstitions about the Devil's doings, handed down from "my rev'rend graunie," are also included. The Devil is at work when the wind howls through the elder bush and the stars cast their eerie light on a clump of rushes, when the butter will not churn, when a young groom knots up his loom, when a traveler drowns as the river unexpectedly thaws, or a drunk sinks into a "miry slough." After offering the Devil a recital of his own adventures, the poet imagines that the Demon must be thinking:

> A certain Bardie's rantin', drinkin',
> Some luckless hour will send him linkin',
> To your black Pit.

He brashly promises to cheat the Devil yet. But the poem ends on a hilarious note as the poet, somewhat less confident than his boast would suggest, asks the Devil to ease up in his mischief against men. There may be an off-chance that salvation in still possible for the Devil if he does, for the poet is distressed at the thought of Hell even as a home for Old Nick himself. Burns implies that Hell is no place for humans either, in spite of what the Calvinists preached. By linking Milton's Biblical Satan with the popular demon of local superstition, Burns subtly but effectively tells us what he thinks of them both.

"THE TWA DOGS": A whimsical and inventive dialogue of rhymed couplets between a pedigree dog named Caesar and a plowman's collie named Luath, "The Twa Dogs" examines the estates of rich and poor and comes to an amusing conclusion.

In a place called "auld King Coil," the two dogs meet and play in the fields. Grown tired of the chase, they rest and converse in a most amiable way. "I see how folk live that hae riches; / But surely poor folk maun be wretches!" Caesar the pampered dog of the rich remarks. He learns from humble Luath, however, that "they're no' sae wretched's ane wad think, / Though constantly on poortith's brink." The poor are so accustomed to poverty that it doesn't frighten them. And they have their comforts too: rest after hard toil, a faithful wife, and "grushie weans" [thriving children], a pint of ale to help them lay aside their own cares and take up those of the state and church, and the comfort of complaining about "patronage and priests" and rising taxes.

Still, it is true, Luath admits, some poor folk are made wretched by a few greedy overseers, trying to impress their absentee masters who are too busy at parliament working for the good of Britain to know what their hirelings are doing. Caesar, however, has lived intimately with the rich and objects to Luath's kindly interpretation of the causes of evil among the poor. The masters are more likely to be gallivanting abroad than making laws for the good of Britain. "For Britain's gude!" he splutters, "—for her destruction! / Wi' dissipation, feud, and faction!"

Luath learns that although the rich never feel hunger, nor the pains of toil, "when nae real ills perplex them, / They make enow themselves to vex them." The worst of it is they are sorely troubled by want of work. The conversation ends as the sun sets and the two dogs rise to leave. Having contemplated the states of men, both rich and poor, they "Rejoiced they werena men but dogs."

"THE HOLY FAIR":   Another of Burns's great satirical poems, this one, included in the Kilmarnock volume, is a galloping tail-rhyme poem with irrepressible wit. Burns describes a religious holiday which was an important event in Scottish Presbyterian life. "The Holy Fair" is the annual communion service held on the second Sunday of each August. Usually several parishes held a joint communion, and this meant that there were crowds of people in attendance, a good deal of confusion, and best of all a festive spirit. In this poem, Burns contrasts the irrepressible spirit of joy in mankind with the stern preachings of the clergy.

> The lads an' lasses, blythely bent
> To mind baith saul an' body,   (both soul)
> Sit round the table, weel content,
> An' steer about the toddy.
> On this ane's dress, an' that ane's leuk, (one's look)
> They're makin observations;
> While some are cosy i' the neuk,   (nook)
> An' forming assignations
> To meet some day.

This earthy zest for life among the people of the taverns and streets contrasts sharply with the noisy portents of damnation preached by the minister in the church:

> Hear how he clears the points o' faith
> Wi' rattlin' an' wi' thumpin'!
> Now meekly calm, now wild in wrath,
> He's stampin' an' he's jumpin'!

Although the poem is satirical, it is basically good-humored. It shows Burns's intense love of life and people, his powers of observation, his fertile imagination, and his joyous appreciation of his colorful native speech. But it is one of Burns's strongest indictments of religious hypocrisy.

"TO A MOUSE":   Burns, the plowman poet, speaks in this piece to a "wee, sleekit, cowrin', tim'rous beastie," a little field mouse, whose home is destroyed because the earth has been tilled above it. He sees his own kinship with the mouse, and in the mouse's disaster, he sees the fate of all men. For men too try to store their gains against the future and are often prevented by unexpected disaster from doing so:

> The best laid schemes o' mice an' men
> Gang aft a-gley,   (often go astray)
> An' lea'e us nought but grief an' pain
> For promis'd joy.

The poem which emphasizes at its beginning the kinship between mouse and man, man's "fellow-mortal," stresses at the end the difference between the two. Unlike man, the mouse is incapable of hindsight or foresight, and so does not share the speaker's regrets and fears and pains:

> But och! I backward cast my e'e   (eye)
> On prospects drear!
> An' forward tho' I cannat see,
> I guess an' fear.

"TO A LOUSE":   These humorous verses are addressed to a louse crawling "Owre gauze and lace" of the bonnet of a country girl who has given herself elegant airs. She is seated in church in front of the speaker, who, as he watches the louse progress along the lady's hat, pretends outrage at its impudence for choosing so fine a place to dwell. A "poor body" or a "beggar's haffet squattle" are better suited to the lowly station of the louse. Nevertheless, the louse aspires to the lady's bonnet.

The next-to-last stanza is addressed to "Jenny," whose simple, common name betrays her true nature. Unheard by the proud beauty, the speaker gives her some friendly advice; she would not put on airs and toss her head so if she knew what was crawling on it. Finally, the speaker draws a general conclusion from the lesson he has learned in church. If only we could see ourselves as others do, we would be saved from many a folly:

> O wad some Pow'r the giftie gie us
> To see oursels as others see us!
> It wad frae mony a blunder free us,
> An' foolish notion:
> What airs in dress an' gait wad lea'e us,
> And ev'n devotion!

What is often overlooked in the otherwise simple reflection is the last line about "devotion." The speaker has been watching a louse in church; he has not been listening to the minister. Whatever he has learned about human nature or whatever moral he has drawn from his observations has come from one of the lowest creatures in nature, the louse, not the minister. We need not take on airs in dress, but neither must we learn morality in church.

"THE COTTER'S SATURDAY NIGHT":   This poem, first published in 1786, has long been one of the most popular of Burn's poems, but in many ways it is disappointing. Whereas the satires have bite and sting and show a truly marvelous ability to get special effects through the use of dialect, and the drinking songs ring in the memory and can be more exciting than the intoxicants they celebrate, and the love songs are sometimes tender, sometimes impudent but always original, "The Cotter's Saturday Night" is very imitative. Burns's inspiration was professedly Gray's *Elegy*. Like Gray, Burns is interested in "The short and simple annals of the poor." Himself a plowman and a proud and defiant man, Burns naturally directed his attention to this subject. In this poem, Burns seems to be trying too hard to be "literary," and the wonderful spontaneity we associate with his best work does not appear here.

Dedicated to Robert Aiken, an Ayrshire friend who is named in line 8, "The Cotter's Saturday Night" is written in the eighteenth-century English "graveyard" tradition. In the original

edition of the poem, Thomas Gray's *Elegy* provided an epigraph
from the stanza beginning "Let not ambition mock," and many
lines in "The Cotter's Saturday Night" are free paraphrases
from Gray's poem. The rustic life of humble folk is glorified in a
sentimental manner which should have embarrassed the poet, a
member of that class. But the sentimentality of the piece is in
keeping with Burns's own nature and with the tenor of the times.
Perhaps the only embarrassment ever suffered over the overweening "goodness" of the Cotter and his family is posterity's.

When the poem opens, the weary cottager is returning from his
chores at the end of a hard work-week. Greeted by his babes
and good wife, he forgets his toils and weariness. His older
children return from their nearby jobs, and last to come is
blooming Jenny with a new dress or, if her parents need it, the
money she has earned that week. As the obedient children listen
to the patriarchal advice of the Cotter, Jenny's new beau knocks
at the door. Fortunately, he is a respectful lad, not one of the
brash young rakes of the neighborhood, and Mother and Dad
welcome him in, to Jenny's relief and delight. "O happy love,
where love like this is found," Burns mawkishly exclaims over
Jenny and her beau. Then, although he was only twenty-six
when he wrote this poem, Burns claims that "sage experience
bids me this declare," that heaven's one gift of pleasure is
virtuous young love. He is a wretch and a villain who would
spoil Jenny's innocence.

A cheerful noisy supper of simple Scottish fare follows. Then
the group circles round the hearth for Bible reading and hymn
singing from the Old Testament or the New, and prayers follow.
The simple ritual is far superior, our poet points out, to all the
showy worship held at church. Then, the babes in their beds and
the older children gone back to their masters, the parents pray
alone for the welfare of their young. "But chiefly," as Calvinists, they pray that God will "in their hearts with grace divine
preside." We are told next that the greatness of Scotland rests
on this noble humble stock, who will get to heaven sooner than
any wretched nobleman. The poem ends with a prayer that
Scotland's noble peasants will never be corrupted by luxury and
that God will continue to bless the land with defenders like
Wallace and patriot-bards (like Burns?).

"The Cotter's Saturday Night" is representative of Burns in his sentimental depths. It is a far cry from the conviviality of his tavern songs, the demonic glee of his goblin poems, the free emotional outbursts of his love tunes, and the acid bite of his religious and social satires. But it would be unfair to say that "The Cotter's Saturday Night" is a hypocritical poem, for Burns was as capable of sentiment as he was of cynicism.

"TAM O'SHANTER": Burns's poems touch upon a wide range of subjects—love, the countryside, the pleasures of the tavern, and a host of others. One of his best-known narrative poems, written in 1790 and published in 1791, is the comic story of Tam o'Shanter. Not more than a mile from the poet's birthplace were the ruins of an old church, Alloway Kirk (kirk is Scottish for church), and many legends and stories of ghosts and witches were associated with this place. The Tam (that is, Tom) of the poem is, of course, a product of Burns's imagination, but there was a certain tenant farmer in a place called Shanter whose fondness for drink may have suggested some of the details in this wonderful story.

On market days in the eighteenth century, people would leave their farms and little villages and go into the nearby larger town to do their shopping. When necessary business had been attended to, friends met with friends and exchanged news and gossip. Sometimes they would find it convenient and pleasant to sit with their friends in a warm tavern. Sometimes men were known to stay in such taverns longer than was prudent. As we sit with our ale, says the poet, getting a bit muddled and very happy, we tend to forget the long Scots miles that lie between us and our home. We may even forget our wives. Burns gives us a memorable picture of the long-suffering and resentful wife at home "Gathering her brows like gathering storm, / Nursing her wrath to keep it warm."

In a tavern in the town of Ayr on one such market day sat honest Tam o'Shanter. Burns speaks affectionately of Ayr, the market town close to his birthplace—

> Auld Ayr, wham ne'er a town surpasses
> For honest men and bonnie lasses.

The comic tone of the poem is intensified by the raciness and homely vigor of Burns's native language. We are reminded that Tam's wife, Kate, had often told him that he was "a skellum [a good-for-nothing], / A bletherin', blusterin', drunken blellum [a blithering, blustering, drunken babbler]." And Kate had often told him too that some dark night he would be seized by witches near Alloway's "auld haunted kirk."

In spite of Kate's constant complaining, here on this particular market day was our hero, sitting in a cozy corner of a tavern with Souter Johnny (Johnny the Cobbler), "His ancient, trusty, drouthy [thirsty] crony." The night wore on with songs and chatter, all the pleasant noises of the tavern, "and aye the ale was growing better." Tam flirted with the landlady who was in the room to help her husband serve the drinks. Johnny told "his queerest stories" and "The landlord's laugh was ready chorus." Outside a storm might "rair (roar) and rustle," but Tam in these pleasant surroundings could not care less.

Pleasures, however, cannot last forever. "The hour approaches Tam maun [must] ride." It was close to midnight. The night was black. The wind howled and the rain was heavy.

> Loud, deep, and lang, the thunder bellow'd:
> That night, a child might understand,
> The Deil [Devil] had business on his hand.

Mounted on his gray mare, Meg, Tam clattered on through puddles and mud, with one hand trying to keep on his head "his gude blue bonnet" (the kind of cap we now in honor of the poem call a Tam o' Shanter) and all the while crooning an old Scots song. The wildness of the night made him more than a little nervous and he kept his eyes open lest bogles [hobgoblins] catch him. He was especially nervous as he approached Alloway Kirk "Whare ghaists and houlets [ghosts and owls] nightly cry."

Stories associated with Alloway raced through his mind. Now, for example, he was crossing the ford where a peddler had once smothered. Now he was going past the birch trees and the great stone "Where drunken Charlie brak's neck-bane" [broke his neck, literally, neck-bone]. He remembered other stories of terrible events, of murders and suicides. The storm grew worse. Lightning flashed. And there was Alloway Kirk, lit up by the streaks of lightning and looking as if on fire.

Whiskey and ale, however, can give a man courage. Tam's horse, called Meg or Maggie, was not so courageous and our bold and drunken hero had to urge her on. "And vow! [wow!] Tam saw an unco [wonderful, strange] sight!"

There before his eyes was "auld Nick" (Old Nick, the Devil himself), presiding over a witches' dance. Old Nick was "in shape o' beast / A touzle tyke [shaggy dog], black, grim, and large." The witches were dancing the wild country dances of eighteenth-century Scotland, "hornpipes, jigs, strathspeys, and reels." Old Nick himself was providing the music, naturally on bagpipes. Open coffins stood round and each corpse held a lighted candle in his cold hand. On the old altar of the church, the "haly [holy] table," were the skeleton of a murderer, two babies who had died without baptism (and who accordingly could not hope for heaven), a thief just cut down from the scaffold, five tomahawks covered with blood, five knives which had been used in murders, a garter "which a babe had strangled, and a blade used by a son to kill his own father."

While Tam looked on, "amaz'd and curious," the dance grew wilder. "The mirth and fun grew fast and furious." Although most of the dancers were withered old hags, there was one young witch who was very pretty. She was wearing a "cutty sark" [a short shift], "in longitude tho' sorely scanty." Tam could not take his eyes off this pretty witch in her fetching cutty sark and finally, unable to contain himself longer, he roared out "Well done, Cutty-sark!" The dance stopped immediately. Maggie galloped away with all the witches in hot pursuit. Tam knew that if he could once get to the bridge across the nearby river he would be safe for witches do not dare cross running water. But just before Meg could get to the middle of the bridge, the point of safety, one of the pursuers grabbed the mare's tail. "The carlin caught her by the rump / And left poor Maggie scarce a stump."

The poet pretends to end this superbly funny little story with a moral:

> Whene'er to drink you are inclin'd,
> Or cutty-sarks rin in your mind,
> Think! ye may buy the joys o'er dear;
> Remember Tam o' Shanter's mare.

The foregoing summary, of course, cannot convey the gusto of the poem itself. Burns is, among other things, one of the greatest comic poets in our literary history.

FRIENDSHIP AND CONVIVIAL SONGS: A songster of infinite variety, Robert Burns created, collected and edited lyrics of friendship, love, nature, brotherhood, and patriotism, which have never lost their human appeal. Wherever friends reunite, "for Auld Lang Syne," the song that Burns restored from the dusty annals of his country's culture is remembered and often sung. Burns's feelings about friendship, however, were expressed in many ways and in many other lyrics. One, which defies classification, but perhaps is best understood as a friendship poem, is "O, Wert Thou in the Cauld Blast." Written to his nurse during his final illness in 1796, the poem projects the gratitude Burns felt for the young lady who cared for him so well. It is singularly revealing of the heart of the poet that Burns's response to friendship and kindness was generosity. He would give his plaid to shield a friend from the cold winds "On yonder lea, on yonder lea." For Burns, a true friend could make a paradise of a desert or would be to him the brightest jewel in his crown if he were king.

Burns drank often in the spirit of friendship and love, and his convivial songs commemorate the joy of companionship over a cup. "Go fetch me a pint o' wine / An' fill it in a silver tassie; / That I may drink before I go, / A service to my lassie" is a cheerful parting song of this type. Others, "Green Grow the Rashes, O," "For A' That, An' A' That" and "Auld Lang Syne," are also drinking songs as well as songs of love, friendship, or brotherhood.

LOVE SONGS: Who in the first blush of young love fails to recall "O, my luve is like a red, red rose, / That's newly sprung in June"? The power of the impetuous male and his sincere commitment to love is felt in the hyperbole of Burns's promise to love "Till a' the seas gang dry, my dear, / And the rocks melt wi' the sun." In another love poem, a less confident, more tender, more romantic lover sighs at the lass's window, hoping for a glimpse of the smiling, gentle "Mary Morison," "Wha for thy sake wad gladly die."

Burns could sing convincingly of many kinds of love. In "John Anderson My Jo," the speaker is an older woman, married and devoted for many a long year to "John Anderson," whom she affectionately calls "my jo." Burns creates a simple and believable character in the wife who recalls her early love when "Your locks were like the raven," and the woman is united with her Highland country when she is made to see life as a hill to be climbed in youth. The fulfillment of love at the end of life is the slow descent:

> Now we maun totter down, John,
> And hand in hand we'll go,
> And Sleep thegither at the foot,
> John Anderson, my jo.

Burns sings also as a carefree lover, cheered by his drink in "Green Grow the Rashes, O" where he confesses with peasant virility that "The sweetest hours that e'er I spend, / Are spent amang the lasses, O." But his sincerity is no less strong because it is of the moment:

> But gie me a canny hour at e'en,
> My arms about my dearie, O;
> An' warly cares, an' warly men   (worldly)
> May a' gae tapsalteerie, O!   (topsy-turvy)

Nor was Burns immune to the tragedy of lost love. In "Highland Mary," the poet is concerned with the death of a young servant girl named Mary Campbell whom he met in the spring of 1786. They parted in May, promising to meet again, but Mary died the following fall. Burns shows that he felt death deeply and intimately understood it in terms of his natural environment:

> But oh! fell Death's untimely frost,
> That nipt my flower sae early!
> Now green's the sod, and cauld's the clay,
> That wraps my Highland Mary!

NATURE:　　Although nature plays an important part in Burns's works, he rarely uses it as his exclusive theme. As he shows in "Highland Mary," he understood human life in terms of nature, and nature in terms of human life. The world of the Highland farmer was intricately bound up in the soil and the seasons of his country, in the rocks of the Scottish hills, which made the farmer's life a hardship, and in the streams which fed the flocks and crops on which his life depended. When Burns thinks of the dead "Highland Mary," he recalls their parting along "Ye banks, and braes, and streams." And with deep affection for both girl and land, he envisions the countryside as a memorial to the girl:

> Green be your woods, and fair your flowers,
> Your waters never drumlie!
> . . . .
> For there I took the last farewell
> O' my sweet Highland Mary.

Nature plays a similar role in "Sweet Afton," where the poet sees the lovely noisy stream which flows between the hilly slopes of Cumnock parish, Ayrshire, as a potential disturber of his beloved Mary's rest: "My Mary's asleep by thy murmuring stream, / Flow gently, sweet Afton, disturb not her dream." In almost all his poems we are made aware of his beloved countryside, nostalgically recalled in "My Heart's in the Highlands" and "Ye Flowery Banks." It is abundantly clear that Burns loved the banks and braes and streams and fields of Scotland and effectively uses its scenery and settings in almost all his poems.

BROTHERHOOD AND PATRIOTISM:　　It was not only his country-side which Burns loved so devoutly, but the humble people in it, and the country which they had built. His love of man and love of country ring out in song after song of Burns's composition. His praise of the poor man is nowhere better expressed than in "For A' That, An' A' That." Poverty is no reason for shame: "Is there, for honest poverty, / That hangs his head, and a' that? / The coward slave, we pass him by, / We dare be poor for a' that!"

Fiercely proud of his Scottish heritage, Burns wrote some of his finest songs in praise of his nation. "It Was A' for Our Rightfu' King" is one, "Fragment of Ode to Prince Charles Edward" another. But Burns's love of country is perhaps best seen in "Scots Wha Hae" in which the warrior spirit of Scotland, Robert Bruce, addresses his army before the Battle of Bannockburn:

> Scots wha hae wi' Wallace bled,
> Scots, wham Bruce has aften led,
> Welcome to your gory bed,
> Or to victorie!

Under Bruce, the Scots won a glorious victory over England at Bannockburn in 1314, and Scotsmen of the eighteenth century who obeyed an English king were proud to recall the power and independence of their ancestors.

CRITICISM: Burns's first volume of verse, *Poems, Chiefly in the Scottish Dialect,* published at Kilmarnock in 1786, was an immediate success. Of the six hundred copies issued in the first edition, three hundred and fifty had been sold in advance, and the rest sold out within two months. Besides gratifying the vanity of the aspiring young poet, the sale of his first volume saved Burns from the terrors of jail with which he was being threatened by Jean Armour's father, and it prevented him from shipping out to Jamaica where he had intended to escape from Armour's legal claims. An account of the reception given to the Kilmarnock volume by an unreliable contemporary named Robert Heron may be exaggerated, but it suggests the spirit in which the poems were greeted: "Old and young, high and low, grave and gay, learned and ignorant, were alike delighted, agitated, transported. . . . I can well remember how even ploughboys and maid-servants would have gladly bestowed the wages they earned most hardly . . . if they might procure the works of Burns." Not only people of his own class, but men and women of rank, like Dugald Steward and Mrs. Dunlop of Dunlop were impressed with his work and asked to meet him. (See Principal Shairp, *Robert Burns,* n.d., pp. 33–34; and Robert Heron, "Original Memoirs . . . ," *The Monthly Magazine and British Register,* London, January-June, 1797.)

The poems were sent by a friend to an Edinburgh poet and began to circulate among appreciative critics of Edinburgh journals. By November 1786, a highly favorable review of the Kilmarnock poems had appeared in *The Edinburgh Magazine.* Henry MacKenzie, the novelist, wrote another for the widely circulated *Lounger* (December 9, 1786), in which he insisted that Burns's original genius was an absolute quality not a relative one and that in judging his verse, allowances need not be made for his class. MacKenzie was deeply impressed by Burns's delineation of manner, emotions, and natural scenery, and proclaimed him a great national poet. The English poet Cowper read and enjoyed the poems, finding them "a very extraordinary production" and calling Burns the first poet of humble rank since Shakespeare. (Shairp, pp. 38, 46–47.)

Burns's death in 1796 was followed by a deluge of biographical accounts, which even in the 1960's are still being written. One of the first of these accounts by Robert Heron gave the public just what it was waiting for; it provided a vivid account of the poet's alleged alcoholism and debauchery and attributed Burns's death to these excesses. Not that Heron's scandal could reduce the public's appreciation of Burns's poems; it did not. But Heron succeeded in surrounding Burns's life with a cloud, which biographers to this day are still trying to disperse. Heron's story was picked up by subsequent biographers, Dr. Currie (1800), John Lockhart (1828), Allan Cunningham (1834), and appears in the otherwise fine biography of Robert Chambers (*Life and Works,* 1851–52).

Early critics who were ostensibly reviewing Burns's poetry could not ignore the character of the poet, because the scandal was by then on everyone's tongue. Francis Jeffrey's review of *Reliques of Robert Burns,* published by R. H. Cromek (1808), was really an essay on the character of Burns. Although Jeffrey appreciated the poetry, he could not get over Burns's lowly origins. To Jeffrey, Burns was both "a great and original genius," and a vulgar and "unlettered plough-boy." (*Edinburgh Review,* XIII, January 1809, p. 249, ff.) In a review of the same book for the *Quarterly Review,* Sir Walter Scott, too, could not forget Burns's peasant stock. He assumed a patronizing attitude toward the Scottish plowman, but he also was the first to praise "The Jolly Beggars" and to analyze with acute perception Burns's method of writing songs. Scarcely a ballad passed through Burns's hands, Scott wrote, "without receiving some of those magic touches which . . . restored its original spirit, or gave it more than it had ever possessed." (I, February 1809, p. 30.)

Later, when Thomas Carlyle reviewed Lockhart's *Life of Burns,* he fell into the same trap as his predecessors, accepting the tradition that Burns was an alcoholic, but showing the utmost sympathy toward his poetry in itself. (*Edinburgh Review,* XLVIII, December 1828, p. 267, ff.)

A few early writers tried to whitewash Burns's reputation, but their efforts were ineffectual. Despite the kind words Jeffrey and Scott had had for Burns's poetic genius, their attitude toward the man himself could not escape notice. Both critics were chastised for their unfair treatment of the poet in the anonymous and hardly influential edition of *Poems by Robert Burns,* 2 vols., Cambridge, 1811. Alexander Peterkin wrote a defensive preface to his new edition of Currie's *Life and Works of Burns*; then he published Currie's *Life,* leaving the Burns scandal intact (Edinburgh, 1815). Another editor, Hamilton Paul, defended Burns against attacks of blasphemy, claiming he saved religion from the fanatics. But he too accepted as fact Burns's immorality and voiced his disapproval of the man. (Preface to *The Poems and Songs of Robert Burns,* Ayre, 1819.)

The numerous publications of lives and works during the nineteenth century attest to Burns's continuing popularity among the later Victorians—the best of these was *Poetry* (1896–7), edited by W. E. Henley and T. F. Henderson. Henley's biographical essay pointed out Burns's place in the popular tradition of Scottish literature and offered a sound description of how Burns reworked old songs. He also showed that Highland Mary was not the ideal lass that legend had made her, and repeated the old saw that Burns's last years were decadent ones. Henley insisted, however, that the real Burns was better than the Burns that Victorian biographers had invented. (See R. T. Fitzhugh, *Robert Burns: His Associates and Contemporaries,* Chapel Hill, 1943, p. 4.) But Henley's biographical attitude turned out to be highly controversial and was censured by enough critics to fill a book. (See *Henley and Burns, or, The Critic Censured,* ed. J. D. Ross, 1901.)

The popularity of Burns continued into the twentieth century for at least three decades; then, gradually, it diminished. A ten-volume edition of the *Works,* edited by John Buchan, appeared in London and Boston in 1929; and Catherine Carswell and F. B. Snyder wrote new lives of Burns in 1930 and 1932, respectively. About the same time De Lancey Ferguson produced a definitive edition of Burns's undoctored letters. (*The Letters of Robert Burns,* 2 vols., Oxford, 1931.) The aim of most of these modern scholars was to restore the "real" Burns to his own biography. Most of them now agree with Henley that the real Burns is better than the legend. As De Lancey Ferguson put it, Burns was not so much a conspicuous sinner as one who sinned conspicuously. Robert T. Fitzhugh, for another, viewed Burns "as a racy, salty, masculine countryman with immense gusto and a shrewd, not to say Rabelaisian, eye for men and their ways." Fitzhugh reminds us that Burns drank but was not a drunkard, that he was not so much a sinner as a passionate man and that his poetry may very well be great because of this nature. (*Robert Burns,* pp. 4–5.)

Of Burns's individual poems, many are too short to merit consideration as great ones, but "Tam o'Shanter," a longer poem, has been singled out as a masterpiece. " 'Tam,' " De Lancey Ferguson wrote, "is not only Burns's greatest single poem but one of the finest short poetic narratives in all litera-ture. . . . In the versified folk-tale 'Tam' stands alone." (*Pride and Passion* [1939], New York, 1964, pp. 264–65.) Aside from the lyrics and songs, "Tam o'Shanter" is the one poem most often studied by critics of our day, and from time to time a new dimension is added to our understanding of the meaning or techniques of this major work. (See M. L. MacKenzie, *Studies in Scottish Literature,* I, 1963, pp. 87–92; and Richard Morton, *Modern Language Quarterly,* XXII, 1961, pp. 12–20.)

Of his lyrics, we have learned much that there is to tell from
Walter Scott, W. E. Henley, and De Lancey Ferguson. Burns's
lyrics were inspired by either an emotion or a piece of music,
and the poet always added to the composition whichever element had not initiated the work. He was an innovator too,
mastering the art of the dramatic lyric and the dramatic monologue long before Browning gave these forms their names.
Although the songs often derive from "personal emotion," they
are not always personal history but often products of artistic
invention. (*Pride and Passion,* pp. 235–36, 250.)

The few critical assessments of Burns which have followed
Ferguson's generally characterize the Kilmarnock volume as
"one of the most remarkable first volumes ever published by a
British poet." (David Daiches, *Robert Burns,* New York, 1950,
p. 104.) No one at present cares to diminish Burns's reputation,
but few critics have felt obliged to advance it. The occasional
full-length studies of Burns which continue to appear tend to
come out of Scotland where the desire to perpetuate Burns's
reputation is entirely understandable. (See Thomas Crawford,
Burns: A Study of the Poems and Songs, Edinburgh, 1960;
E. S. Rae, *Poet's Pilgrimage: A Study of the Life and Times of
Robert Burns,* Glasgow, 1960; and R. D. Thornton, *James
Currie, the Entire Stranger, and Robert Burns,* Edinburgh and
London, 1963.) Once in a rare while, a new edition of Burns's
poems appears, such as J. C. Weston's edition of *The Jolly
Beggars: A Cantata* (Northampton, Mass., 1963). A few biog-
raphers are still at work on the restoration of the "real" Burns,
such as R. D. Thornton (see above) and David Daiches ("The
Identity of Burns," *Restoration and Eighteenth-Century Litera-
ture,* XVII, 1965, pp. 323–40).

Perhaps, if the new biographers succeed in separating the poet
entirely from his legend, this generation will have little more to
say about Burns. Despite the paucity of Burns essays and
articles in recent years, his tribute continues to be paid whenever a sweet singer chants one of his songs, or a new reader
laughs at his satirical poems, or an old one, recollecting the
early pleasure of reading Burns, returns to his verse for re-
freshment.

WILLIAM WORDSWORTH

William Wordsworth did perhaps more than any other poet of his time to implement the Romantic revolution in English letters which took place during the nineteenth century. Along with his good friend Samuel Taylor Coleridge, Wordsworth published the first poetry of the new era in the *Lyrical Ballads* of 1798. Two years later in a preface to the second edition of the *Lyrical Ballads,* Wordsworth presented the manifesto of Romantic poetry, releasing to the public a whole new set of principles by which Wordsworth's and the next generation of poets would be writing. Although few poets consciously imitated Wordsworth, and although even his best friend Coleridge tore his poetic theory to ribbons, no one was willing or able to push back the Romantic tide which Wordsworth let loose.

LIFE: Born in Cockermouth, Cumberland, in the Lake District of northwestern England on April 7, 1770, William Wordsworth was orphaned at an early age. Sent to Hawkshead School at the age of eight, Wordsworth was left free to wander about the countryside of northern England, which is noted for its impressive scenery, lovely lakes, beautiful waterfalls, awesome mountains, picturesque castles, churches, and Roman ruins. Here Wordsworth developed the love of nature which sustained him all his life. In 1787, he entered St. James College, Cambridge. After a promising start, his interest in study gradually declined, and he received a degree without honors in 1791. What interested him more were his long vacations. He would return to Hawkshead, visit his sister Dorothy at Penrith, or take walking tours through the English countryside and in Europe.

A walking tour through France, Italy, and Switzerland in 1790 aroused in the young poet an interest in the French Revolution. Wordsworth soon became an ardent republican and his revolutionary fervor prompted many of his early poems. Two years later, Wordsworth was back in France. He fell in love with Annette Vallon, a young Frenchwoman of good family, who became the mother of his child. Recalled to England by his guardians, Wordsworth was prevented from returning to Annette when war between England and France broke out in February 1793. For several years, reunion was impossible, and the result of this separation was estrangement. The two never married. He saw her again in 1802 and made arrangements for the support of his daughter before marrying Mary Hutchinson whom he had known for many years. Receiving a small bequest from a friend in 1795, Wordsworth settled with his sister Dorothy in a cottage at Racedown, Dorset. There he met Samuel Taylor Coleridge, and the friendship which proved to be of such great significance for both poets began to develop.

In 1798, the two poets published *Lyrical Ballads,* containing poems mainly by Wordsworth, a few by Coleridge. The following year, Wordsworth, Dorothy, and Coleridge set off for a brief tour of Germany. Upon their return, Wordsworth and Dorothy settled in Dove Cottage, Grasmere, in Westmoreland. Except for brief excursions, Wordsworth spent the remainder of his life in the Lake Country. He married in 1802 and had five children. In 1813, he was appointed stamp-distributor for Westmoreland, a position which considerably eased his financial burdens. After this time, his reputation as a poet gradually improved, until, in 1843, he became Poet Laureate of England. He died in 1850 at the age of eighty.

TWO PERIODS: Although it is possible to divide Wordsworth's life into four periods—1) the happy motherless days in the Cumberland Hills, 2) the revolutionary period, beginning with the first visit to France in 1790, 3) his most creative poetic period, 1798–1815, 4) the period of decline, 1815–1850—it is customary to speak of Wordsworth's poetic career as having only two periods. The earlier period is generally regarded as the more successful one, when Wordsworth wrote most of his great poetry, when his politics were liberal, his religion ambiguous. The later period, beginning about 1807, after the publication of *Poems in Two Volumes,* is usually counted as the period of his gradual decline as a poet. Wordsworth wrote a great deal of occasional verse during this later period and spent much of his time reworking, polishing, and finishing poems started in the earlier years. Because the later period saw the fulfillment of work long since begun, it is considered by some critics, not as a period of decline, but as a period of maturity during which the promise of his early years was fulfilled. The second period is also marked by a change in Wordsworth's political and religious views. Whereas in 1793 he had been a revolutionist, by 1798 (perhaps even sooner) his attitude toward France with Napoleon in power began to change, and by 1802, his political opposition to Napoleon was explicit. By 1813, when he became stamp-distributor, he was clearly conservative. In his earlier years, he had displayed no interest in the church, and his poetry seemed almost pagan in tone; in the later years, however, he became a pillar of the Anglican Church, writing the *Ecclesiastical Sonnets* and other poems which signified his new frame of mind. He had come to believe that man's wild spirits needed taming by the church.

PHILOSOPHY: Wordsworth believed that it was through the permanent forms of nature that God was revealed to man. His best poetry is the lofty and sublime expression of the divine solace and comfort which he found in nature.

Not a deist, Wordsworth is nevertheless linked with deism because he infers a Creator from his creation. Not a transcendentalist, Wordsworth is associated with that group because he believed that the soul, instructed by the senses and by nature, transcends both and becomes assimilated with a divine totality. Wordsworth's philosophy of nature had always incorporated within it necessities of change from joy to pleasure to quietism, and to a large extent, these changes explain what critics have chosen to call his "decline."

In Wordsworth's thinking, man's life is divided into three stages. The awareness of the child is totally sensuous and unself-conscious. But his experience of the world is more spiritual than he knows, more unified, and more joyful because his senses respond to experience in a pure and innocent way. As the child matures into youth, he becomes more self-conscious. The joy is tempered by a sense of loss, and his perception is no longer unified, but disturbingly dualized. The youth sees and remembers the things that have once produced his sense of joy. He still finds pleasure in experience, but he is conscious of the missing element of joy, and begins to ask why. As the youth matures, he develops wisdom. He learns in his maturity to understand the triple stages of man's life and, through the wisdom achieved in maturity, he experiences a new kind of happiness. It is not the unconscious joy of the child, or the pleasure of awareness which the young man feels, but the contentment of wisdom of the older man. It is in the final stage of life that man can re-identify with nature, not with his senses alone as the child knew it, not with the conscious pleasure of the youth, but with his soul as only the mature man can understand it. Wordsworth's later poetry reflects the contentment and mature wisdom of his philosophy. It no longer expresses the conflict and perplexities of a youthful searcher. Because the passion for life and the conflict which the earlier poetry reflects often do not appear in the later works, critics have often judged the "quietism" Wordsworth achieved in his later years as a mark of "decline."

Throughout this explanation, the word "nature" has been used —a word which Wordsworth uses frequently and which has laid him open to charges of paganism. What Wordsworth meant in his philosophy of nature is not that God *is* nature, but that nature is a *manifestation* of God's creation in its purest, most uncorrupted form. It is through nature that man communicates with God, learns about God, and enjoys the holy and awesome feelings which are religious feelings. In this sense, "nature" is a metaphor for God in Wordsworth's poetry, not a synonym. Wordsworth's poetry of nature, however, is susceptible to more than one interpretation. Wordsworth has been seen as a pantheist who views nature as God himself, or as a concrete idealist who believes that ideal truth is manifest in visible, tangible, phenomenological aspects of reality.

Wordsworth's concept of the child, an important figure in his philosophy and in his poetry, is derived from Rousseauvian and Platonic philosophy. Rousseau had taught the divine nature of the child, and Plato had supplied the doctrine of pre-existence and immortality which Wordsworth incorporated into his own thinking. He believed in immortality, in the idea that the soul lives forever. This meant, to Wordsworth, that the pure soul exists before birth as well as after death. During life, the secrets of the soul are hidden to humans. But the child, because he has lived for so short a time, is still close to the state of pre-existence. His birth into human form has erased from his conscious memory the pre-life of his soul, but there is still an unimpaired subconscious memory of eternal bliss, which allows the child, through his human senses, to respond to nature and the world with instinctive joy and with the innocence of a pure soul. The child, then, Wordsworth believed, has a special kind of wisdom to which men can turn for instruction. In addition, because childhood perceptions are remembered in youth and later maturity, the mature man can use this memory to learn of the continuity of his own existence. He can acquire a sense of wholeness within himself and a sense of identification with God. In 1802, in "My Heart Leaps Up," Wordsworth wrote:

> The Child is father of the Man;
> And I could wish my days to be
> Bound each to each by natural piety.

WORKS: Although Wordsworth's poetry received little critical acclaim until after 1820, he continued to write all during his life and produced a quantity of poetry too numerous to list or discuss in this brief survey. Among the titles published during his life were: *An Evening Walk* (1793); *Lyrical Ballads* (1798; 1800; 1802; 1815); *Poems* (1807); *The Excursion* (1814); *Collected Works* (1815); *The River Duddon* (1820); *Yarrow Revisited and Other Poems* (1835). *The Prelude* (1850) was published posthumously as was *The Recluse, a fragment* (1888).

Among the individual poems appearing in the various collections, the more famous ones are: "Written in Very Early Youth" (1786); "Dear Brook, Farewell" (1787–89); "Lines" (1795); "The Reverie of Poor Susan" (1797); "We Are Seven" (1798); "The Thorn" (1798); "Goody Blake" (1798); "Her Eyes Are Wild" (1798); "Simon Lee" (1798); "Lines Written in Early Spring" (1798); "To My Sister" (1798); "Expostulation and Reply" (1798); "Tintern Abbey" (1798); "Nutting" (1799); The "Lucy Poems" (1799); "Matthew" (1799); "Lucy Gray" (1799); "Michael" (1800); "My Heart Leaps Up" (1802); "Resolution and Independence" (1802); "Westminister Bridge" (1802); "It Is a Beauteous Evening" (1802); "To Toussaint L'Ouverture" (1802); "London, 1802" (1802); "The Solitary Reaper" (1803); "She Was a Phantom of Delight" (1804); "I Wandered Lonely as a Cloud" (1804); "The Affliction of Margaret" (1804); "Ode to Duty" (1805); "Elegiac Stanzas" (1805); "Nuns Fret Not" (1806); "The World Is Too Much with Us" (1806); "Ode: Intimations of Immortality" (1802–6); "Composed upon an Evening of Extraordinary Splendour" (1818); "To a Skylark" (1825); "A Poet!—He Hath Put His Heart to School" (1842).

"WRITTEN IN VERY EARLY YOUTH": This early sonnet with its unusual rhyme scheme (abba, acca, ccdd, ad) was first published in 1802. It contains a number of ideas and images of nature, which Wordsworth continued to use in his later and more important poems. In addition, the sonnet reveals the inner turmoil of the young poet, who finds momentary peace and comfort in nature. Later in his life, the comfort was to become more enduring. The image of the wheel, which Wordsworth used for the moving universe, appears in a state of rest in the first line of the sonnet: "Calm is all nature as a resting wheel." The idea of resting nature is amplified in the first six lines. Nature's healing powers for the troubled man are asserted in the next four-and-a-half lines, and the poem concludes with an address to friends who have tried to comfort the poet in vain, for only nature can provide the solace he seeks.

LYRICAL BALLADS, WITH A FEW OTHER POEMS

The friendship and collaboration of Wordsworth and Coleridge (and Dorothy Wordsworth) led to the publication in 1798 of a book that marks the "official" opening of the English Romantic period. Although the book opened with Coleridge's justly famous "The Rime of the Ancient Mariner" (which will be discussed in a later chapter) and closed with Wordsworth's now recognized masterpiece "Lines Composed a Few Miles above Tintern Abbey" ("Tintern Abbey"), it was not well received by critics of the time. Not all the poems in *Lyrical Ballads* are successful ones, and there is some justification in the adverse criticism, but much that was remarkably good was overlooked because it was new and highly experimental, and the critics were not quite ready for change.

Despite its poor critical reception, the book sold fairly well, and in 1800 Wordsworth prepared a second edition, to which he added a second volume of his poems. He signed his name to this edition (although neither poet had signed the first one), and, encouraged by Coleridge, he wrote a Preface in which he explained what he and his friend were trying to do in this experiment.

THE PREFACE: Wordsworth's Preface was a "defense of the theory upon which the poems were written." The first edition of poems had been a conscious experiment in which he and Coleridge had set aside conventional poetic diction, the language of neoclassical poetry. The poetry of the new era would speak "as far as was possible . . . language really used by men." It would present ordinary incidents and situations in an imaginative way, and would deal with man's reactions to life "in a state of excitement." To declare the lives of common men fit subjects for poetry, to proclaim their language proper diction for poems, and to insist on emotional excitement as the proper psychological state for the poet's attention was to defy all the major tenets of the neoclassical code. Nature to Augustan poets had meant "human" nature, and the best human types were those in the court and in the cities where the most urbane subjects could be found. Their language naturally would be literary, elegant, sophisticated, and their emotional state would be, at its best, temperate, well modulated, and restrained. The truths these great subjects would reveal were the truths of ancient Rome. They were not the human truths for which Wordsworth sought and which he believed he could only find in "humble or rustic life." To Wordsworth, it was the simple man, living close to nature, unrestrained in feeling and speech by the tempering influences of an urbane society, who would express the essential truths of humanity which are "beautiful and permanent forms of nature."

Hopefully, the reader was to find that each of the poems had high purpose, a purpose not always directly stated, but one which was carried along by the noble feelings of the poet. The poetry thus produced would be "the spontaneous overflow of powerful feelings." This did not mean an emotional outburst contrived on the spur of the moment, but "emotion recollected in tranquillity," feelings experienced in the past and contemplated later by the poet until those feelings were imaginatively recalled. In a way, the poet would experience a double sensation and convert that imaginative experience into verse.

The objects which excited these emotions were to be ordinary ones: a tree, a mountain, an old man. For Wordsworth believed that he could serve the reader by helping him develop his powers of thought through contemplation of the real and the ordinary. There was altogether too much sensationalism in the Gothic literature of his day, Wordsworth felt. The excitement of this literature was kindled through external strangeness, not through inner thoughtfulness. It was toward the cultivation of the latter that Wordsworth aimed.

The style selected for the new poetry was also to be simple. "Personifications of abstract ideas" were mainly avoided by the poet in order to imitate "the very language of men"; he also chose to avoid what is called "poetic diction," describing his subjects from life, not in imitation of traditional literary types in conventional phrases and figures of speech. Wordsworth did not mean, however, that he planned to imitate life as a portrait or landscape painter might, but that he would look at the object steadily until he was able to understand its essential nature and thus simplify and generalize his description. The language, except where the meter required it, was to differ "in no respect . . . from the language of good prose."

Wordsworth's definition of poetry and his description of the poem which appeared in the Preface are often overlooked. But these reveal Wordsworth's personal aims and attitudes and have a close bearing on his poetic theory. Wordsworth believed a poet is "a man speaking to man," but he is a more feeling and more sensitive man, one "who rejoices more than other men in the spirit of life that is in him." Wordsworth affirms the Aristotelian classification of poetry as "the most philosophic of all writing," whose object is not a specific truth but a "general and operative" truth, and he argues that the poet is free in all respects but one. He must give pleasure. In accepting this requirement, the poet indirectly acknowledges "the beauty of the universe." He pays homage "to the native and naked dignity of man" when he agrees to provide the pleasure through which man acquires knowledge. Thus, in Wordsworth's opinion, the poet "binds together by passion and knowledge the vast empire of human society, as it is spread over the whole earth, and over all time."

Wordsworth's poetic practice did not always coincide with the poetic theory of his Preface, nor were his statements always valid. He did not solve the problem of language, for example; the "language really used by men" can be tedious, and often dull and prosy, as Wordsworth's sometimes is. Furthermore, Wordsworth's own poetic language is not consistent. He often, quite properly, uses elevated language, especially in reflective passages, which is far removed from the language of everyday life. He is mistaken in citing Milton as a poet whose language differs "in no respect . . . from the language of good prose." Milton's syntax is usually consistent with good prose syntax; his diction, however, is often literary, sophisticated, and ornate; his personifications and other figures of speech are numerous. Wordsworth is correct in recognizing the greatness of Milton, but he does not seem to know why he is great.

Although parts of Wordsworth's theory are vague and inconclusive, there is little doubt as to his purposes. He saw that poetry was becoming increasingly remote from the concerns of men, was becoming increasingly artificial in some respects, overly sensational in others. Many poets were merely repeating their predecessors and had run out of important things to say. Wordsworth (and Coleridge) proposed to put poetry back on the right track, to restore its spiritual and moral significance, and to relate it to the permanent concerns of men.

"WE ARE SEVEN":   This is one of Wordsworth's fullest statements of his conception of the child. In sixteen quatrains and a final emphatic five-line stanza, Wordsworth describes a "little cottage girl," one of his simple children of nature, who at eight experiences life through all the senses, "feels its life in every limb." Intuitively, she sees into the heart of things. She is aware of the continuity of life through death and insists that although two of her siblings are dead, "we are seven." Her adult companion patiently tries to reason with the child by explaining the facts of life and arithmetic. "If two are in the churchyard laid, / Then ye are only five." But the simple child insists, "O master! we are seven." "But they are dead; those two are dead!" the older man cries in exasperation, even as he realizes that it is like throwing words away, for the child patiently repeats, "We are seven!" The adult speaker who ascribes "willfulness" to the child is, in Wordsworth's view, the stubborn one. He fails to comprehend the essential unity of the human experience in death as well as in life, and he refuses to be guided to truth by the instinctive wisdom of the child.

"THE THORN":   In twenty-two stanzas of eleven octosyllabic lines, formed by irregular and varying rhyme schemes, the poet tells an old story of a woman's suffering. The betrayed woman grieves by a mound which looks like an infant's grave. The mound is a beautiful, many-hued, mossy hillock beside which grows an aged thorn, a thorn so old it has no prickles left, nor leaves, but only a "mass of knotted joints." No one knows why the woman goes to the hillock on the mountain top. But they do know that twenty years ago she was betrothed to a man who forgot his vow and married another. For six months, Martha Ray (as she was called) climbed the mountain top; "She was with child and she was mad." The neighbors are sure that the babe is buried there, but when they tried to dig it up and bring its mother to justice, the whole mound stirred. No one tries to disturb the grave any more, nor can the strange stirring be explained. But this much is certain, that the thorn is entwined with the grave moss, which tries "to drag it to the ground," and that Martha can be heard crying on the mountain top, "Oh misery! oh misery!"

The story of Martha and the thorn deals with a situation common among ordinary men and women (the betrayed mother theme), and the pain of grief the abandoned mother feels is, in Wordsworth's eyes, a fundamental human passion, symbolized by the ancient and grotesque thorn. The stirring of the ground over the infant's grave belongs to a pattern of folk superstition that is also a part of humble life. But Wordsworth, whose "scientific" eye rarely misunderstood natural phenomena, supplies enough information for the naturalist's conjecture that the moss covering the grave and spreading wide over the ground is certain to stir when any part of it is disturbed. Overly sentimental and sometimes ludicrous (note Martha's language, "Oh misery," etc.), the poem is redeemed by its mood descriptions of the thorn, mound, and mountain, which reflect the feelings of the grieving woman and supply appropriate, if Romantic, atmosphere for the feelings of awe and sympathy over the human condition.

"GOODY BLAKE AND HARRY GILL":   Subtitled "a true story," the poem tells a moral tale of Goody Blake, a poor old crone who, when she was cold, would steal sticks for her fire from the hedge of rich Harry Gill. But Harry suspected and begrudged the poor woman's thefts and lay in wait for her night after night. One night, trapped by the selfish farmer, Goody invoked a curse of eternal coldness upon Harry Gill. From then on, Harry was never warm again. The poem ends with the moral:

>Now think, ye farmers all, I pray,
>Of Goody Blake and Harry Gill!

Modern readers have all but lost their taste for stories of this kind, although children still enjoy tales with explicit meanings. Nevertheless, the Gothic element of the curse enforced by a mysterious power for the purpose of punishing evil has a lasting appeal to that part of us which will always be a child.

"SIMON LEE":   A tale that is no tale, the point of "Simon Lee" is a feeling not an idea—the feeling of profound sadness over the excessive gratitude of Simon for a trivial favor. Wordsworth is fully aware that his lengthy introduction, in which Simon and his early life are described, seems to be leading to a story. Therefore, he cautions the reader more than midway through the poem that there will be no story, at least none of the usual kind, "but should you think, / Perhaps a tale you'll make it." Sorely misunderstood by many readers, "Simon Lee" is actually one of the "experiments" Wordsworth described in his Preface. It provides a simple description of a simple man, with the aim of provoking thought and arousing the sympathetic passions of the reader. Wordsworth consciously refuses in this poem to supply any of the mysterious external sensations (such as the stirring grave of "The Thorn" or the supernatural curse of "Goody Blake and Harry Gill") to excite the passions of his readers. Instead, he asks the reader to "think" and hopes that, in contemplation of the "ordinary" behavior of Simon, the reader will discover, as the poet did, certain human truths and moral point.

"LINES WRITTEN IN EARLY SPRING": Another poem in which the poet is saddened by thoughts of human alienation, this is also one of Wordsworth's most beautiful statements of his philosophy of nature: "I heard a thousand blended notes, / While in a grove I sate reclined." Wordsworth's ability to find solace and pause for reflection in nature is stated in the second stanza: "To her fair works did Nature link / The human soul that through me ran." His reflections, however, concern humanity, which has turned away from nature: "And much is grieved my heart to think / What man has made of man."

As he observes the primrose tufts, and the periwinkle, the birds, and budding twigs, he is convinced that in each natural object "there was pleasure there." The idea that inanimate objects can feel pleasure, if correctly understood as "Nature's holy plan," explains why the poet must lament "what man has made of man." Lines 21 and 22 juxtapose "heaven" and "Nature," which should caution the reader to observe that Wordsworth acknowledges heaven before nature. He ʾlizes that his knowledge and his beliefs are drawn from his observations of concrete and material nature, but he supposes that his thoughts about nature may be heaven-sent.

"TINTERN ABBEY": Perhaps the best introduction to Wordsworth's ideas may be found in the meditative poem which closed the first edition of the *Lyrical Ballads*. Pretentiously entitled "Lines Composed a Few Miles above Tintern Abbey, on Revisiting the Banks of the Wye During a Tour, July 13, 1798," the poem is more popularly known as "Tintern Abbey," although the abbey is not described in the poem at all. The

poem expresses the three states of awareness, which Wordsworth believed accompanied the three stages of human life:
childhood, youth, maturity. It reflects the poet's emotions and
associations, his belief in the soothing and tutelary powers of
nature, and in the power of the imagination to color ordinary
situations.

In 1793, Wordsworth had visited the Wye valley in Monmouth-
shire near southeastern Wales. He was twenty-three when he
made his first tour of the region. Five years later, a more
experienced, wearier, more disillusioned man, he returned with
his sister Dorothy for "a ramble of four or five days." By this
time Wordsworth had been to France, had met Annette Vallon,
and had spent many months in the disquieting city of London.
England had been at war with France for five years, Napoleon
had risen in power, and France had become an aggressor nation
to the disappointment of many of her former advocates. With a
small inheritance, Wordsworth had managed to send for Dorothy and settle with her in a country house in Racedown where
he slowly began to recover from his worldly depression. The
short ramble along the Wye came at about the end of this
period of dejection.

The poem begins by noting that five years have passed since he
last beheld "these steep and lofty cliffs" which have a power
over nature and the poet. They create "a wild secluded scene."
Visible to the eye and to the poet's inner mind, the cliffs link the
divers parts of nature, "and connect / The landscape with the
quiet of the sky." The vista which spreads before the poet is
rich in natural beauty. Seen from the distant bank on which the
poet stands, the fruit trees are diminutive "orchard-tufts," their
green foliage and green fruits blending into the green landscape.
The hedgerows look like "little lines" which thread unevenly
across the pastures like "sportive wood run wild," and smoke
rising through the trees (perhaps from cottages hidden by
foliage) suggests that a lone vagrant or hermit is dwelling in the
woods.

These are the natural formations which the poet has remembered during his five years' absence from the Wye valley and
which he now sees again (and sees still a third time through

recollection and imagination as he composes the poem). These are the objects of memory which elevated his mind and restored his peace when, wearied by "the din / Of towns and cities," the poet turned inward to draw upon the resources of his memory and imagination.

Nature has a special significance for Wordsworth. It does more than give temporary pleasure; it affects his whole being. The poem itself is a "recollection in tranquillity" of the 1798 visit to the Wye; it includes, in addition, the memory of the 1793 visit, and the memories retained during the five-year interval. One vision is associated with another, and all are joined harmoniously within the poem. But nature has still another value for Wordsworth. It has the power of transmitting "feelings too / Of unremembered pleasure," moral feelings which are "that best portion of a good man's life," moral feelings which derive from forgotten events, or go back to a pre-existent state when the entire soul was pure, an innocent and moral essence. These feelings too, although "unremembered," constitute the "best portion of a good man's life."

Above all, Wordsworth believes the "beauteous forms" of the Wye landscape bestow

> another gift,
> Of aspect more sublime; that blessed mood,
> In which the burthen of the mystery,
> In which the heavy and the weary weight
> Of all this unintelligible world,
> Is lightened. . . .

Nature provides solace for man; it lightens his burden of humanity. The "beauteous forms" of nature lull the human passions into a state of repose so that the poet may "become a living soul," a pure soul which can penetrate the corporeal forms of things and "see into the life of things." It is through a power in nature, then, that the poet transcends nature's material forms and contemplates a higher, more divine state of being.

His belief in the transcendent powers of nature, however vain they may be, is, nevertheless, true for him, the poet asserts:

"How often has my spirit turned to thee." With Kantian logic, Wordsworth reasons that his beliefs in higher powers are based on his needs; therefore, although his beliefs may be doubted by others, they are, nevertheless, true for him. The evidence of his need for solace in nature and the feelings of comfort received from nature is sufficient for his belief that nature actually has these comforting powers. Having dealt with the effects of nature on the feeling of the poet, Wordsworth next turns to the thoughts which the scene, now dimly perceived, has introduced. The thoughts are of pleasure. Not only does the poet find present pleasure in the actual viewing of the scene, but he has a happy and mature awareness that the memory will last,

> That in this moment there is life and food
> For future years.

The poet's description of the three stages of man's life and his three states of awareness is given in the next lines (65, ff.). During his first visit to the Wye, he had been a youth, still much like a child in its first state of awareness. His response to the scene was sensual, almost erotic, "when like a roe / I bounded o'er the mountains." But as a youth he also had a second state of awareness; he was restless and troubled—"more like a man / Flying from something that he dreads." The 1798 visit is made by an older, wiser, quieter man "who sought the thing he loved." He now knows the pleasures of youth ("my boyish days") are "coarser pleasures," experienced by the senses only, characterized by "animal movements," with thoughtless and undifferentiated responses:

> To me was all in all.—I cannot paint
> What then I was. The sounding cataract
> Haunted me like a passion: the tall rock,
> The mountain, and the deep and gloomy wood,
> Their colours and their forms, were then to me
> An appetite. . . .

The later visit to the Wye is made by a more mature man at the beginning of the third state of awareness. The "aching joys" and "dizzy raptures" of boyhood are gone. But "for such a loss," there is "abundant recompense."

> For I have learned
> To look on nature, not as in the hour
> Of thoughtless youth; but hearing oftentimes
> The still, sad music of humanity.

The powers of awareness accompany maturity, and a sympathetic understanding of the saddening condition of man is acquired. A new "sense sublime" replaces the corporeal fire; through it is apprehended the great soul of the universe, a power which dwells in "the light of setting suns, / And round the ocean and the living air." Therefore, the third stage of life carries pleasure with it, pleasure in the knowledge that the soul is activated by nature and the experiences of the senses, which together instruct and guide the moral being of the poet.

Turning next to his sister Dorothy, whom he addresses as "My dear, dear friend," Wordsworth acknowledges his sense of loss and prays that his younger sister, whose pleasure in nature is still carefree and wild, may help him remember "former pleasures" a little while longer. He affirms his belief that nature is so designed as to lead man from "joy to joy" and protect him from evil. Therefore, he may wish that Dorothy's youth be blessed with nature's joys. Later, "these wild ecstasies shall be matured / Into a sober pleasure; when thy mind / Shall be a mansion for all lovely forms / Thy memory be as a dwelling-place / For all sweet sounds and harmonies. . . ." But now, in her "wild eyes," there can be seen still the instinctive joy of the soul newly arrived in the human world—"these gleams / Of past existence." Later, these memories of early joy will comfort the girl grown old. Wordsworth urges his sister to remember always that the woods and cliffs of the Wye valley were even more dear on his second trip than on his first, for the mature pleasure which the poet found in nature itself and for the memory of "former pleasures," which Dorothy's "wild eyes" recalled to him.

OTHER LYRICAL BALLADS: Although "Tintern Abbey" is unquestionably the best and most important of Wordsworth's contributions to the *Lyrical Ballads,* there are other poems that deserve notice. In one, called "To My Sister," the poet calls upon his sister Dorothy, who lived with him most of his life, to enjoy with him "the first mild day of March." He says "there is a blessing in the air" and asserts the superiority of feeling and experience in nature over reason:

> One moment now may give us more
> Than years of toiling reason:
> Our minds shall drink at every pore
> The spirit of the season.

The poem represents an early expression of a favorite Wordsworthian theme—the importance of "wise passiveness." The poet is saying that if we listen to nature, we can learn more in a moment than we can learn by our intellectual efforts over many years. Wordsworth's devaluation of reason is another of the characteristics which set him apart from neoclassical poets of the preceding generation, but he was not entirely exempt from the attractions of reason. As we learn in *The Prelude* (see below), Wordsworth had turned to the powers of reason after his disillusionment with the French Revolution. His flirtation with rational philosophy led to the period of despair mentioned in "Tintern Abbey" (above) and in *The Prelude* (below). Dorothy ministered to him during this depressed time and helped him back to his former health by transmitting her unimpaired love of nature to her poet brother. During his "convalescence," Wordsworth learned the wisdom of a passive response to nature.

"EXPOSTULATION AND REPLY":   The phrase "wise passiveness" appears in another of the *Lyrical Ballads*. According to Wordsworth, the poem "arose out of conversation with a friend who was somewhat unreasonably attached to modern books of moral philosophy." The poet's friend (perhaps William Hazlitt) scolds him because he is dreaming away his time instead of reading and availing himself of the intellectual accomplishments of others. In his reply, the poet declares that

> there are Powers
> Which of themselves our minds impress;
> That we can feed this mind of ours
> In a wise passiveness.

"THE TABLES TURNED": A companion piece to "Expostulation and Reply," this poem contains the famous stanza in which Wordsworth again asserts that direct experience of nature is preferable to the "wisdom" of the ancients, which one learns from books.

> One impulse from a vernal wood
> May teach you more of man,
> Of moral evil and of good,
> Than all the sages can.

THE "LUCY" POEMS: Wordsworth added a new volume of poems to the second edition of the *Lyrical Ballads*. Of special importance in this volume were the so-called "Lucy Poems." They are five in number and all touch upon the early death of a young lady, Lucy. The identity of Lucy has never been satisfactorily established. It may well be that she is entirely a fictional character, though the mood of the poems may have been influenced by the poet's close association and deep affection for his sister Dorothy. It is even possible that these exquisite poems on love and grief may owe something to the poet's renewed friendship with Mary Hutchinson, who later became his wife. They were written at a time when Wordsworth and Dorothy were spending a winter in Germany, and the prevailing melancholy of the poems may reflect a nostalgic longing for the poet's native countryside.

The first of the "Lucy Poems" tells of a visit and a premonition. "I to her cottage bent my way, / Beneath an evening moon." The poet falls into a reverie while looking at the sinking moon.

> My horse moved on; hoof after hoof
> He raised, and never stopped:
> When down behind the cottage roof,
> At once, the bright moon dropped.

The sinking moon is symbolic of the ebbing of life, and the poet's love for Lucy is expressed in terms of his fears that he may not find her alive.

The second poem tells us that Lucy "dwelt among the untrodden ways / Beside the springs of Dove." Lucy lived a quiet, rustic life, close to nature. The third and final stanza of this lovely poem startles the reader by its sudden revelation of Lucy's death.

> She lived unknown, and few could know
> When Lucy ceased to be;
> But she is in her grave, and, oh,
> The difference to me!

There is nothing more to be said. The poet could have elaborated on his grief, but he prefers the simple statement that Lucy's death made a "difference" to him. This reluctance on the part of the poet to say all the things that might have been said about the death of a loved one is called "understatement." "Understatement" is an effective rhetorical device because it forces the reader to translate the experience of death into his own terms.

The third poem tells of the lover's effort to recover from his grief. "I wandered among unknown men, / In a land beyond the sea." He found himself homesick. "Nor, England, did I know till then / What love I bore to thee." Back in England, he finds a kind of peace in the sights and sounds of his native land. He finds consolation in the fact that "She I cherished turned her wheel [that is, her spinning wheel] / Beside an English fire."

The fourth poem in the cycle is the lover's remembrance of his love. Once again the final stanza acquires exceptional emotional force by unadorned, direct statement:

> She died, and left to me
> This heath, this calm, and quiet scene;
> The memory of what has been,
> And never more will be.

The fifth and last of the "Lucy Poems" exhibits Wordsworth's philosophic serenity. He comes to an understanding of the cyclical nature of life. He knows that all things must die, but he realizes that we are all part of a vast, unending universe. The concluding statement is unforgettable:

No motion has she now, no force;
She neither hears nor sees;
Rolled round in earth's diurnal course,
With rocks, and stones, and trees.

THE PRELUDE, OR, GROWTH OF A POET'S MIND

Begun in the spring of 1798, *The Prelude* was intended as an exercise in anticipation of a major work on a great theme which Wordsworth hoped to write. It was to serve as the introduction to *The Recluse,* a philosophical epic which was never completed (a fragment of it was published in 1888), and was to precede *The Excursion* (published in 1814), a poem in nine books illustrating the feelings and thoughts of a poet in seclusion. *The Prelude* is a personal history which traces Wordsworth's development as a poet, and, by analogy, examines the relationship of man to nature. It is also an exposition of the process by which man achieves serenity. In effect, it is a portrait of the artist as a young man, covering twenty-eight years of his life from childhood to the *Lyrical Ballads.*

The Prelude, as it turned out, became the work of a lifetime. The first version, completed in 1805–6, he considered unsatisfactory or perhaps too personal to publish. Instead of offering it to the public, Wordsworth kept it at his side, polishing, changing, deleting, and adding to the poem, perhaps until 1850. Finally published a few months after his death, *The Prelude* of 1850 was considerably altered from the manuscript of 1805–6. The style of the later version was more literary, less crude and simple; early ambiguities were clarified and loose repetitions amended. Tender references to Coleridge as "most loving soul" in 1805 were modified after 1810 when the friends became estranged. The manner and address were shifted from the personal "I" to an impersonal manner and pronoun construction. The naked truths of the first version were disguised in the later, and the state of awareness was changed in early and later versions from the youthful to the mature: "I loved and enjoyed," for example, became "Content to observe, to admire, to enjoy." (See Helen Darbishire, *Wordsworth,* London, 1950;

and R. D. Havens, *The Mind of a Poet,* Vol. II, Baltimore, 1941, for full discussions of the two versions of *The Prelude.*)

In both versions, however, the poem contained fourteen books and more than eight thousand lines. The first two books recount Wordsworth's childhood and early schooling in the awesome Lake Country where he learned a "solemn fear of nature" through such outdoor sports as swimming, poaching, stealing a boat, and ice skating. Even as a child, his experiences were mystical, and he felt "Presences of Nature" make "The surface of the universal earth / . . . Work like the sea." At Hawkshead Grammar School, he learned not too much from books but a good deal from the sun, which he watched "lay / His beauty on the morning hills." As he passed the seasons, days and nights, sleeping and waking, "thought / From sources inexhaustible, poured forth / To feed the spirit of religious love / In which I walked with Nature." For as a child, he "still retained / My first creative sensibility," the instinctive unifying powers of the child (see "We Are Seven").

Book III follows Wordsworth to Cambridge at the age of seventeen. His love of nature increased here; "to every natural form . . . I gave moral life." But his development as a student of nature was often impeded by college diversions such as getting drunk in the room once used by the poet Milton. "Submissively idle" in college, Wordsworth passed some pleasing months and looked forward to the summer vacation at Hawkshead in 1788, which is described in Book IV. The visit fulfilled the joy of anticipation, but now all was seen "with another eye," and "with new delight," and with some regret: "a pensive feeling," and "shadings of mortality." The trivial diversions of Cambridge had conspired "to lure my mind from firm habitual quest / Of feeling pleasures, to depress the zeal / And damp those yearnings which had once been mine—"

Book V is a Rousseauvian digression on books and education. Wordsworth is pleased that his mother had let him read what he liked, so that he developed his natural tastes in literature. He especially approves of tales of magic and wonder for children because these help them to appreciate the wonderful in nature and to cultivate their imaginations. He states the Rousseauvian belief that education ought to develop the "natural instinct" of the child rather than eliminate or replace it. The book also contains the famous lines beginning "There was a boy: ye knew him well ye cliffs," which were composed late in 1798 and published in 1800.

In Book VI, Wordsworth's return to Cambridge is followed by a walking tour in 1790 through France and Switzerland with his Welsh friend Robert Jones. His poetic career now a firm hope in his heart, Wordsworth reacts deeply to the splendors of the Simplon Pass, a description of which is the high point of Book VI. His revolutionist sympathies, absorbed as he journeys through France, are also described, and the new spirit of fraternity among the common men of France is noted. Book VII opens with his return to London in 1791 and tells of his excitement at the sounds and sights of the city. His feelings of distress and disquiet because the city distracts him from his quiet contemplations are also evident.

A natural outgrowth of Book VII, the next is a reflective one called "Retrospect—Love of Nature Leading to Love of Man." Still in London and dissatisfied with his life there, Wordsworth recalls the glories of Mount Hellvellyn and its valley, whose rustic inhabitants are tutored in moral virtue by the splendor and beauty of their natural surroundings. Nature and men of humble life are glorified at the expense of rationalism: "Ye who pore / On the dead letter, miss the spirit of things."

Books IX, X, and XI describe Wordsworth's second visit to France from the winter of 1791 to the winter of 1792. His affair with Annette Vallon, the mother of his child, is not mentioned. This conspicuous omission of biographical material in an autobiographical work has been the cause of considerable speculation on the part of critics of *The Prelude*. Perhaps Wordsworth felt that Annette was not implemental in his development as a poet, which is the central theme of the poem, or that his relationship with Annette was too personal for the general purposes of the poem, to describe "the growth of a mind," not specifically Wordsworth's. On the other hand, many readers have felt that the omission of Annette was an act of dishonesty on Wordsworth's part and that the poet was excessively concerned with sustaining a false image of himself as a completely virtuous man. These critics, however, might do well to explain other omissions, such as discussions of adult education and reading, or his study of Italian, or details of his last three years at Cambridge, or his visit to Wales during a college vacation, or the last part of his European tour in 1790. These French books do deal openly with Wordsworth's view of the revolution. At first he was unimpressed by the new republic, for he had always taken the rights of man for granted. But he became acquainted with a noble French patriot and began to see the revolution much as Blake had: "To Nature then, / Power had reverted." In the 1805–6 version of *The Prelude*, Wordsworth wrote that he was forced to leave France because he had run out of money. The later version gives no reason for his return, and the older Wordsworth simply thanks Providence for his early departure from France.

In Book XI, Wordsworth's love for the French Revolution is a "pleasant exercise of hope and joy!" And he begins to court Reason which "seemed the most to assert her right / . . . to assist the work" of the revolution. Then in "open war / Britain opposed the liberties of France," and Wordsworth's sentiments were changed "into their contraries." The French meanwhile had become oppressors, waging aggressive war against Spain, Italy, Germany, and Holland. Disappointed and resentful, Wordsworth attacks France harshly, then turns to rationalism more completely: "This was the time, when . . . / speculative schemes— / That promised to abstract the hopes of Man / Out of his feelings . . . / Found ready welcome." Thus begins a period of despair and unrest which probably lasted until 1797, when the legacy of Raisley Calvert enabled Wordsworth to rent a home in Racedown and settle there with Dorothy. Through her aid, his spirits were restored.

Books XII and XIII are called "Imagination and Taste, How Impaired and Restored." Book XII opens in the mood of despair, but at its deepest pitch, Wordsworth recalls "a maid / A young enthusiast" whose "eye was not the mistress of her heart," who still responded to nature with innocent delight. She was as Wordsworth had been before he left his native hills, when he "loved whate'er I saw," and loved intensely. In contemplation of this maid (Dorothy), Wordsworth shook off despair "and again / In Nature's presence stood, as now I stand, / A sensitive being, a creative soul." Thus, with Dorothy's aid, Wordsworth discards rationalism and returns to nature with a new sense of awareness. The mystery of man still puzzles him, but he senses that its grandeur is based on simple childhood. He glimpses "the hiding-places of Man's powers" and decides to give his feelings "substance and life" by "enshrining . . . the spirit of the Past / For future restoration." That is, he decides to record his memories and feelings in poetry.

He asserts in Book XIII that the humble people he had known as a child in the Lake Country were the most innocent and noble of men and decides to devote himself to a study of these men and their country: "Of these, said I, shall be my song / . . . —my theme / No Other than the very heart of man."

The final book of The Prelude is a survey of Wordsworth's spiritual journey, including, in the later text, a certain Christian orthodoxy, which is missing in the early version. The poem ends with Wordsworth's spiritual restoration and his determination to dedicate himself to "This love more intellectual [which] cannot be / Without Imagination."

The magnificence of The Prelude cannot be reproduced in any account of it, no matter how detailed, nor can the comments of admiring critics explain it. But the attempts they have made are noteworthy. H. W. Garrod found in The Prelude "the conscious language of the saints—only those speak thus who carry within them an inalienable assurance of their own poetic salvation" (Wordsworth: Lectures and Essays [1923], London, 1954, p. 26). Ernest De Selincourt called it "a masterpiece" whose unity sprang "from the poet's own inner life" (Introduction in The Prelude, London, 1926, p. xxxix). R. D. Havens saw "greatness" in the poetry describing his early life, in a style "none too elevated for the theme—how Nature framed 'a being destined for no common tasks.'" (Mind of a Poet, Baltimore, 1941, II, p. 286.)

POEMS, 1807

The poems published in this volume were written for the most part between the years 1802 and 1807. They represent more than any other collection Wordsworth's greatest achievement in his craft. The poems contain the fullest and clearest expression of his favorite themes: the holiness of nature, the beauty of a flower, and the wisdom to be learned from simple men.

"MY HEART LEAPS UP":   This is a capsule statement of his entire moral philosophy, his ideas of the continuity of life, and the relation among the three stages of human development. The poem ends with the famous lines:

> The Child is father of the Man;
> And I could wish my days to be
> Bound each to each by natural piety.

"TO A SMALL CELANDINE":   This poem glorifies the early spring flower, a modest bloom, as "Prophet of delight and mirth," and "Herald of a mighty band."

"RESOLUTION AND INDEPENDENCE":   This was written early in 1802 after an uncreative period during which Wordsworth began to fear that his poetic powers were leaving him. The stanza form is an unusual one for a Romantic poet, for it is the Rhyme Royal or Troilus Stanza which Chaucer had created and which few other poets have managed to use successfully. Chatterton, who is mentioned in the poem, was one of the few. The stanza consists of seven decasyllabic lines of which the last line is an alexandrine (twelve syllables). Wordsworth had recently translated a portion of Chaucer's *Troilus and Criseyde* and the medieval allegory *The Cuckoo and the Nightingale,* which he believed was by Chaucer. Several of Wordsworth's lines echo these medieval poems and suggest the Chaucerian joy in nature, the Romantic despondency of Chaucer's Troilus, and the trancelike mood of *The Cuckoo and the Nightingale's* allegory. Wordsworth's poem reflects the doubts about his poetic creativity which the poet felt at this time and describes the self-confirmation he gained from converse with the simple leech-gatherer.

The poem opens with a description of morning woodland joy following a raging storm at night, which is unsurpassed in Wordsworth's or any other nature poetry:

> All things that love the sun are out of doors;
> The sky rejoices in the morning's birth;
> The grass is bright with rain-drops;—on the moors
> The hare is running races in her mirth.

"I was a traveller then upon a moor," Wordsworth continues. He is so pleased by the woods and waters that all the melancholy ways of men are entirely forgotten—for a moment. Then as if he had reached the bounds of joy and could go no farther, he sinks to utter dejection. His mood is in direct contrast to the scene about him. His mind plays upon its fears of future sorrow as he reflects upon his life which he has devoted to pleasure. How can he expect others to care for him who has taken no care for himself, he wonders. He thinks of other poets whose lives have been unfulfilled: Thomas Chatterton the boy poet who forged "medieval" poems and committed suicide when his deception was discovered; Robert Burns the plowman poet who was overworked in youth and died at 37 of heart disease.

> We Poets in our youth begin in gladness;
> But thereof come in the end despondency and madness.

In the course of these depressing reflections, the poet suddenly comes upon "a pond by which an old man was." (Wordsworth pointed out in a letter to friends that the old man neither "stood" nor "sat" but "was.") Motionless beside the unshaded pool, the figure blends into the scenery so as to be almost indistinguishable from his surroundings. In a memorable simile with profound implications, Wordsworth associates the vision of the old man with a boulder perched atop a mountain, and the boulder is associated with some sea-beast that had crawled out of the sea to sun itself on the ledge for all eternity. He also examines the reaction of the spectator to the object when the viewer is uncertain whether it is a creature or boulder. A sense of the earth's ancient past is incorporated into the present in the image of the rock formation. By association, the bent old man is one with the durable and timeless forms of nature. (Coleridge criticized Wordsworth for making the image of the old man both ethereal and present in the here and now, but the modern reader tends to appreciate the multidimensional image.)

The old man ekes out a meager living, roaming from pond to pond, collecting leeches. As he tells the poet of his way of life, the poet ceases to listen and imagines as in a trance that the old man is a heavenly messenger sent "to give me human strength, by apt admonishment." Because of his reverie the poet fails to hear what the old man says, but the old man patiently repeats his tale: Leeches are scarce these days, though once they could be found in abundance. The poet, however, returns to his reverie, this time envisioning the old man as an eternal wanderer who paces "About the weary moors continually, / . . . alone and silently." Impressed by the firm mind of the old man, the poet gains insight into his own weakness and resolves, as an antidote for future despair, to remember "the leech-gatherer on the lonely moor."

In an excellent and comprehensive study of this poem, Anthony E. M. Conran describes its theme as the poet's escape from the gates of a Romantic hell of wasted imagination. Conran points out the dialectical method employed in the poem, a method in which one symbolic event is set against another, and the contraries are resolved in a third event. Thus, the contrast of the stormy night and the fine morning resolves in the fresh growth and new life of the woods; the joyous mood of the woodland creatures contrasts with the poet's dejection and resolves in the appearance of the old man; and in the poem as a whole, the dejected poet and the cheerful old man are reconciled in the rebirth of the poet's spirit, in the poet's resolution to be content with his lot. (*PMLA*, March 1960, pp. 66–74.)

The poet's own explanation of the poem, which appeared in the letter to friends dated July 14, 1802, states in part: "I describe myself as having been exalted to the highest pitch of delight by the joyousness and beauty of nature; and then as depressed, even in the midst of those beautiful objects, to the lowest dejection and despair. A young poet in the midst of happiness of nature is described as overwhelmed by the thoughts of the miserable reverses which have befallen the happiest of all men, *viz.* poets. I think of this till I am so deeply impressed with it, that I consider the manner in which I was rescued from my dejection and despair almost as an interposition of Providence." The old man was a real person, Wordsworth affirms, and though his own imagination is a strong one, the old man was not a product of poetic invention, for Wordsworth could not have conceived "a figure more impressive than that of an old man like this, survivor of a wife and ten children, travelling alone among the mountains and all lonely places, carrying with him his own fortitude, and the necessities which an unjust state of society has laid upon him." (Christopher Wordsworth, *Memoirs of William Wordsworth,* 1851, I, pp. 172–73.)

"ODE TO DUTY":   Written in 1805 after the death by drowning of his brother John, this poem also appeared in the 1807 volume of poetry. The poem records a crisis in Wordsworth's spiritual life when he turned his back on "unchartered freedom" and vowed to the "Stern Lawgiver" (Duty) no longer to defer "the task, in smoother walks to stray," that is, no longer to defer his duty to man for a life of solitude and pleasure. True liberty, the poem states, lies in service to the laws of the universe and in service to mankind. The poem ends with a prayer to the "awful Power":

> Give unto me, made lowly wise,
> The spirit of self-sacrifice.

As has been pointed out by Hoxie Fairchild (*The Romantic Quest*), Wordsworth paradoxically bows in submission to a "new control," the laws of life. In doing so, however, he triumphs. Fairchild believes the poem reflects Wordsworth's deep philosophic conservatism, marked by his belief that the individual will find salvation in retreating from the world and returning to nature. On the other hand, N. P. Stallknecht has detected in the poem Wordsworth's new philosophical orientation toward Stoicism which Wordsworth acquired through his acquaintance with the moral philosophy of Kant, a philosophy which centers "about a doctrine of duty or rational obligation that is said to surpass all other values in human life." (*Strange Seas of Thought* [1945], Bloomington, 1962, p. 276.)

"INTIMATIONS OF IMMORTALITY":   Fully entitled "Ode: Intimations of Immortality from Recollections of Early Childhood," this poem was written between 1802 and 1804. It is perhaps the finest poem published in the 1807 volume. In an eloquent lyrical examination of the theme, Wordsworth expands upon his philosophy of human growth which had been stated in part in "Tintern Abbey" and *The Prelude*. The form employed for this purpose differs from that of the earlier poems. Wordsworth chose the ode, specifically the "irregular" or "Cowleyan" ode which Abraham Cowley had invented in 1656 as a variation on English imitations of the ancient Greek Pindaric ode. Cowley allowed the thought of each stanza to determine its length and rhythm, and the idea of each line to determine its meter. This was the example Wordsworth was following in "Intimations of Immortality," but in doing so he far surpassed his model and produced what is commonly regarded as the finest ode in the English language.

The first stanza states the central problem faced by the poet. In childhood everything seems fresh and new, "Appareled in celestial light." When we grow up our sense of glory becomes much less acute. "The things which I have seen I now can see no more."

The second stanza provides illustration of the first. We are given examples of those beauties that are peculiarly stirring:

> The Rainbow comes and goes,
> And lovely is the Rose.
> The Moon doth with delight
> Look round her when the heavens are bare.
> Waters on a starry night
> Are beautiful and fair;
> The sunshine is a glorious birth.

Then the stanza ends with the poet's sad confession that even though he still recognizes the beauty of external nature, something has happened. "But yet I know, where'er I go, / That there hath passed away a glory from the earth."

In the third stanza the poet celebrates the holiday spirit of spring, not as a thoughtless, instinctive child, but as a man to whom alone amid the joyous scenes "there came a thought of grief." But the poem is not simply about the contrast between youth and age, for in spite of his "thought of grief" the poet finds solace in "a timely utterance." The ode is in part auto-biographical, and Wordsworth may well have found a release from despondency in the act of creating a particular poem, "the timely utterance." One need not know, however, what poem he had in mind if, indeed, he had one poem in mind. The meaning is clear. Artistic creation heals, restores. The artist cannot share the uncomplicated joys of childhood but he can find another kind of pleasure.

The fourth stanza makes it clear that the act of creation does not take place without stimulus from the outside world. Though no longer a child, the poet can watch and hear with sympathetic eyes and ears. There is still, however, an aching consciousness "of something that is gone." He asks

> Whither is fled the visionary gleam?
> Where is it now, the glory and the dream?

This brings us in the fifth stanza to Wordsworth's much-discussed use of Plato's theory of pre-existence. In this theory the soul is thought to have had an existence prior to its entrance into this world. The theory helps to dramatize the bright innocence of childhood, for the child retains for a time his consciousness of heaven. "Not in entire forgetfulness . . . / But trailing clouds of glory do we come / From God, who is our home." Youth, therefore, is "by the vision splendid . . . on his way attended." Gradually the vision of heaven dies away and "fades into the light of common day."

It is not, we are told in the short sixth stanza, simply a matter of leaving heavenly radiance for earthly darkness, for "Earth fills her lap with pleasures of her own." If we are exiles from our true home, Earth at least acts as a kindly foster mother.

The seventh stanza places "the Child" among his "new-born blisses," that is, the pleasures proffered by his foster mother, and shows how he learns to play various roles in this world. The poet is emphasizing the part that imitation has in our lives. Even the child does not live entirely according to his instincts, says the poet. He is, from an early age, "growing up." Although Wordsworth held childhood in general in high esteem, he has a particular child in mind in this stanza. It is Hartley Coleridge, born in 1796, who was in 1802 "a six years' Darling." Hartley was a gifted and much adored child in Wordsworth's and Coleridge's circle and is the subject of numerous poems and letters by his father and his father's friends. (See C. M. Bowra, *The Romantic Imagination,* New York, 1950, pp. 93–94.)

The stanza about "the little Actor" is followed by the poet's impassioned celebration of childhood. The child is the "best Philosopher . . . mighty Prophet." The poet asks the poignant question that lies at the heart of the ode:

> Why with such earnest pains doth thou provoke
> The years to bring the inevitable yoke?

The stanza serves as a necessary preparation for the surging final stanzas of the ode.

The first of these (stanza 9) begins exultantly:

> O joy! that in our embers
> Is something that doth live,
> That nature yet remembers
> What was so fugitive!

Even though we grow old and lose the innocence of childhood, we do not lose it completely. We always have our memories. "The thought of our past years in me doth breed / Perpetual benediction." The poet feels blessed because childhood, "shadowy recollections" of heavenly glory, are "the fountain light of all our day," "the master light of all our seeing."

The excitement rises in the tenth stanza:

Then sing, ye Birds, sing, sing a joyous song!
And let the young Lambs bound
As to the tabor's sound!
We in thought will join your throng,
Ye that pipe and ye that play,
Ye that through your hearts today
Feel the gladness of the May!

The poet has found a way of participating in the holiday spirit memorably described in the third stanza. The opening three lines of the tenth stanza actually echo the opening lines of the third and compel us to compare the two and to see that the poet has made progress in solving his problem. He felt that he was not part of the spring he first looked upon. Now, conscious of the fact that he cannot really share the joys of youth, he is nonetheless far from being a stranger to youth. The teachings of the "best Philosopher" are still there.

The eleventh and final stanza closes with lines that emphasize the persistence of our powers of sympathy. The poet now can no longer live beneath "the more habitual sway" of nature. As an adult he has cares, anxieties, obligations. As a child he could roam the woods and fields at will. In one of his most popular lyrics, "My Heart Leaps Up" (written in 1802, published in 1807 in *Poems in Two Volumes*), Wordsworth wrote:

The Child is father of the Man;
And I could wish my days to be
Bound each to each by natural piety.

He used these lines as a motto for "Intimations of Immortality." And the final lines of the great ode remind us that in spite of age we retain values learned in childhood.

Thanks to the human heart by which we live.
Thanks to its tenderness, its joys, and fears,
To me the meanest flower that blows can give
Thoughts that do often lie too deep for tears.

Sometimes Wordsworth is thought of as a rather simple poet who "wandered lonely as a cloud" and looked at "golden daffodils." He is actually a poet with an immense range of interests and one who is constantly challenging our habitual ways of seeing things. He forces us to look at the world afresh.

CRITICISM: Until at least 1820, Wordsworth's poetry was poorly received by his contemporaries. Southey's review of the *Lyrical Ballads* was unsympathetic; his friend Coleridge's evaluations of these poems contained high praise but were often captious. *The Excursion* was severely attacked by the *Edinburgh Review*'s critic Francis Jeffrey in the famous line, "This will never do." He was also parodied and mocked by the younger Romantics, Byron, Reynolds, and Shelley, and was charged with apostasy by William Hazlitt and Robert Browning. There was a brief period of interest in his poems before his death, when even the ill-famed *The Excursion* was read with some approval. Matthew Arnold tells us that "Wordsworth had never either before or since been so accepted and popular, so established in possession of the minds of all who profess to care for poetry, as he was between the years 1830 and 1840, and at Cambridge." But by 1880, there were very few "believers and witnesses" left. "Even in 1850, when Wordsworth died, this diminution of popularity was visible," Arnold wrote. Wordsworth's reputation, nevertheless, managed to endure, if only in the esteem of a few persistent admirers. (See *The Portable Matthew Arnold,* New York, 1949, pp. 331–33.)

In 1903, Walter Raleigh urged a revival of interest in Wordsworth, asking that he be read without unfavorable predispositions, so that it would be seen that Wordsworth "is not the purveyor to established tastes but a shaping and compelling force, a light thrown on the dark places of changeful human experience." (*Wordsworth,* London, 1903, p. 225.) Paul Elmer More, however, refused to go along with this suggestion. Instead, he revived Jeffrey's statement (although Jeffrey himself had changed his opinion and regretted the line) and added some poison from his own pen. The *Lyrical Ballads* wavered between "silliness and pathos," More wrote; Wordsworth had no sense of humor, and worse, he lacked native vitality. (*Shelburne Essays,* First Series, New York, 1904.) But Raleigh found an adherent in A. C. Bradley, who in 1909 recommended Raleigh's fresh approach to Wordsworth. Wordsworth has a "unique way of seeing and feeling," Bradley believed, and he brings his readers "peace, strength, exaltation." (*Oxford Lectures on Poetry,* London, 1909, p. 101.) This favorable view of Wordsworth became more prevalent, especially in connection with *The Prelude,* after Ernest De Selincourt declared the work a "masterpiece" in his edition of the poem. (London, 1926, p. xxxix.) Wordsworth's reputation further increased when F. R. Leavis remarked that the chief virtue of Wordsworth's poetry was its "firm hold upon the world of common perception." (*Revaluation,* London, 1936, p. 175.)

Wordsworth's later poems, however, continued to suffer the unkindly darts of critics who, charging him with apostasy and with premature aging, found in the poems of the second period a decay of his poetic powers. Against these charges, defense was made in 1933 by Edith C. Batho who argued that "he was to the end passionate against injustice and wrong, but he saw that the roots of them went deeper than he had realized in the years of the French Revolution, and that the remedies must be more profound." Miss Batho also described his later thought as "a consistent development, not a swing to the left followed by a swing to the right; and . . . his religious development was equally consistent." (*The Later Wordsworth,* New York, 1963, pp. 232–33.) Her opinion has been shared by others like Carlos Baker who recently wrote, "Too much has probably been made of the alleged shrinkage of power in Wordsworth, as if, after forty, his stature had suddenly declined to that of a dwarf. . . . This is a 'despondency' about Wordsworth that needs to be corrected. . . . His power ripened gradually, reached a peak in his middle and late thirties, and thereafter very gradually declined." (In *English Romantic Poets,* ed. M. H. Abrams, New York, 1960, p. 109.) In the Forties, the later works were being read with more sympathy; and in the Fifties, even *The Excursion* began to receive favorable attention. Although it is a later work, J. S. Lyon found in it "clear evidence of several important strides forward in the poet's mental development." It is "more profound, more serene, and wiser" than most of the previous works. (*The Excursion: A Study,* New Haven, 1950, p. 139.)

It is a mistake to think that the earlier poetry was universally approved. Douglas Bush, for example, felt that the poetry of the great decade might have been greater if more of it had been born of conflict between the ideals of "unchartered freedom and order." (In *Wordsworth Centenary Study,* ed. E. L. Griggs, Princeton, 1951, p. 20.) It is this lack of conflict and Wordsworth's concern for the humble, spiritual, quiet life, which accounts for his high reputation inside the universities and his low one outside, Lionel Trilling believed. (*Kenyon Review,* Summer 1950, pp. 478, 497.)

Mixed opinions of Wordsworth do not only occur among separate critics; they sometimes are found within a single reader. John Crowe Ransom explains the case admirably: "My own idea is that many of us for the first time when we were young, discovered in the poetry of Wordsworth what poetry was; but turned from him as we became experienced in other poetry of greater virtuosity; and through some need felt in our maturity have finally come back to him with admiration for the purity of his style." (*Kenyon Review,* Summer 1950, p. 507.)

Perhaps it is his pure style, perhaps his philosophy of quietism, which makes Wordsworth endure. Or, perhaps it is another quality, as F. W. Bateson thinks, his "intuitive artistry." Of the *Lyrical Ballads,* "We Are Seven" and "The Idiot Boy," Bateson wrote, "Grotesque though the stories may be they remain indelibly fixed in the memory—a fact that is an unconscious tribute to Wordsworth's intuitive artistry. Somehow or other he hit upon themes that satisfy a profound psychological hunger in the modern mind." (*Wordsworth—A Reinterpretation* [1954], New York, 1956, p. 138.)

SIR WALTER SCOTT

Much better known today for his novels than his poems, Scott is the author of several verse narratives that enjoyed great popularity when they first appeared and which are still considered worthy of critical attention. There is no question that Scott made significant contributions to the formation of Romantic habits of mind in British, American, and Continental readers.

LIFE: The story of Scott's life, apart from his poetry, has an appeal of its own. Scott was born in Edinburgh in 1771. When he was only two years old he was stricken with infantile paralysis and was lame for the rest of his life. He never allowed this disability to stand in the way of his full participation in life. His courage displayed itself in other ways. His father was a lawyer, and after leaving the University of Edinburgh, Scott studied law in his father's office. He was admitted to the bar in 1792.

From boyhood he was intensely interested in Scotland's past. He liked to spend his holidays traveling through the country collecting stories and legends and ballads about the Scottish past. His enthusiasm had been awakened by Bishop Percy's *Reliques*. Romanticism, it should be noted, was not an exclusively English phenomenon. At this time changes in taste similar to those taking place in Britain were to be observed on the Continent. Scott knew French, Italian, and German literatures, and his readings in these further stimulated his interest in the Border tales of his own country.

In 1809 he became a silent partner in the publishing firm of John Ballantyne and Co. This proved to be a grievous mistake and within a few years Scott was virtually bankrupt. At this time he happened to come upon a manuscript in his papers which contained the opening chapters of a novel he had begun some years before and had set aside. Now, desperate for money, he sat down and completed the novel. Entitling it *Waverley,* he published it anonymously in 1814. Thus was launched one of the most distinguished novel-writing careers in English literary history.

Essentially a noble character, Scott had his little vanities. Shortly after his first successes as a narrative poet, he began to plan the construction of a great estate at Abbotsford. He wished to recreate for himself and his family the splendid way of life of the feudal lords. He fulfilled his dream, but again it forced him to show his moral fiber. For in 1826, Scott and the Ballantyne Company were once more in serious difficulties. Scott personally owed an enormous sum of money. Determined to save Abbotsford, he resolutely set to work to clear the debt by his pen. He succeeded, but he probably shortened his life by his efforts.

Scott's novels need not be discussed in an account of English Romantic poetry. The fact that he turned from the writing of narrative verse to what proved to be the more congenial task of writing novels must be mentioned. And a word may conveniently be said about the general character of the novels.

There were twenty-seven novels in all, several of which tell stories set in the Middle Ages. Although unquestionably a leading exponent of the new Romantic spirit, Scott was at the same time a lover of the eighteenth century. The largest number of his novels (eleven) have to do with Scottish life in the eighteenth century. Romanticism must be looked upon as a kind of revolt against the eighteenth century, but Scott succeeded in "Romanticizing" the eighteenth century.

More than any of the other Romantic poets Scott was a man of the eighteenth century. Although his themes and style were Romantic, he was not, as Blake and Burns and Wordsworth were, in revolt against the neoclassical age. That an almost typical eighteenth-century gentleman could be one of the most important shapers of Romantic sensibility reminds us how many-sided English Romanticism is.

Scott's industry was remarkable. In addition to his narrative poems and his immensely successful historical novels, he published (in 1808) an edition of the works of John Dryden, the greatest of the Restoration poets, and in 1814 an edition of the works of Jonathan Swift.

Honors were showered upon Scott throughout his life. In 1813 he was offered the honor of being the British Poet Laureate. He declined the honor and recommended that the post be given to Robert Southey.

Having overtaxed his strength in his heroic efforts to meet the debts he incurred in 1826, in 1830 Scott suffered a stroke. In failing health he cruised the Mediterranean on a vessel provided by the British government. He died in 1832, and his death is a kind of symbol of the end of the Romantic period.

WORKS: Scott produced more volumes of verse and prose than it is convenient to name in a brief review. This representative list of his literary output includes poems, novels, biographies, and collections: *Minstrelsy of the Scottish Border* (1802–3); *The Lay of the Last Minstrel* (1805); *Marmion* (1808); *The Lady of the Lake* (1810); *Rokeby* (1813); *The Bridal of Triermain* (1813); *Waverley* (1814); *The Lord of the Isles* (1815); *The Antiquary* (1816); *Old Mortality* (1816); *Harold the Dauntless* (1817); *Rob Roy* (1818); *The Bride of Lammermoor* (1819); *Ivanhoe* (1820); *Kenilworth* (1821); *The Pirate* (1822); *The Fortunes of Nigel* (1822); *Quentin Durward* (1823); *Redgauntlet* (1824); *The Talisman* (1825); *Lives of the Novelists* (1825); *Woodstock* (1826); *Life of Napoleon* (1827); *The Fair Maid of Perth* (1828); *Anne of Geierstein* (1829); *Letters on Demonology and Witchcraft* (1830).

MINSTRELSY OF THE SCOTTISH BORDER: In 1802–3 Scott published in three volumes his important ballad collection, *Minstrelsy of the Scottish Border*. The collection contained some of his own ballads, written in imitation of those he had heard from his fellow countrymen in his travels. In 1804 he made still another contribution to our knowledge of the past by editing and publishing *Sir Tristrem,* an English medieval romance.

THE LAY OF THE LAST MINSTREL: His first considerable original work appeared in 1805. This was *The Lay of the Last Minstrel,* a story about Border raids led by Scottish chieftains against the English, about blood feuds, magic, and the triumph of love over various obstacles. It is set in the Border country (the region where England and Scotland meet) of the mid-sixteenth century.

A lay is simply a story told or recited or sung by a minstrel. The minstrels thought of themselves as "professional" men who alone knew the "proper" way of telling or singing a story. They handed down from generation to generation the secrets of their craft. They were wanderers, stopping in this great house or that great castle, certain of a warm welcome, of a good meal and gifts. Minstrelsy in one form or another is to be found in most societies. It is not something peculiar to Scotland. Homer was a minstrel. Almost all European countries throughout the Middle Ages had their wandering minstrels. But minstrels are usually found in primitive societies or societies that were quite recently primitive.

The teller of this lay, accordingly, is a romantically pathetic figure. An old man, he is the last of the minstrels who once in large numbers roamed the Border region. This fact alone gives a Romantic melancholy to Scott's tale.

The story is about the love of Margaret, daughter of the leader of the Buccleuch (modern English, Buckley) clan, and gallant Lord Cranstoun. Margaret's father is dead, killed in a fight in which Cranstoun was on the side of his foes. His widow is set on revenge and sends a friend to Melrose Abbey to get a book of magic that will help her toward the accomplishment of her desires.

The visit to Melrose Abbey is not especially important to the plot. It brings into the story the Romantic appeal of the strange and wonderful. The book was resting in the tomb of an old wizard whose very name, Michael Scott (an ancestor of Sir Walter?) was supposed to produce chills and delicious fears. Melrose Abbey is a real place, accounted the finest of the old ruins of Scotland. In it is now resting the heart of the great Scottish hero, Robert Bruce. The popularity of *The Lay of the Last Minstrel* in part proceeded from Scott's use of such story elements as magic and from his awareness of how memorials of the past and the Scottish landscape touch the heart and stir the emotions.

Returning from his errand, the friend, Sir William Deloraine, meets Lord Cranstoun. They fight and Deloraine is wounded. Cranstoun has an elfin page, that is, a page with magical powers, a page who belongs to the "other" world of folklore, and the page manages to return Deloraine to Branksome Hall, the seat of the Buccleuchs. He also, out of a spirit of mischief, lures away from Branksome the young brother of Margaret.

Unhappily the boy falls into the hands of an English enemy of the Buccleuchs. The Englishman and his followers march on Branksome and propose a single combat between Deloraine and one of the English warriors, Sir Richard Musgrave. Deloraine seems to be victorious in the ensuing encounter, but then it is revealed that Cranstoun with the help of his page has assumed the form and arms of Deloraine, who, of course, could not accept the English challenge because of his wounds.

The conditions of the duel had been that Margaret's brother, the future chief of the Buccleuchs, was to go to the victor. Margaret's mother is so happy to have her son back that she no longer opposes the marriage of the two lovers.

Not only were all the ingredients of Romantic story present to satisfy and to influence popular taste but the form of the story also was responsible for its favorable reception. Scott used a predominantly four-stress line but achieved a pleasing freedom or irregularity by varying the number of syllables in many lines. Some lines have as few as seven syllables, some as many as twelve. Woven into the narrative are several songs. They help Scott to avoid the danger of monotony in his telling of his story and they have a bouncy rhythm that makes them worth reading even when detached from the story.

MARMION: *The Lay of the Last Minstrel* was followed, in 1808, by *Marmion*. Here Scott retells the tragic story of the overthrow of Scottish knighthood at Flodden Field. In this battle, fought between the Scots and the English in 1513, the Scots risked all and lost all. Scott's *Marmion* contains what has come to be recognized as a magnificent account of that battle.

Marmion is the most wildly Romantic of all of Scott's narratives in verse. The hero, Marmion, is a cynical villain, but he also has noble qualities. He prepares us for some of Byron's heroes, as we shall subsequently see. (In this connection, it is said that the growing popularity of Byron was one of the chief things that turned Scott from poetry to prose, from his verse narratives to novels.) Not only is the villain "Romantic," but the events are calculated to produce the shudders that the new age found so delightful. Marmion loves and is loved, for example, by Constance, a nun who has "escaped" from her convent. The view that nuns were not voluntary seekers after spiritual perfection but the pitiful victims of ecclesiastical cruelty was a common view in Protestant nineteenth-century England. It is found in many of the fashionable tales of terror. Constance, as an escaped nun, finds it necessary to assume a disguise. She follows Marmion dressed up to look like his page. This disguise theme is still another stock element in Romantic story. Forged letters enter into the plot of the story, and the Constance-Marmion story culminates in a betrayal that returns the fugitive nun to her convent, where she is, in suitable deference to "Gothic" taste, walled up alive.

The story of Marmion and Constance is complicated by his love of the Lady Clare. He tires of Constance early in the story (this, of course, is the cause of her tragic history) and pursues Clare. The complications are unbelievable. Lady Clare runs from him, at one point, and hides in a convent. Disguise story follows disguise story. The appeal of this story rests heavily on its complicated plot.

Four features of *Marmion* are worth the student's notice: (1) the Gothic trappings, the sensational elements that link it to the tradition encouraged by Walpole's *Castle of Otranto;* (2) the author's ability to revitalize history, to recreate the past; (3) the memorable songs woven into a narrative conducted in a more regular four-stress meter than *The Lay of the Last Minstrel*; (4) the verse introductions to the individual sections of the poem. A word must be said about these introductions.

Marmion was written at the time when Napoleon was trying to become master of all Europe. Scott's introductions take the form of verse epistles to friends. Although not directly related to the story of Marmion, they are interesting by virtue of the martial spirit they exhibit. They provide us with a valuable insight into the temper of England at the time of the crucial war with France. *Marmion,* then, is not only a stirring story about the sixteenth century, about Flodden Field; it is also about the courage and hardihood that men who love their country must always display.

THE LADY OF THE LAKE:　　The next of the verse narratives to be published, *The Lady of the Lake,* is widely regarded as Scott's best poem. The tone is completely different from that of *Marmion.* Whereas *Marmion* responded to the contemporary demand for chills, *The Lady of the Lake* is notable for the normality, the solidity, the healthiness of its characters.

It tells the story of Roderick Dhu, a fierce Highland chief, and of James Fitz-James, a knight who finds hospitality in the home of Roderick. Both Fitz-James and Roderick love Ellen, the daughter of an outlaw, Lord James of Douglas. Ellen, however, is in love with Malcolm Graeme.

The story is set in the turbulent age that followed the Scottish defeat at Flodden. The leaders of the Highland clans resisted all efforts to curtail what they considered to be their hereditary rights. The king of Scotland, on the other hand, felt that the nation had to be unified. In Scott's story, accordingly, there is a report that the king is moving against Roderick Dhu. The outlawed Lord James of Douglas, feeling that he is the cause of the impending battle, sets off to the royal court. James Fitz-James proposes to escort his beloved Ellen to a place of safety. She refuses his offer, confessing that she loves another man. Fitz-

James gallantly yields to his rival and at the same time gives Ellen a signet ring which, he tells her, will, if shown to the king, bring her any boon she should ask.

A quarrel breaks out between Roderick Dhu and Fitz-James. They fight and Roderick is wounded and carried off to the king's court at Stirling.

Ellen arrives at Stirling, displays her signet ring, and begs the royal pardon for her father. She discovers that the king is none other than James Fitz-James. The king grants Ellen's request. Roderick dies of his wounds. Ellen and Malcolm Graeme marry.

The Lady of the Lake is notable for its story. The plots of the two earlier poems are somewhat confused. The plot of this poem is well managed. *The Lady of the Lake* is also notable for its magnificent descriptions of Highland scenery. A few years before his death Scott prepared an introduction for this poem in which he wrote:

> I had also read a great deal, seen much, and heard more, of that romantic country, where I was in the habit of spending some time every autumn; and the scenery of Loch [Lake] Katrine was connected with the recollection of many a dear friend and merry expedition of former days. This poem, the action of which lay among scenes so beautiful, and so deeply imprinted on my recollection, was a labor of love; and it was no less so to recall the manners and incidents introduced.

As in the earlier poems, Scott's talents as song-writer display themselves in *The Lady of the Lake*. One of the most famous of the interspersed songs is the coronach, "a wild expression of lamentation, poured forth by the mourners over the body of a departed friend." A conventional Gaelic poetic form, it commended itself to Scott by reason of the fact that it had fallen into almost complete disuse in his time.

Also famous in *The Lady of the Lake* is the spirited boat song, "Hail to the Chief who in triumph advances." And the "Rest,

Warrior, Rest" and the "Hymn to the Virgin" (Ave Maria! maiden mild! / Listen to a maiden's prayer") are also much admired.

LAST POEMS: *Rokeby,* a complicated story of a conspiracy to win lands and treasure, full of melodramatic themes (the heroine faces the problem of choosing a disagreeable marriage or having her father executed; a valiant page is discovered to be the lost son of the man against whom the conspiracy was formed), invites comparison with Byron's narratives. *The Bridal of Trier-main,* published in the same year (1813), is the earliest nineteenth-century experiment with Arthurian story.

Scott wrote two more narrative poems, *The Lord of the Isles* (1815) and *Harold the Dauntless* (1817), but he had already turned his creative energies to prose fiction.

CRITICISM: After *The Lady of the Lake* (1810), interest in Scott's poetry declined rapidly. Scott had stolen the scene from Wordsworth, and soon Byron was to do the same to Scott. Perhaps sensing his imminent poetic decline, Scott turned to the novel, publishing *Waverley* anonymously in 1814. Thereafter, he wrote few poems. His own opinion of his verse was cavalier. His talent was for storytelling, and he judged himself wisely when he turned to the prose novel.

After more than a century of exposure to public estimate, Scott's self-evaluation has held true. In perhaps the most thorough modern study of Scott's art, Karl Kroeber summed up its value: "None of his writing bears the impress of intense artistry." His "enormous importance in the history of European literature" lies in his ability to blend " 'real' history with imaginative romance. In *The Lady of the Lake,* Scott's best narrative poem, the mingling of these elements is handled in masterly fashion." (*Romantic Narrative Art,* Madison, 1960, pp. 169, 172.)

Although critics of our century have generally agreed that Scott lacked poetic artistry, they have willingly conceded the merits he has. "In prosodic music," George Saintsbury wrote in 1910, "there have been few apter scholars." Scott is also a great master of metrical variety and excellence, Saintsbury felt, but considered that in the later poems "Scott allowed himself to slip too much into the unbroken octosyllabic." He displayed in later poems only a "slipshod and monotonous fluency." (*A History of English Prosody,* New York, 1961, III, pp. 77, 79.)

Scott's virtue as an entertainer was noted by Oliver Elton in 1912. But Elton believed that only at rare moments did Scott write first-rate poetry: "Scott . . . is so great and good an entertainer, that we have to be on the alert for the moments when he is something more than that and rises into high, at times into consummate, literature." (*Survey of English Literature, 1780–1830,* London, 1955, p. 298.)

Scott's ballad meter, which his early public enjoyed so much, was well suited to the matter of his narratives, Samuel Chew thought, "but combined with his inexhaustible memories and affluent imagination it produced stories and descriptions that are almost always too long." Even in his mysteries, Scott told too much and repeated too much. Only in his lyrics did he achieve "a condensed poignancy." (In *A Literary History of England,* ed. A. C. Baugh, New York, 1948, p. 1210.) Ernest Bernbaum agrees with Chew that the lyrics were successful. But in respect to the narrative poems, he allows Scott three rather than one masterpiece: *The Lay of the Last Minstrel* and *Marmion* in addition to *The Lady of the Lake.* Like other critics, Bernbaum regards the last as "the best of his narrative poems." And he shares the opinion of others on the later poems which lacked "the vigor and beauty" of the early ones. Bernbaum does not stint, however, his praise of the epic poems. These, he believes, are like a "trumpet call," spontaneous, swift, and animated, "reminding readers, more than any other English narratives in verse, of *The Iliad.*" (*Guide Through the Romantic Movement,* New York, 1949, p. 141.)

SAMUEL TAYLOR COLERIDGE

Coleridge's theories of literature not only did much to promote the spirit of Romanticism but they also have had a considerable influence on later writers and critics. Many people today think that Coleridge is the most provocative of all English critics. Coleridge's ideas have attracted so much attention that his poetry has to some extent suffered. He is, of course, known to everyone as the author of that unforgettable experiment in the ballad manner, "The Rime of the Ancient Mariner," and his two strange and stirring uncompleted poems, "Christabel" and "Kubla Khan," have always had many admirers. Much of his other poetry deserves more attention than it is usually given. It is, however, true that his poetic powers weakened early and his theories about literature have had a much greater and more permanent effect on English literature than his poetry has had.

The importance of Coleridge's association with other Romantic poets has already been suggested in the chapter on Wordsworth. Coleridge was also a friend of Charles Lamb, the great master of the literary form known as the familiar essay, and he was for a time a very close friend of Robert Southey who, in his own day, enjoyed a considerable reputation as a man of letters. Southey's reputation has greatly declined, and today he is rarely read. But Coleridge is still important in the history of English Romanticism not only for what he wrote but also for what he did.

LIFE: Born in rural Devonshire in 1772, Coleridge inherited his bookish tastes from his father, a learned (and eccentric) clergyman. Coleridge as a boy lived almost entirely in a world of books and ideas. After his father's death, he was sent, in 1782, to a famous charity school in London, known as Christ's Hospital. It was in this school that he met Charles Lamb. Life in a charity school is never especially pleasant; neither Coleridge nor Lamb was particularly happy. But they did receive a good education. Coleridge, for example, here became a first-rate student of the Latin and Greek classics and also read widely in the earlier English authors.

Coleridge next won a scholarship to Cambridge University, where he studied at Jesus College. At Cambridge he began to exhibit a certain instability of character that was to show itself throughout the rest of his life. Finding himself (through his own imprudence) desperately in debt, he rushed off to London and enlisted in the Army under the wonderful name of Silas Tomkin Comberbach. He hated army life and was terrified of the cavalry horses; so when his brothers contrived to have him released, he gladly returned to Cambridge.

Shortly thereafter, he visited Oxford and met Robert Southey. Both wild-eyed young idealists, aflame with the revolutionary spirit that was in part encouraged by the success of the American War of Independence and was in the 1790's being given a new impetus by the French Revolution, Coleridge and Southey worked on a harebrained scheme which they called "Pantisocracy." As the name implies, this was to be a Utopian society in which the powers of government were to be shared by all. The "Pantisocracy" of Coleridge and Southey came to nothing. Throughout his life Coleridge was better at drawing up plans than at putting them into practice. American readers should be especially interested in "Pantisocracy" because the young English idealists hoped to establish their ideal community in the new United States.

OPIUM: His head full of Utopian dreams, Coleridge left Cambridge without taking a degree. Never the easiest man in the world to get on with, he soon quarreled with Southey, and in 1795 took place the momentous meeting with Wordsworth. In the same year he married Sarah Fricker. The marriage was to prove unhappy. In the following year he suffered from a violent attack of neuralgia and, seeking relief from the almost unendurable pain, began taking opium. At the time this drug had medical respectability; nonetheless Coleridge's use of it had disastrous consequences. He became, unwittingly, an addict, and his addiction fatally affected the rest of his literary career.

COLERIDGE AND THE WORDSWORTHS: The really close association of Coleridge and William and Dorothy Wordsworth began in 1797. Now began that extraordinarily fruitful exchange of ideas and communication of enthusiasms that led to the publication of *Lyrical Ballads*. Coleridge's ideas had an electrifying effect on Wordsworth; on the other hand, Wordsworth's almost mystical feeling for nature inspired some of Coleridge's best poetry. At this time he probably wrote all three of his most famous poems ("The Rime of the Ancient Mariner," "Christabel," and "Kubla Khan"). He also wrote, among other poems, a group in blank verse that are Wordsworthian in their detailed evocations of nature and in their emotional intensity. These poems, called the "Conversation Poems," are "This Limetree Bower," "Frost at Midnight," "Fears in Solitude," and "The Nightingale." During this so-called "wonder year" Coleridge also wrote a notable poem, "France: an Ode," which expresses his disenchantment with France because of its unprovoked invasion of Switzerland. This ode marks the beginning of his conversion from fiery political radicalism to a political conservatism that he was to exhibit the rest of his life.

GERMANY: While at Cambridge, Coleridge had abandoned traditional Christianity for Unitarianism. The Unitarians denied the divinity of Christ. At the time of the association with the Wordsworths Coleridge briefly thought of becoming a Unitarian minister but changed his mind. Instead he decided to visit Germany to become more intimately acquainted with the new, invigorating ideas there gaining currency.

Accompanied by Wordsworth and his sister, Coleridge went to Germany in 1798. The Wordsworths settled down in Goslar. Coleridge, on the other hand, spent his time in Ratzeburg and Gottingen, became proficient in the German language, and was deeply influenced by German philosophy.

Back in England after ten months in Germany, Coleridge again visited the Wordsworths. At this time he brought further woes into his already troubled life by falling in love with Sarah Hutchinson, the sister of Wordsworth's future wife.

Ill-health, addiction to opium, and his unhappy marriage almost completely destroyed his poetic powers. "Dejection: an Ode," addressed to Sarah Hutchinson who, in the poem, is simply called "Lady," is Coleridge's moving recognition of his failing health, of his growing misery, and of the waning of his creative abilities.

His difficulties continued. In 1807 he separated from his wife. In 1810 he quarreled with Wordsworth. Although in time there was a reconciliation, the old intimacy was never restored. He suffered from grievous financial difficulties.

LECTURES AND TALK: In spite of all this, Coleridge continued to play an active part in the world of literature and ideas. He delivered important lectures which gave currency to his many important ideas. He prepared and gave an exceptionally challenging series of lectures on Shakespeare. He began his most significant prose work, *Biographia Literaria*. The title of this classic among English critical writings is best explained by Coleridge's subtitle: "Biographical Sketches of My Literary Life and Opinions." What he had completed of this rambling but thought-provoking work was published in 1817. Nothing further appeared during his life.

As Coleridge grew older he found happiness in the general acceptance of his eminence as a thinker. He continued to write on various subjects. Perhaps more influential than his writings were his conversations. It must be remembered that Coleridge made an impact on his generation by the restless energy of his talk. At one time in his life, as we have noted, Coleridge thought of becoming a minister. There is a story that he once said to his friend Charles Lamb, "Charles, have you ever heard me preach?" Lamb replied, in effect, "I have never heard you do anything else."

Coleridge died in 1834.

WORKS: Much of Coleridge's work was left unfinished and unpublished during his life. Among those which were known to his contemporaries were various "Conversation Poems " (1795–1802); "France: an Ode" (1798); "The Rime of the Ancient Mariner" (1798); "Love" (1799); "Christabel" (1816); *The*

Friend (1809–10; revised 1818); *Biographia Literaria* (1817); Lectures (delivered 1808–10); *Aids to Reflection* (1825).

"THE RIME OF THE ANCIENT MARINER" We shall now concentrate our attention on Coleridge's three "golden poems": "The Rime of the Ancient Mariner," "Christabel," and "Kubla Khan."

The story of the Ancient Mariner is told in the style and meter used in many traditional ballads. Most of the stanzas are of four lines, alternately of four stresses and three stresses. The rhymes also alternate, a b a b. Variety is obtained by introducing occasional six-line stanzas. One stanza is nine lines long.

It is, perhaps, the finest "literary" ballad in English literature. A literary ballad, in contrast to a folk ballad, is one written by a known author in conscious imitation of the old traditional ballads whose authorship is not known. These earlier ballads were probably composed in connection with the experiences of a particular community—murders, tragic betrayals, heroic exploits—and were transmitted orally.

It has been demonstrated that the poem reflects Coleridge's amazingly wide reading. In what has become a classic of literary detective work, Professor J. L. Lowes has traced the poet's reading and has shown how materials concerning the polar regions, the equatorial regions, guardian spirits, the Scriptural story of Cain, legends about the Wandering Jew, all came together in his imagination and shaped this hauntingly beautiful and profoundly moving poem. His book entitled *The Road to Xanadu* was published in 1927, expanded in 1930.

The story tells of the unnecessary and wanton shooting of an albatross. The Ancient Mariner, a chillingly mysterious figure who almost forcibly detains a young man on his way to a wedding feast to listen to his narrative, tells of a storm that carried his ship to the seas of the Antarctic. Terrified by the snow and ice, utterly isolated from the world of living things, the crew is overjoyed when an albatross appears. The Ancient Mariner pauses in his story and the "Wedding-Guest" is startled by his appearance:

"God save thee, ancient Mariner!
From the fiends, that plague thee thus!—
Why look'st thou so?"—"With my cross-bow
I shot the Albatross."

At first his shipmates are angry at him because of his rash and meaningless act. When the fog and mist lift, however, they decide that the shooting of the bird has brought them luck and they applaud the crime of their companion, thus becoming, as it were, his accomplices.

Racing north toward the equator, the ship is becalmed in the torrid sea. Suffering from unbearable heat and from thirst, the crew is terrified by the approach of a skeleton-ship, carrying Death and Life-in-Death. On the skeleton-ship a grisly dice game takes place, and Life-in-Death wins. The Mariner's shipmates all die, and he is left hopelessly alone with his physical agony and his consciousness of guilt.

There comes a moment, however, in his terrible loneliness when the glint of moonlight on the brightly colored creatures of the deep so affects the Ancient Mariner that he thanks God for all living things. After his pointless slaughter of the albatross, he is once more able to profess his allegiance to life, to realize the sacredness of life.

Released from the awful punishment that his crime demanded, the Mariner returns to his native land. The consequences of his evil-doing, however, cannot be ignored. It is his fate to wander, presumably for all eternity, throughout the world, telling and retelling his frightening story.

It should be obvious that this is not a cautionary tale about being kind to animals. It is a psychologically profound study of guilt, of remorse, of the nature of evil.

"The Rime of the Ancient Mariner" was first published in *Lyrical Ballads* and is one of the most notable results of that feverish communication of ideas on poetry between Coleridge and the Wordsworths that took place in 1797 and 1798. In his stimulating account of his life as a man of letters, his *Bio-*

graphia Literaria (1817), Coleridge tells us about the relationship of his famous ballad to the poems his friend Wordsworth was contributing to the epoch-making volume:

> During the first year that Mr. Wordsworth and I were neighbours our conversations turned frequently on the two cardinal points of poetry, the power of exciting the sympathy of the reader by a faithful adherence to the truth of nature, and the power of giving the interest of novelty by the modifying colours of the imagination. The sudden charm, which accidents of light and shade, which moonlight or sunset diffused over a known and familiar landscape, appeared to represent the practicability of combining both. These are the poetry of nature. The thought suggested itself (to which of us I do not recollect) that a series of poems might be composed of two sorts. In the one, the incidents and agents were to be, in part at least, supernatural; and the excellence aimed at was to consist in the interesting of the affections by the dramatic truth of such emotions as would naturally accompany such situations, supposing them real. And real in *this* sense they have been to every human being who, from whatever source of delusion, has at any time believed himself under supernatural agency. For the second class, subjects were to be chosen from ordinary life; the characters and incidents were to be such as will be found in every village and its vicinity, where there is a meditative and feeling mind to seek after them, or to notice them when they present themselves.

In the light of what actually happened in the preparation of the *Lyrical Ballads,* it is clear that Wordsworth tried to make his readers aware of the wonderfulness of everyday life; Coleridge tried to show the relevance of the strange and mysterious to our consciousness of reality.

"CHRISTABEL": Like so many of Coleridge's compositions, "Christabel" (1797–1800; 1816) was never brought to completion, because, as Coleridge said, he knew what he wanted to do and how to do it, but he did not feel he could execute the end of the work as successfully as the beginning. A tale of enchantment intended to run four cantos in length, the poem as it now stands contains only two parts, the conclusion to the second part bearing little relation to it. It is a story of witchery which is remarkable for its recreation of the strange and distant world of the Gothic or medieval romance, but it is also a highly suggestive tale of good and evil. The eternal conflict between these two moral forces is dramatized in the relationship between Christabel (whose name suggests Christ) and Geraldine, an inhuman creature, who is a witch or vampire.

The meter of this poem is especially interesting, for as a revival of the old Anglo-Saxon four-stress line, it helps to create an ancient and Gothic atmosphere. Coleridge wrote in his original preface to the poem that the irregular meter was "founded on a new principle: namely, that of counting in each line the accents, not the syllables. Though the latter may vary from seven to twelve, yet in each line the accents will be found to be only four." There are occasional variations from this pattern, but on the whole the four-stress rule prevails. Each verse, then, is to be scanned according to the four accented syllables in each line, with a pause or caesura at the half line. For example,

> 'Tis the middle of the night / by the castle clock,
> And the owls have awakened / the crowing cock.

As can be seen, a certain amount of alliteration is used (words having the same initial sounds as in "crow" and "cock") when Coleridge finds it is convenient, but he does not try to follow the more restrictive alliterative requirements of Anglo-Saxon verse.

The story opens at the midnight hour. The owl is shrieking. The dog is baying. She seems to be restless, and superstition has it that dogs can sense the presence of spirits. "My lady's shroud," representing the dead wife of Sir Leoline, Christabel's father, suggests that the spirit of Christabel's dead mother may be wandering abroad. There is a full moon tonight, partly hidden by the gray clouds. The month is April (the season of resurrection and rebirth), but it is too chilly for a real spring, which comes late in this northern part of the world.

On this eerie night, Christabel of Langdale Hall has been restless too. Having dreamed that her lover may be in danger, she has gone to the woods to pray for his safety. The woods and an old oak tree are strange places for a Christian to pray and Coleridge is perhaps suggesting an ancient time when pagan ideas had not yet been effaced from the beliefs of early Christians. Alone and frightened, Christabel meets a mysterious stranger, "richly clad" and "beautiful exceedingly." The lady identifies herself as the noblewoman Geraldine, who has been carried off, in typical romance fashion, by five strange warriors. She asks Christabel to take her hand and help a damsel in distress. Upon receiving Christabel's hand and offer of hospitality, Geraldine is now able to rise. But she is unable to move quickly. She seems to be walking slowly, against her will, as in a dream. She also has an uncanny knowledge of Sir Leoline's poor health and makes a strange request to spend the night secretly in Christabel's bed.

As they reach the castle and Christabel works at the wicket lock, the lady Geraldine sinks to the ground as though in pain. Christabel is forced to lift her over the threshold. The suggestion here is strong that Geraldine is an evil spirit who cannot cross the threshold of a Christian unless the Christian carries it across. Hints that Geraldine is a supernatural creature begin to mount as the lady, feigning weariness, refuses to pray to the Virgin as Christabel suggests. The mastiff, who has never growled in the presence of Christabel, now moans in her sleep, and the flames of the dying firebrands shoot up as Geraldine passes, as if a gust of air not a solid body had passed the flames. Christabel looks into the lady's eyes and sees nothing else, except "thereby" the engraving of her father's shield which hangs nearby. Are Geraldine's eyes empty because she has no soul? Is Christabel protected from the lady's evil eye because she sees her father's emblem, which is perhaps a cross? The passage is intentionally ambiguous so that the reader may imagine the eerie experience in his own way.

As the two make their silent way through the Gothic corridors of Sir Leoline's castle, the atmosphere of suspense and mystery is heightened. At last, they are safe in Christabel's chamber, which is ornamented by the curious carved figures Gothic sculptors were accustomed to design in a theme appropriate to the occupant of the place. Christabel's ornaments, which are "strange and sweet," and apparently include cherubs and angels, are meant to suggest her own innocence and angelic qualities. In the angelic atmosphere of the chamber, Geraldine once more sinks to the floor. She learns that Christabel's mother is dead and pretends to wish the mother were present with them. Apparently her wish has the power of being fulfilled, for in the next moment, Geraldine "with altered voice" calls, "Off, wandering mother." The guardian spirit of the mother has made its appearance, and Geraldine has the "power to bid thee [the mother] flee." The poet interpolates at this point to make his meaning clear, "Can she the bodiless dead espy?" The answer seems to be yes.

Geraldine is restored by a sip of "wild-flower wine," the innocent nectar which is kept for Christabel's use. Told to undress and go to bed, Christabel obeys, while Geraldine says her "prayers." And what prayers they are. She bows, rolls her eyes, then disrobes. The sight of the naked Geraldine is something "to dream of, not to tell!" We may only guess that beneath the bright robes of the fair Geraldine, the hideous body of a witch is concealed. Christabel has witnessed the disrobing, but she will never be able to tell of it. For Geraldine, taking the girl in her arms, casts a spell over her, which will force her to reveal only part of the truth, that she found a lady in the woods and brought her home to protect her.

The conclusion to the first part of the poem describes the change which has taken place in Christabel. One moment she was a fair maiden praying under her magical oak tree; the next, she is entranced, sleeping with open eyes and dreaming fearfully, while the lady Geraldine slumbers as peacefully as a mother with her child. As the morning star rises, Christabel relaxes from her trance, closes her eyes, and has sweet dreams mingled with sad thoughts. Her innocence returns to her, but it is no longer pure. Now it is blended with sadness acquired through an unremembered encounter with evil.

Part II takes place the next morning. The opening lines focus on Sir Leoline who rises at the sound of the matin bell. He is a bereaved knight who has regretted life daily, ever since he rose and found his wife dead many years ago. A new character is introduced: Bracy the Bard. Bracy has heard the matin bell too, and knows that the sacristan is slowly saying his prayers between each toll. He thinks it is a good thing that the prayers are being said, for he knows well how many evil spirits occupy the lower regions of the air, "the space between" heaven and earth. The scene next shifts to Christabel's chamber, where the lady Geraldine, refreshed from her sleep, rises and dresses. She looks more lovely than ever before. Christabel awakens with a sharp sense of guilt. She imagines she may have sinned, but she thanks heaven if all be well. Although her mind is perplexed, she does not know what has happened and sweetly greets Geraldine.

Next, Christabel introduces Geraldine to her father, and the old Baron pales as he learns that his guest is the daughter of Lord Roland de Vaux of Tryermaine. The pain of memory has crossed the Baron's mind. He and Lord Roland had been loving friends in youth. But they had parted in anger long ago, ever to regret the breach which had come between them and the loss of friendship which no other could replace. (Coleridge who had quarreled with his friend and brother-in-law Robert Southey may have had that personal experience in mind.) In memory of his old friend, Sir Leoline vows to make it up to Geraldine and embraces her joyfully. As he does so, Christabel has a fearful vision of Geraldine's bosom, which she had seen the night before. The Baron notices Christabel's disturbance, and Geraldine, pretending she has offended the child, asks to be sent home immediately. The Baron will not hear of this. He sends for Bracy, the Bard, and charges him to take a young assistant to Tryermaine. Describing the route to him, in terms of Lake District scenery, the Baron explains that Lord Roland's castle is near the Scottish border. Bracy is to ask Lord Roland to come to Langdale Hall for his daughter, and when he arrives, the Baron plans to apologize for their ancient feud.

Bracy falls to the ground and clasps the Baron's knees to ask a boon. He would like to delay the trip for a day in order to clear the woods of some unblessed thing which seems to be lurking there. He tells the Baron that in a dream, he saw a dove, meaning Christabel, being strangled by a snake, and upon awakening,

vowed to wander through the forest with music and saintly song
to rid the woods of the unholy thing.

The Baron, who is completely enchanted by Geraldine, interprets the dove as a symbol of Geraldine not Christabel. He
promises that he and Geraldine's father, when he comes, will
kill the viper in the woods, whom he takes to be the five
kidnapers. Geraldine feigns the manners of a shy and chaste
maiden. But beneath her lowered lids, she looks askance at
Christabel, who sees the small shrunken eyes of a snake in
Geraldine's face, and falls into another dizzy trance. When
Geraldine turns to Sir Leoline, however, her eyes are large and
bright and divine, while Christabel's face, in full view of her
father, has been distorted into an image of the hated thing she
has just seen. A malicious and hateful expression appears on
her face. When the trance passes, Christabel implores her father
to send Geraldine away, but as she is under a spell she is unable
to explain her reasons.

The Baron is enraged at his daughter's uncharitable and inhos-
pitable request. He forgets the devotion which he and his wife
had shared for each other and the prayer his wife made for the
Baron and her child as she lay dying in childbirth. He orders
Bracy to be on his way, and turning his back on Christabel,
leads lady Geraldine away on his arm.

The conclusion to Part II did not appear with any of the three
manuscripts of the poem, and may not have been meant for this
poem at all. The lines describe a parent's supreme delight in and
strong emotional reactions to his child, which may be expressed
in terms of rage and pain because they are so often excessive.
The feeling described here may have been suggested by the
emotional tension with which the fragment of "Christabel" ends,
when the father has turned away in rage from his daughter who
was ever the light in his life.

The plan for the remainder of the poem which, of course, was
never written, was described by Coleridge's friend Dr. Gilman,
with whom Coleridge spent his declining years. The plan was to
follow the Bard to Tryermaine where the Bard would discover
that Lord Roland's castle had been washed away in a flood.
Geraldine, who had occult knowledge of the Bard's doings,

would disappear when she learned of Bracy's plan to return with the news that would give her away. She would reappear for a while to fill the Baron with further anger and jealousy against his daughter, with passions to which he had always been susceptible. When the Bard was about to arrive, Geraldine would take the form of Christabel's absent lover and court the young maid. Christabel would be unable to explain her new feelings of revulsion for her supposed lover. But in the end she would have to agree to marry the young knight as her father insisted. On the wedding day, the real lover would appear, and Geraldine would be forced to exit. The wedding of the real lovers would take place, and as the dead mother had predicted, the castle bells would toll, the mother's voice would be heard, and all would rejoice as father and daughter explained their behavior and became reconciled.

The supernatural paraphernalia which was to resolve the tale had at least partly been prepared for in the first two parts of the poem. Twelve bells at midnight, form-changing, the allegorical dream of the Bard were all elements of popular romance and medieval superstition which Coleridge learned from the people and from his reading. The suggestions that Geraldine is a symbol of evil and that Christabel symbolizes good are too clear to be overlooked. It seems clear, also, that evil which is introduced by the acts of an innocent cannot enter the lives of Christians unassisted. The Baron, a man of excessive pride and passion, embraces evil (literally as well as figuratively) to the possible destruction of himself and his loved ones. The proud man forgets former loyalties too easily and refuses to listen to the truth of the Bard, a prophet by tradition, whose allegorical dreams explain reality. In these ways, the Baron's willfulness and Christabel's naïveté—in short, human nature—have as much a share as the supernatural in the near-tragedy of "Christabel."

"KUBLA KHAN; OR, A VISION IN A DREAM": In the preface which appeared at the publication of this poem in 1816, Coleridge described the conditions under which the "dream" had been created. Suffering from neuralgia, he had taken some opium which sent him into a three-hour sleep or reverie (his story varied). During that time, he dreamed or "composed" visions enough for several hundred lines of poetry. Upon awakening, he sat down to write and had finished fifty-four lines when business called him away. He was never able to recapture the images which were then dissipated by the intrusive caller. Before he fell asleep, Coleridge had been reading Purchas's *Pilgrimage,* which contained the lines, as Coleridge recalled them, "Here the Khan Kubla commanded a palace to be built, and a stately garden thereunto. And thus ten miles of fertile ground were inclosed with a wall." These lines apparently inspired the first vision: "In Xanadu did Kubla Khan / A stately pleasure-dome decree." The sources of the images which follow have been studied minutely by a number of scholars, for whom J. L. Lowes paved the way and provided the method in *The Road to Xanadu.*

The images and "meaning" of the poem, if such can be attributed to a composition which is more like an "experience" than a poem with a specific rational meaning, will be discussed shortly. It may be pointed out first that the poem has an unusual and distinctive "method," which should be recognized if understanding is to take place. Coleridge, whose word is not always to be trusted, did apparently record an actual dream, as he said. But it is not to be supposed that the poem is merely a series of disorganized and unrelated fragments. It is an artful composition, which is self-contained and has a unity of its own. Whatever his state of mind, whether in sleep or reverie, Coleridge's genius enabled him to recapture the qualities of a dream, which like a surrealistic film, moves from image to image, as the reel unwinds in slow motion. The materials which make up the images rose up into the current of his sleeping mind from the subterranean vaults of his memory. Some of the images in the storehouse of his subconscious came from his reading, others from his ideas and experiences. Still other materials, Maud Bodkin has shown, reflect suprapersonal "archetypal" patterns which are common to all mankind. In fact, emotional forces acted upon "the selections or the fashioning of the material of the poem" and must also be taken into account. (*Archetypal Patterns in English Poetry* [1934], London, 1951, p. 40.) With these "emotionally selected" materials, both personal and suprapersonal, Coleridge created a new world, one of enchantment, rich with emotional experience, romance, glamour, adventure, and sheer magic. The poem is intentionally inexplicit, for Coleridge wished to enhance the mystery of the poem. In connection with this poetic mystery, Coleridge stated some years after "Kubla Khan" was written and before it was published:

> The grandest effects of poetry are where the imagination is called forth, not to produce a distinct form, but a strong working of the mind . . . ; the result being what the poet wishes to impress, namely, the substitution of a sublime feeling of the unimaginable for a mere image. (Lecture VIII, "On Shakespeare and Milton," 1811–12.)

The images of "Kubla Khan" do just that. They suggest to each reader his own eternal and exotic world of sublime feelings which is far more mysterious and unimaginable than the individual images and the sum of those parts can possibly be. It is hoped that the student will allow for "a strong working of the mind" as he examines the images of "Kubla Khan."

Since some limit must be set on the amount of detail which can be examined here, "Kubla Khan" may be divided for present convenience into twelve images. The first image is of the magnificent palace and grounds built long ago in far off Xanadu (a region in Tartary) by the emperor Kubla Khan (the monarch who founded the Mogul dynasty in the thirteenth century and who is famed in history and legend for his resplendent court). The names "Xanadu" and "Kubla Khan" in themselves suggest the exotic orient, a distant place, and a distant time. The "sacred river" (its name "Alph" suggests the beginning of things as in "alphabet," and it flows "measureless" beneath the realm of Kubla) augments the impression of distance and eternity. At the same time the sensual description of the grounds of Xanadu makes present experience of the scents and sights of that magnificent faraway land.

The second image also deals with the lands around Xanadu. But "that deep romantic chasm" works as a contrast to the living greenery and sunny lights of the emperor's garden. It is a "savage" place in contrast to the civilized walls and towers and fertile grounds of the first impression. It is a place of darkness and moonlight. It is a place suggestive of impassioned and unearthly evil spirits, a "woman wailing for her demon-lover." The passage is pure enchantment and constitutes the "five little lines" of which Rudyard Kipling wrote, "These are the magic. These are the vision. The rest is only poetry."

Within this chasm is a third remarkable sight, a gusher or geyser heaving out of the ground, thrusting forth from the bosom of the earth, hail or grain or pebbles like "dancing rocks," and the living springs of Alph, the sacred river, which marks the beginning of all things.

Next, in a panoramic vista, the river is followed for five miles. Slowly and lazily, it meanders through the fertile land where the pleasure dome is built. Then, in a "tumult" or wild waterfall, it disappears into "a lifeless ocean."

The focus moves, at this point, to Kubla himself. Kubla at the "tumult" hears from deep within it an ancient prophecy of war. We not only see Kubla hearkening to the sounds of the river, but we also glimpse his thoughts as he listens and interprets the prophetic voice of the sacred stream: a war, an eternal conflict is foreshadowed. Is it the unending conflict of man within himself? Or is it the forecast of social conflict?

The image of Kubla fades, and a new one appears. "The shadow of the dome of pleasure," a shade within the dream not the dome itself, is seen upon the waves of the Alph as it meanders five miles through the pleasure grounds before it disappears. And beneath the waves or from the waves are heard echoes of its unknown underground passage and of the fountain source from which the river springs. A "sacred," indefinable past and unknown, unimaginable places are mysteriously suggested by the invisible source of the "measureless" river. The pleasure-dome is now thought of as a "miracle." Its dome is sunny, yet there are "caves of ice" beneath. Free play of the fancy will suggest many meanings for this image. For example, the dome as a shadow on the water is "sunny" on its surface, but cold and icy as the stream beneath the shadow. Symbolically, the "miracle" dome may be seen as the ideal work of literature, a perfect poem, which Coleridge always hoped or expected to write. The poem would be beautifully imagistic on the surface, clearly intellectual and deeply suggestive of eternal qualities beneath. The surface of this ideal poem would be seen as "sunny," its intellectual substrata as "cold."

(See Arthur Clayborough, *The Grotesque in English Literature,*
London, 1965, pp. 195–99.)

The image of the sunny dome with its caves of ice disperses to
admit a vision of an Abyssinian maid, another exotic creature,
who plays an ancient and obsolete instrument. As she plays her
dulcimer, she sings of Mount Abora, a romantic name invented
for the purposes of the poem, or a poetic translation of Mount
Amara in Abyssinia, regarded in legend as the seat of the
earthly paradise. The extraordinary Abyssinian maiden is most
probably emblematic of poetic inspiration. In the same way that
the song of Wordsworth's Highland reaper suggested thoughts
of eternal passions to the poet of ordinary life, the exotic
African maiden may have been employed by Coleridge as the
inspiration for his genius which tended toward the arcane, the
bizarre, and the mysterious. She seems to be the symbolic muse
of his visionary and prophetic chants.

The image of the maiden blends with the next one, as we hear
the voice of the poet expressing his desires and dreams. "Could
I revive within me," the poet says, the inspired poetry, suggestive of things eternal of which the maiden sings, then he too
would (or could) create a perfect poem. That is, inspired by the
Abyssinian muse, Coleridge could build a "dome," an ethereal
palace "in air." That dome (or poem) would be "sunny" with
pleasure on the surface, but its "caves of ice" beneath would
reach profoundly into the cold, permanent atmosphere of absolute art.

An image of the poet's audience flashes by briefly as we see
them gaze in awe at the poet-architect of the pleasure-dome in
air. We also hear them cry "Beware! Beware!" Our eyes move
to the center of their attention, the inspired poet, possessed like
a madman or prophet with "flashing eyes" and "floating hair."
We see the poet at the end, surrounded by his enchanted
listeners as they magically "weave a circle round him thrice,"
and close their eyes in awe at the sight of the powerful spirit
who, having partaken of the foods of paradise, has returned to
teach them of other worlds and of unimaginable, spiritual
things.

An examination of the images of "Kubla Khan" should make it
apparent that purely rational meanings cannot easily be attached

to the poem. Subjective responses, such as Maud Bodkin's, or symbolist interpretations such as Humphry House's, serve Coleridge much better. For in either case, "a strong working of the mind" is required of the reader who is impressed by the archetypal suggestions, the mysterious effects, or the symbolic meanings of the poem. Miss Bodkin, for example, has seen in the poem memories of man's unconscious first awareness of his experience in the womb. And Humphrey House has read "Kubla Khan" as a poem about the artistic creation, a subject which preoccupied Coleridge most of his life. (*Coleridge* [1951–52], London, 1953, p. 114, ff.) To these interpretations, Arthur Clayborough has added new ideas. He sees Kubla as the poet, the sounds of war as the conflict between the creative powers and the intellectual energies, and the sunny dome with caves of ice as the ideal work of art "with submerged intellectual content" and "habitual and instinctive knowledge." (*The Grotesque in English Literature,* pp. 195–99.) It is equally possible that at the time of writing "Kubla Khan," Coleridge had already felt the waning of his poetic powers, which he tells about in "Dejection: an Ode" (1802), and was expressing a desire for their return.

"DEJECTION: AN ODE":   Written April 4, 1802, this ode was an extremely personal address to Sarah Hutchinson, sister of Wordsworth's wife Mary, whom Coleridge had met and grown to love a few years after his marriage to Sarah Fricker. Other versions of the poem are addressed not to Sarah but to Wordsworth, other friends, and finally to "O Lady." The manner of the ode is rather like his early conversation poems in which the poet's feelings were addressed to a friend who seemed to be present. Published in *The London Morning Post* on Wordsworth's wedding day, October 4, 1802, the ode is believed to be a tribute to his friend.

The ode is related to Wordsworth's "Resolution and Independence," written in the same year on the same theme (the poet's dejection over his lost muse, that is, the failure of his poetic powers and imagination). Though the poems were written almost simultaneously (Coleridge's was begun earlier and was finished later than Wordsworth's), the marked difference between the statements of the two poems is in the poets' response to the mood of despair; Coleridge yields to it, while Wordsworth rejects it.

The reasons given for Coleridge's lost muse have varied considerably. His physical condition was poor, his use of opium had become slavish, his marriage was in trouble, and his love for Sarah Hutchinson was hopeless. He was perhaps depressed by Wordsworth's forthcoming marriage, and it is probable that he had been feeling the loss of his poetic powers for some time, resolving at this point to abandon poetry forever. The impact of the decision was apparently powerful enough to allow Coleridge to write one more excellent poem.

The ode is more tightly structured than many of the poems he had written before. The storm, for example, which is forecast at the beginning, does come off near the end. And the complete surrender of joy in the final stanza encloses the stormy moment of passion between the becalmed beginning and the passively hopeless ending. As a unit, the poem sustains its single mood of dejection, yet it provides variety of feeling within that mood. In other respects too, the poem is structurally tight. The nature description of the opening stanza is tied in with the poet's personal reflections, and the natural scenes described throughout are consistently made to reflect the poet's state of mind. The calm night is Coleridge's passive imagination, his desire for the storm is his desire for the return of active imagination. The storm itself is the momentary reactivation of his imagination, which expresses feelings of agony and pathos when revived. The wind dies down as his imagination does, and the only joy that remains in the final stanza belongs not to the poet but to the "Dear Lady." (See M. F. Schulz, *The Poetic Voices of Coleridge,* Detroit, 1963, p. 33, ff.)

The opening of the poem is preceded by a stanza from the ballad "Sir Patrick Spens," in which the new moon is seen with the old and the coming of a storm is feared. It is typical of Coleridge to see nature in literary terms, that is, in terms of something he has read. The poem proper begins with reflections on the ballad which is also used as a springboard for his own description of the tranquil night. Coleridge cannot respond to nature and wishes for a storm to rouse him and "send his soul abroad." For now his mind, the Æolian harp, responds to nature only faintly, as to a slight draft, with "moans and rakes." His "genial spirits" fail; his creative powers are lost. "Joy," which comes from the inner being, is no longer with him. "I see not feel," the poet complains.

As a transcendental philosopher, Coleridge asserts the existence of a world outside men, a world which may be seen through the active, creative mind. It is creative activity, Coleridge believes, which gives nature its being and significance. He also recognizes the psychological reality of nature, a reality in which men attribute to nature their own deepest moods: "O Lady! we receive but what we give, / And in our life alone does Nature live."

Coleridge next accounts for his loss of poetic power, his "shaping spirit of imagination." Once he could recover from despair. When he still had hope, he would bury his gloom in research until the mood passed away. But through this habit of prose thinking and prose writing, he eventually lost his poetic powers. Now "abstruse research," the knowledge of philosophy, brings him only care and steals his powers of joy.

But now the wind is howling, the creative spirit is calling. In agony, he turns away from the "viper thoughts" of philosophy for a little while. He hears in the howling of the wind, sounds of pain and sounds of grief and screams of fear. All are projections of his own mind, and he cannot sleep. Finally, he turns his thoughts to the pure lady again, wishing that she may never hear those tortured sounds of the wind and that she may keep her joy in life forevermore.

It is ironic that Coleridge's consciousness of his loss of creative power was so strong that it enabled him to recover the power long enough to write this ode. A few more poems issued from his pen after 1802, but Coleridge never recovered the poetic powers he had had in the 1790's.

BIOGRAPHIA LITERARIA: In a brief survey of English Romantic poetry we cannot enter into the complexities of Coleridge's theories. It may be pointed out, however, that in his conversations with Wordsworth and in his wide reading he developed a theory about the poet's imagination that has proved to be exceptionally influential. He emphasized the relationship of the imagination to the entire process of artistic creation. He denied that the imagination was the mere reshaping of images originally produced by sense impressions and thus was able to make a more profound contribution to our understanding of artistic originality than was made by any neoclassical or pre-Romantic theorist.

Related to his ideas on the imagination is his healthy awareness that a poem is an organic whole. It is, in other words, like all living things, more than the sum of its parts. One can, of course, analyze parts of a poem, such as the diction, the meter, the rhymes, and the like. But true criticism must ultimately go beyond analysis and examine the poem in its totality.

Most of Coleridge's ideas on literature are to be found in his *Biographia Literaria*. Many of the specific critical comments in this rambling, uneven, and frequently cloudy book are worth attention. For example, his remarks on Wordsworth show a perceptive understanding of that poet's greatness. At the same time that he praises Wordsworth, he takes issue with Wordsworth's oversimplified views on poetic diction and he shows that Wordsworth does not always follow his own stated principles.

CRITICISM: The body of Coleridge criticism and scholarship in our time is vast. It would be well under the circumstances to confine this survey to the criticism of those works generally acknowledged as his best. What will barely be evident here is the wide interest currently being shown in Coleridge's prose (critical, political, philosophical). Although some brief reference has been made above to Coleridge's *Biographia Literaria*, his prose is not the subject of this book, and the arduous task of reviewing criticism in that area has been reluctantly dismissed.

Aside from humanist critics like Irving Babbitt, who wrote "it is impossible to extract any serious ethical purport from 'The Ancient Mariner,'" Coleridge's poem has been regarded universally as a serious, ethical, and artistic creation, one of the most important poems of the Romantic movement and of all time. Babbitt's charges made in 1929 and earlier that "the poem lays claims to a religious seriousness that at bottom it does not possess" have been answered again and again by critics who have found in the Mariner's "crime, punishment, and reconciliation" a serious artistic creation or a deeply religious theme of "One Life." (See Babbitt, *On Being Creative,* Boston, 1932, pp. 118–20.)

The first of these defenders was J. L. Lowes, who in *The Road to Xanadu* (1927; 1930) answered the moralist Babbitt by insisting that Coleridge's intentions were neither philosophical nor Christian but superstitious and legendary, and that the poem itself is an artistic structure, "a complex design wrought out through the exquisite adjustment of innumerable details." (Boston, 1964, p. 425.) Lowes paid the poem perhaps the highest tribute it has ever received when he made a full-length study of it to recover the original materials that went into the making of "The Ancient Mariner." Lowes traced the pattern of the poet's imagination as expressed in the poem and learned that the "structure of the voyage is . . . as austerely true to fact as an Admiralty report. Yet the stark outline . . . is itself a compendium of premonitory dreams, and the imaginative vision and the intrepid daring of two-score generations." Upon the voyage frame, Coleridge's imagination wove a magic pattern, which Lowes found to be "deep-rooted as the continents themselves, and permeated with the elemental experiences of humanity" (p. 53).

The same fundamental "experiences of humanity" as Lowes had found in the poem were also discovered there by Maud Bodkin who studied the *Archetypal Patterns in English Poetry* (London, 1934) and judged "The Ancient Mariner" to be one of that body of poetry which "affords us a means of increased awareness and of fuller expression and control of our own lives in their secret and momentous obedience to universal rhythms" (p. 89). That the experience of "all humanity" is one of the deep meanings of the poem was also asserted by G. H. Clarke who saw, in addition, personal and religious meanings. " 'The Ancient Mariner,' " Clarke wrote, "who is at once Coleridge himself, Coleridge and all humanity—having sinned, both incurs punishment and seeks redemption." That is, he becomes "aware" of the God of Law (the sun) and subconsciously seeks forgiveness of the God of Love (the moon). (*Queens Quarterly,* XL, February 1933, pp. 29–30.) D. W. Harding read essentially the same meaning into the poem. The Mariner is

Coleridge, Harding believed, but he is also symbolic of all "human experience," for "the suffering he [Coleridge] describes is of a kind which is perhaps not found except in slightly pathological conditions, but which, pathological or not, has been felt by a great many people." (*Scrutiny,* IX, March 1941, pp. 334–35.) The intensely personal nature of the poem was also felt by George Whalley, who described the "suffering, perplexity, loneliness, longing, horror, fear" of Coleridge's "nightmare land" as the personal horror which gives the poem its "haunting quality." (*University of Toronto Quarterly,* XVI, June 1947, p. 382.)

A second major view of the poem came in 1945, when Robert Penn Warren, tracking the symbols in the poem, discovered two themes, both deeply significant, one religious, one philosophical. Warren traced the theme of "One Life" which he called "the sacramental vision" through the symbols of the poem and explained the killing of the albatross as a reenactment of Original Sin. At the end "the angelic troops wipe out the crime (i.e., the 'criminal' ship and the dead bodies). . . ." Warren also found symbols for a second and equally important theme of Imagination which coincides, he believed, with the theory of Imagination Coleridge later systematized in his *Biographia Literaria.* (*Selected Essays,* New York, 1948, pp. 234–50.)

We are cautioned, however, from accepting Warren's symbolic interpretations by E. E. Stoll who facetiously calls "The Ancient Mariner" the "happiest hunting ground for symbolists." Stoll reminds us of the answer J. L. Lowes made to the moralist critic Irving Babbitt and urges us to apply that answer to Warren's analysis. "The Ancient Mariner" is an exquisitely structured poem first and foremost. (*PMLA,* LXIII, 1948, pp. 214, 225–26.) Humphry House, though, expresses gratitude for Warren's illumination of the "One Life" theme. He takes exception, however, to Warren's understanding of the second theme of Imagination. House believes that "The Ancient Mariner" is part of the experience which led to Coleridge's later theories but not the "symbolic adumbration of the theoretic statements themselves." (*Coleridge,* p. 113.)

The attacks against symbolist criticism are numerous, but Warren has a number of supporters. E. B. Gose, Jr., also found the poem deeply symbolic and religious: "The Mariner's act is . . . an attempt to negate God's principle." For such a crime, Gose wrote, it is fitting punishment that the Mariner is left alone surrounded by the soulless bodies of his friends, who are reminders that the albatross was "like a Christian soul," symbolically "repudiated." The sinning Mariner is redeemed; he regains "harmony with God first and decisively in the blessing scene. . . . But not until he mixes with the mortals of this earth is he enabled to do bodily penance for his violation of the one life." (*PMLA*, LXXV, 1960, pp. 239, 244.) Also confirming this religious symbolic view of the poem is R. L. Brett who believes that "the events of the poem show a pattern of what might be called orthodox religious experience." Brett states that "the voyage of the Mariner has been a dark night of the soul, in which he has wandered from God and sinned against Him." (*Reason and Imagination*, New York, 1960, pp. 102, 106.)

Similar religious symbolic insights into the poem are shared by Harold Creed and M. F. Schulz. Creed, who adapts Warren's analysis to his own reading of the poem, states that "the albatross . . . [is] the key symbol in the poem." Coleridge believed in the "oneness" of the world; the murder of the albatross was a selfish and willful sin of "arrogant pride"; and his punishment was fitting to his crime. (*The English Journal*, XLIX, 1960, p. 221.) Schulz's position provides us with an apt summary of modern opinions of Coleridge's great poem: the Ancient Mariner's "awareness of good and evil and man's oneness with the external world adds moral and metaphysical dimensions to an otherwise stark recital of fearful occurrences." (*The Poetic Voices of Coleridge*, Detroit, 1963, p. 64.) There seems to be no modern critic who shares the opinion Babbitt expressed almost forty years ago that "The Ancient Mariner," an "enthralling" fiction and "good in its own way—almost miraculously good," was a poem that had no "human substance." (*On Being Creative*, p. 71.)

Although "Christabel" has received its fair share of critical attention, and a number of bewitched readers have tried to solve the puzzle of the fragment, it is "Kubla Khan" (along with "The Ancient Mariner") which has successfully upstaged the second of Coleridge's "golden poems" in the theater of criticism. Coleridge called "Kubla Khan" an opium dream, but his statement of his experience has more than once been called into question by critics who are familiar with Coleridge's unpleasant habit of distorting the truth. To those who doubted the poet's veracity over the facts of composition of "Kubla Khan," J. L. Lowes tried in 1927 to provide a definitive answer. "Nobody in his waking senses could have fabricated those amazing eighteen lines." For the poem bears "the infallible marks of authenticity"; its "dissolving panorama," its "vivid incoherence," its "illusion of natural and expected sequence," are all "distinctive attributes of dreams," Lowes wrote. (*The Road to Xanadu*, p. 331.) M. H. Abrams, who studied the marks of opium in several poems written by known users, also established the authenticity of Coleridge's opium dream. (*The Milk of Paradise*, Cambridge, Mass., 1934.) However, we are wisely cautioned by Elisabeth Schneider not to mistake the great dream poem as a product of opium alone, for opium does not have the power to elicit from the writer a genius he does not possess. The poem, although envisioned as an opium dream, was a product of Coleridge's own creative powers. (*PMLA*, LX, 1945, p. 784, ff.; and *Coleridge, Opium, and Kubla Khan*, Chicago, 1953.)

Although the validity of the dream and an understanding of the true effects of opium were the critics' first interest, there has also been a continuous concern with the meaning of the poem. "The trouble" with "Kubla Khan," J. B. Beer wrote, "is not that the poem has no meaning but that it has too much." (*Coleridge the Visionary*, London, 1959, pp. 266–67.) Lowes understood the poem as a dream sequence in which the relation of the parts is "inconsequential." The caves of ice appear and are gone; then suddenly the Abyssinian damsel is there. The whole is "a bafflingly complex involution—dreams within dreams, like a nest of Oriental ivories, 'sphere in sphere.'" (*The Road to Xanadu*, p. 409.) In a certain sense, however, the imagery is not "inconsequential" as Lowes thought. According to Maud Bodkin, the images are "psychophysiological echoes," some of them reminiscent of "the first conscious reaction to dark enclosed places" felt by the infant. She believed the images of Coleridge's romantic dream poem arose "directly from the inner experience of the poet": although they first appear to be random constructions, upon analysis they seem to be "ordered and penetrated by the same familiar patterns" one finds in classical literature. (*Archetypal Patterns,* pp. 114–15.)

Coherency of another kind was found by Humphry House who felt that Lowes was prejudiced by Coleridge's statement that the poem was a dream. Actually, the poem has coherent meaning, House states: "the whole poem can be made to appear to be about the failure and frustration of the creative power," or it can be stating "the very possibility of creative achievement." House has "no hesitation in taking the second alternative," for he feels "Kubla Khan" is "biographically relevant" and that at the time of its writing, Coleridge still had hopes his poetic creativity would last. Kubla, House believed, is the poet in action. (*Coleridge,* p. 115.) Similarly, J. B. Beer declared that "Kubla Khan" "reflects the intense subterranean energy of a mind which could not rest in its endeavour to apprehend all experience and reduce it to one harmony." Kubla is a man of genius who tries to realize that harmony. (*Coleridge the Visionary,* pp. 226–29.)

M. F. Schulz, who agrees essentially with House and Beer, adds that Kubla is also "the dreamer who creates, or gives actuality to, his reveries." Xanadu was a palace, which according to legend Kubla constructed after a dream. Most probably, Schulz conjectures, Coleridge "thought of Xanadu and the pleasure-dome as the epitome of all that man visualizes in his dreaming moments and longs to realize in life." In the poem Xanadu is the raw material which must be shaped into poetry. (*The Poetic Voices of Coleridge,* p. 115.)

One need only glance at the bibliographies of Coleridge criticism to see how influential Coleridge's ideas and poems have become. A prophet without honor in his own time, he has few detractors in ours.

GEORGE NOEL GORDON,
LORD BYRON

The most aristocratic, flamboyant, and notorious of the great Romantics, Lord Byron was a popular figure in his own day and an important influence on the literature which came after him. He devised and was himself the prototype of a new Romantic hero, the social exile, the cynic, and the melancholy man, brooding over a secret sin and suggesting depths of soul which attracted men and women alike.

LIFE: Notorious for his immoral behavior, Byron may have inherited his wildness from his father, "Mad Jack" Byron, who married the Marchioness of Carmathen, a divorcee, by whom he had a daughter, Augusta, in 1783. Catherine Gordon, "Mad Jack's" second wife and Byron's mother, was an unstable woman with aristocratic pretensions, given to fits of hysteria and moodiness. The offspring of this unpromising pair was born in London in 1788, handicapped from birth by a deformed leg. When he was only three, his father died in France, where he had gone to evade his English creditors. The boy was raised by his mother under impoverished and unstable conditions. At ten, however, he inherited the title and estate of his great-uncle William, Lord Byron. Three years later, his mother enrolled him in Harrow, a school for aristocrats, which ranks with Eton and Winchester as one of England's great "public schools." At Harrow from 1801 to 1805, he showed a talent for friendship which he was to exhibit throughout his life and which is one of his most attractive characteristics. He also excelled in sports, especially in swimming, in spite of the fact that he had been born with a club foot. Proud, rebellious, and mischievous, he was not a good student but he managed to find time for a great deal of reading, and it was obvious to his masters and school-fellows that he possessed unusual talents.

In 1805 he entered Trinity College, Cambridge, and lived there so recklessly that he was soon heavily in debt. In addition to living extravagantly at Cambridge, Byron continued to show his determination not to allow his lameness to interfere with his manliness. He continued his swimming and he took up boxing and fencing. He also dabbled in poetry.

Restless, after a few terms he withdrew for a time from the University. In 1806 he published his first collection of poems, *Fugitive Pieces,* some of which were indiscreet. He was persuaded to suppress the book. The following year, a revised and expurgated selection of these early poems appeared under the title *Poems on Various Occasions.* A few months later he reissued this work, calling it now *Hours of Idleness.*

He returned to Cambridge and in spite of his undisciplined life received his M.A. in 1808. While in Cambridge he read in the *Edinburgh Review,* one of the most influential literary journals of the nineteenth century, a sarcastic review of his *Hours of Idleness.* Byron retaliated with a rambunctious satirical poem, *English Bards and Scotch Reviewers.*

THE GRAND TOUR: In 1809, Byron and one of his college friends, J. C. Hobhouse, set out on an extended tour of Spain, Portugal, Albania, and Greece. One fruit of this expedition was the poet's *Childe Harold's Pilgrimage,* the first two cantos of which were published in 1812, the third in 1816, the fourth in 1818.

Back in London by 1811, Byron became one of the most talked-about men of his time. Notorious for his many love affairs, for his dissolute living, his political radicalism, he nevertheless found it possible amid all of his other activities to produce a series of verse narratives that established him as a new star in the literary firmament.

MARRIAGE: Early in 1815 he made one of the gravest mistakes of his career. He married Anne Isabella Milbanke. Not only was Byron temperamentally unsuited to marriage, but he was also peculiarly unsuited to marriage with Anne Isabella. She was foolish enough to think that she could reform the wicked Lord Byron, but her smugness and self-righteousness only made her husband all the more determined to live his own kind of life.

The unhappy couple separated in the following year, but not before Lady Byron had borne him a daughter, Augusta Ada.

EXILE: The separation caused a great deal of malicious gossip. Angry at the talk and vexed that his efforts toward a reconciliation with his wife were unsuccessful, Byron and some friends, including Hobhouse, left England. The poet never returned to his native land.

In Geneva he struck up a friendship with Shelley, another poet who found it impossible to accept the conventions of society. In 1814, although still married to his first wife Harriet Westbrook, Shelley had eloped with Mary Godwin, the seventeen-year-old daughter of William Godwin, the author of radical books and pamphlets on government and morality. Residing with Shelley and Mary was Mary's half-sister, Claire Clairmont. Byron had an affair with Claire and by her had a daughter, Allegra.

In 1817 Byron published his best poetic drama, *Manfred*. The following year saw the publication of *Beppo,* an experiment in the flippant style that was to characterize his satirical master-piece, *Don Juan,* a long, rambling narrative poem on which he worked from 1818 to 1824. During this period he was involved in his last famous love affair, that with Teresa Guiccioli, the young wife of an aged Italian count.

For some years Greece had been tyrannically governed by the Turkish Empire. In 1821 the Greek War of Independence broke out. Throughout Europe the revolutionary spirit was high, and many people rallied to the support of the Greeks. An enthu-siastic supporter of the Greeks, Byron joined the insurgents, but at Missolonghi he contracted a fever and died.

WORKS: In addition to the works already named, and almost equally well read, the *Turkish Tales* (1813–14); *Hebrew Melo-dies* (1815); *Mazeppa* (1819); *The Island* (1823); *The Vision of Judgment* (1822).

ENGLISH BARDS AND SCOTCH REVIEWERS: In iambic pen-tameter couplets, the poem is an obvious imitation of the satirical manner of Pope. The bite and the bounce of the verse make the poem entertaining even when Byron's opinions about his victims are most outrageously unfair. As an exhibition of literary swordsmanship, it is superb.

It has been remarked that the satire was occasioned by an unfavorable review of Byron's *Hours of Idleness.* It is to be expected, therefore, that the editor of the *Edinburgh Review,* where the offending critical notice appeared, would be one of Byron's targets. In this poem, however, the arrogant young man attacks the entire Romantic movement. Scott, Wordsworth, and Coleridge are accused of being dull, obscure, and silly. Of all the great Romantic poets, Byron is most in sympathy with neoclassicism. *English Bards and Scotch Reviewers* is important not only for what it satirizes but also for its lively advocacy of the virtues of such poets as Dryden and Pope.

CHILDE HAROLD'S PILGRIMAGE: Largely autobiographical, inspired by the tour of the Mediterranean countries and the Near East begun by the poet in 1809, this long poem in Spenserian stanzas established Byron's European reputation. It describes the travels and the reflections of a pilgrim (Childe Harold, the archaic title "childe" signifying a youth of gentle birth) who has turned from an empty life of pleasure and is now seeking spiritual rebirth. The first two cantos were published in 1812. They describe travels through Portugal, Spain, the Ionian Isles, and Albania. In the light of Byron's subsequent participation in the Greek struggle for freedom, the conclusion of the second canto, a lament that Greece is subject to the tyranny of the Turks, has a special interest.

Canto III appeared in 1816. It brings the pilgrim to Belgium, the Rhineland, and Switzerland. In each place, he reflects on historical associations. Byron, for example, visited the battlefield at Waterloo where on June 18, 1815, Napoleon's ambitions were finally frustrated.

The passage in which Harold recreates the celebrated battle is one of the best-known passages in the poem. The description of Alpine scenery in this canto is also deservedly admired. The opening lines of the canto have a peculiar pathos, addressed as they are by Byron to his little daughter whom he had not seen since she was five weeks old and whom he was never again to see.

It is clear through the first three cantos that Childe Harold is Byron himself. In the fourth canto, the poet abandons the pose and speaks in his own person. The evocation of Italian scenes and a deep love of Italy, an appreciation of Italy's art and literature, make the canto notable.

One most important feature of *Childe Harold's Pilgrimage* is the fact that here for the first time we meet the so-called "Byronic Hero." This was Byron's special contribution to Romanticism. The Byronic hero is a man in rebellion against society, a lonely individualist, proud and willful. Beneath his cynicism and disdain, however, are an aching sadness and a pathetic feeling of hopelessness.

Childe Harold's Pilgrimage is Romantic in the lavishness of its descriptions and in its emotionalism. It is also Romantic in its emphasis on individualism. Childe Harold and Byron are at odds with the world. They suffer. They are blessed (or cursed) with a sensitivity denied to ordinary mortals. The poem gives us exceptionally valuable insights into Byron's special ways of responding to the world. It must be noted, however, that Childe Harold—and the poet who tells us of the travels of Childe Harold—is a consciously "literary" creation. Putting it another way, in *Childe Harold's Pilgrimage* we encounter a Byron who is inclined to take himself seriously. He even uses the stanza employed by Edmund Spenser in his delightful but basically serious *The Faerie Queene*. This "Spenserian" stanza is made up of nine lines. The first eight are iambic pentameter; the ninth line is iambic hexameter (six metrical feet predominantly patterned on the sequence of unstressed syllable followed by stressed syllable). The rhyme scheme is a b a b b c b c c.

TURKISH TALES: The Byronic hero appears again and again in three long, melodramatic verse tales that Byron wrote between 1813 and 1814. The settings of all of these tales are in the Orient. The first, *The Giaour* (pronounced "jour," means "infidel"; it was a term applied by Turks to Christians, "infidels," from the point of view of Moslems), is about incidents in the chambers of a caliph (a Moslem ruler). *The Bride of Abydos* is a story of a pirate, as is *The Corsair*. The tales appealed to popular taste and were so enthusiastically received that Scott gave up his verse narratives and turned to novel-writing. Another verse tale, *Lara,* is a sequel to *The Corsair*. The story, however, is located in Spain.

Extravagantly admired in their time, the "oriental tales" are still read today. They form an essential part of the story of how Byron captured the imagination of his contemporaries on the Continent as well as in his native land.

MANFRED: Published in 1817, this dramatic poem is Byron's experiment with the Faust legend. The legend tells of a famous scholar who sells his soul to the Devil. The subject of a play by Christopher Marlowe, one of the greatest of the Elizabethan dramatists whose work is thought to have had a great influence on Shakespeare, it was also explored by Goethe, the most important of all German writers, in what is regarded as his finest poem.

In Byron's story, we meet Manfred, a man who has committed some dreadful but unnamed crime. The crime is so hideous that he knows that he can never atone for it. He lives alone in the Alps, an outcast from society, tortured by remorse.

In his agony, Manfred summons the spirits of the universe and begs for oblivion. They refuse to grant his request. He summons the witch of the Alps, to no avail. Tempted, he refuses to submit to the spirits of evil. Then he has a vision of Astarte, the woman he has truly loved, and in the vision she foretells his death on the following day. When the fatal hour arrives, demons come to claim Manfred. He denies that they have power over him, and they depart. Manfred then finds release in death.

Here again is the Byronic hero and the Romantic manner. Even though Byron admired Dryden and Pope and thought that many of the attitudes of poets like Wordsworth and Coleridge were cloudy and absurd, he was influenced more than he realized by the changing tastes and feelings of his time.

DON JUAN: Byron's most enduring achievement is his vast, sprawling comic poem, *Don Juan*. The theatricality of the "oriental tales" and of *Manfred* have, in some measure, lost their appeal, while *Don Juan* speaks to readers of the twentieth century more effectively than it spoke to its original readers.

During his residence in Italy, Byron became interested in Italian poets of the Renaissance. He became particularly interested in their ability to alternate from the jaunty and gay to the sentimental. He observed how the Italians used the lively language of everyday speech but interspersed it with deliberately "poetic" language. He recognized that the Italian ottava rima was suitable to the expression of his own devil-may-care, defiant, cynical but emotion-fraught view of the universe. *Don Juan* owes much to Italian poetry. It also owes something to the work of a contemporary English poet named John H. Frere who anticipated Byron in seeing the possibility of imitating in racy English the Renaissance Italian poems and adapted the ottava rima to English verse.

The Italian ottava rima is similar to the Spenserian stanza of *Childe Harold*. It is also predominantly iambic pentameter. It dispenses, however, with the expanded ninth line and thus it achieves a rapidity and raciness that the Spenserian stanza deliberately avoids. The rhyme scheme of the ottava rima is different from the Spenserian stanza in that its pattern of rhymes runs a b a b a b c c. It proved to be a stanza admirably suited to Byron's mocking, sardonic view of life.

His first experiment in this new technique was *Beppo*. A lighthearted story about a carnival, a lady, her lover, and the unexpected return of her husband, *Beppo* is important not so much for its story as for its revelation of Byron's sure instinct for comedy. After the completion of *Beppo*, Byron began planning his greatest comic masterpiece, *Don Juan*. He was to work on this for the rest of his life. He never completed it. What he has left us, however, is a very long poem, running to sixteen cantos and part of a seventeenth.

The story of *Don Juan* is not nearly so important as the poet's comments on the events of the story and on life in general. The story is about a young man of Seville, Don Juan, who has a love affair with an older (and married) woman. His pious mother, accordingly, sends him abroad to keep him from further indiscretions. He is shipwrecked but, naturally, survives. He and his few fortunate companions finally come to a Greek island and there he is comforted by Haidée, the beautiful daughter of a pirate. When Haidée's father discovers that Juan and his daughter are in love he has Juan put in chains and sent away on one of his ships. Haidée goes mad and dies. Juan is sold into slavery in Constantinople. His purchaser is a sultana who has fallen in love with his manly beauty. His troubles, however, are far from over. The sultana becomes jealous and orders Juan's death. The boy manages to escape and joins the Russian army. His gallantry and handsomeness attract the favorable attention of Catherine the Great, who was notorious throughout Europe for her amorousness. Catherine sends Juan on a political mission to England. This is the point at which the story halts.

The poem is mockingly dedicated to Robert Southey. At the time, Southey was considered one of the most important of the Romantic poets. In 1813 he was made Poet Laureate, a traditional honor given by the Crown. The fact that the king extended this honor to Southey shows not only that his poetry was highly regarded but (and this is more important) that his political ideas were acceptable to the Government. He was safe. Like Wordsworth and Coleridge, with whom he had been friendly and with whom he made up that band of poets called the "Lake Poets," Southey once had advocated revolutionary ideas. Like them he later changed his mind and became a conservative. And as such, he attracted Byron's withering scorn. Also ridiculed in this savage but clever and amusing dedication are Wordsworth and Coleridge.

Don Juan was meant to shock its original readers. But social changes that have taken place since it was written make it far less shocking today. Although Byron's own behavior was often scandalous, his young rake, Don Juan, is fundamentally a hero. He is, of course, far from being a model of virtue, but he is not a monster of vice. We recognize his instincts as fundamentally healthy.

In a certain sense, indeed, *Don Juan* can be read as a comic poem that has beneath its surface some profoundly valuable things to be said about life. The tone is irreverent; however, the irreverence stems from the poet's hatred for hypocrisy, smugness, and sickening sanctimoniousness. The portrait of Donna Inez, the mother of Don Juan, in the first canto provides an illustration of this coming together of the amusing and the serious. As one reads the sketch one cannot help but sense that Byron is enjoying himself hugely, is relishing the absurdities of Donna Inez. At the same time, one notices that painful memories of his life with the virtuous Anne Isabella Milbanke helped to give substance to his satire. He is saying, in effect, that some of the self-styled good people in the world cause an awful lot of trouble.

The dazzling variety of incidents, scenes, and moods makes this poem a masterpiece. The inexhaustible energy of the ottava rima stanzas is another reason for the poem's popularity. And Byron's comments on an almost endless number of subjects— love, selfishness, generosity, heroism, cowardice, jealousy, politics—add to the importance of a work that only pretends to be light and frivolous.

Byron was an astonishingly prolific writer and apparently was able to compose with remarkable speed. There is a kind of deliberate carelessness about his writing. He often seems to be saying to his readers, "I write to please myself and have no intention of taking great pains to please you."

Byron contributed to the Romantic movement in many ways. In *Childe Harold's Pilgrimage,* for example, he created a melancholy hero, moved to reflection by picturesque scenes, a brooding man poignantly conscious of his aloneness, of his isolation from society. In the *Turkish Tales,* Byron appealed to the popular demand for "tales of terror" and showed his "Gothic" imagination. In *Don Juan,* the author poses as an anti-

Romantic, a man who is completely down-to-earth, completely honest. His pose is that he despises the affectations of poets like Wordsworth and Coleridge. He wants to have nothing to do with misty theorizing. On the other hand, the author's determination to speak his own mind, to speak fearlessly, to record his unique encounter with life is essentially an expression of Romantic individualism. The pose in *Don Juan* is very different from that in *Childe Harold's Pilgrimage*. Both poses, however, were struck by a poet who responded to the new Romantic emphasis on self rather than on society.

The complexity of Byron's character and the complexity of Romantic ideas and feelings must never be minimized. Byron hated affectation—yet he made himself a legend. Byron was a wicked man (and wickedness was part of the legend he created)—yet he forced his contemporaries and later generations to re-examine the nature of true morality and the definition of goodness. The whole Romantic age is full of similar paradoxes. Romantic poets were inclined to take their own emotional pulses in public. This behavior would have been considered bad form in the neoclassical period. But preoccupation with self in the Romantic age never interfered with the poets' other concerns. All of the important Romantic poets were passionately involved in the crucial social and political movements of their time. Some of the Romantic poets who were revolutionists in their youth became more conservative as they grew older, as was the case with Wordsworth and Coleridge. Others like Byron and Shelley died young and remained rebels to the end. But all of them in one way or another attacked the old order and searched for a way to establish a new one.

CRITICISM: From the very first volume of verse he published as an anonymous young lord, Byron attracted attention to his person as well as to his poems. It was probably the aristocratic anonymous signature of the inconsequential *Hours of Idleness* which invited the notice of the *Edinburgh Review*'s Henry Brougham (January 1808) in the first place, but it was the mock modesty of the preface which provoked Brougham's sarcastic attacks not only on the poetry ("The poesy of this young lord belongs to the class which neither gods nor men are said to permit") but also on the author himself (" 'It is highly improbable, from his situation and pursuits hereafter,' that he should again condescend to be an author. Therefore let us take what we get and be thankful"). It was this review which inspired Byron to write *English Bards and Scotch Reviewers,* the satire on contemporary poetry which attracted even more attention than *Hours of Idleness,* and made not a few enemies for the young poet.

The tone of the *Edinburgh Review* (this time with Jeffrey not Brougham behind the pen) altered considerably with the publication of *Childe Harold* I and II. And as the *Turkish Tales* began to appear (1813), Jeffrey, in his inimitable fashion, continued to praise the popular young poet. He especially admired the diction and verse and "moral sublimity" of the author. In the December 1816 review of *Childe Harold* III, Jeffrey went even further. He found the diction and sentiment of that poem superior to that of Scott, Campbell, Crabbe, and Moore, the leading lights of contemporary poetry. But he objected to the Byronic hero of *Childe Harold,* who was too guilty and too gloomy for Jeffrey's taste.

Jeffrey's view of the Byronic hero was shared by many critics of the time. Sir Walter Scott, reviewing the third canto in the *Quarterly Review* (October 1816), was fascinated. He was the first critic to recognize that Byron had created an important new character. But he identified the character with the poet himself and may have helped Byron create the myth of himself. Analyzing both poet and character as men fascinated by forbidden things, Scott described them as melancholy figures who lived with the guilt of an unnamed disaster in the past. Although the Byronic hero had a strong sense of sin, he also had noble virtues, Scott felt. He was, in addition, a rebel, a wanderer, a misanthrope, and a lover who was at the same time disillusioned by women. Scott recognized the restless and tortured spirit of the poet and confessed his own attraction to this figure, a fearful attraction shared by many later poets too. Nevertheless, Scott advised the young poet to seek peace of mind. He failed to see that he was asking the poet to tear the heart out of the Byronic hero.

When the fourth canto of *Childe Harold* appeared, *Blackwood's* reviewer (possibly John Wilson, May 1818) was enthusiastic about the power and force of its poetry. But, like Scott, he found the hero's tyrannical passions dangerous, especially to young readers, and suggested modifications of those emotions. Like Scott, this reviewer failed to see that the real power of the poem lay in the strong passions of its hero.

Contemporary critics were in substantial agreement about *Don Juan*. *Blackwood's* (August 1819; July 1823) recognized the greatness of the poem but condemned it as immoral because it exalted decadence. Its publisher John Murray refused to have anything to do with it after the fifth canto, and John Hunt published the remainder of the poem. In fact, one of the few defenses (a lame one at that) of *Don Juan* was made in *The Examiner* by Hunt's brother, Leigh Hunt, who insisted the poem was not immoral. He objected to it on other grounds, however, because it "trifles with our feelings" and because as satire, it couldn't achieve greatness. These critics' objections to *Don Juan* were not shared by the general public, and the work was extremely popular among poets on the Continent as well. Goethe thought *Don Juan* "a work of boundless genius" (*Kunst und Alterthum,* 1821) and Shelley admired its "originality" (Letter to Byron, October 21, 1821). There was an attraction about Byron and his poems which even his most ardent opponents were obliged to confess. After Byron's death, Hazlitt recanted the "peevishness" of his attacks against Byron, which had appeared in *The Spirit of the Age*; and Walter Savage Landor, whose anti-Byron remarks were about to appear in *Imaginary Conversations,* added a commendatory statement about the poet who had died in the cause of liberty.

A good deal of Byron criticism has been biographical rather than literary. The scandal which accompanied Byron's marriage to and separation from Anne Isabella Milbanke, and his alleged incest with his sister Augusta, have been major concerns in many biographies of Byron. Still another reason for so much interest in the life of Byron has been the critics' desire to understand the school of "Byronism," which the poet had unknowingly initiated. A whole body of "decadent" literature dealing with melancholy, tortured, and guilty souls and with forbidden subjects emerged, especially in France, years after Byron's death. Mario Praz attributed the movement to the Frenchman's fascination with the Byronic hero, combined with excessive interest in the madly "divine" Marquis de Sade. (*The Romantic Agony* [1933], New York, 1956, p. 81.)

Whether to indulge in the scandal or to penetrate the mystery of Byronism, Byron's biographers have proliferated ever since it became clear that Thomas Moore had destroyed some of Byron's papers and had failed to publish the "whole truth" in his *Letters and Journals of Lord Byron* (1830). There had been, in 1828, a peevish exposé of the "real" Byron by Leigh Hunt who had clashed with the lord in Italy. Other contemporary accounts of Byron had been written by friends: Thomas Medwin in 1824, John Galt in 1830, and Teresa Guiccioli in 1868. It was perhaps the Countess' book which at last broke Anne Isabella Milbanke's long silence about her side of the marriage, and in 1869, she permitted Harriet Beecher Stowe to publish an article vindicating Lady Byron; a book by the same author on the same subject appeared the following year.

Stowe's book was an open declaration of war against Byron's reputation, and two camps formed, one siding with Anne Isabella, the other with the poet. Ralph, Earl of Lovelace, represented Lady Byron's camp in a book called *Astarte* (1905). He described Byron as a bitter, fierce, vindictive, and sadistic man, almost maniacal: "A display of moral baseness, of human infamy caught in the act, stirred him to fierce transports of delight," the earl wrote. (*Astarte,* p. 3.) He insisted that Byron purposefully imitated the hero he had invented, that his "Byronism" was a pose of the fallen or exiled being of Oriental literature who lived under a curse, and that the pose "resembled a delusion." Worst of all, he provided evidence that Byron had committed incest with his sister Augusta.

The idea that Byron was a "poseur" was accepted by many, including Byron's admirers. But the idea of Byron's incest was hard to take. A year after Lovelace's book, John Murray offered an antidote to the poisonous *Astarte* in *Lord Byron and His Detractors*. Richard Edgcumbe tried to save Byron's reputation in an unconvincing argument that Augusta had adopted Byron's illegitimate child by another woman. (*Byron: The Last Phase,* 1909.) Sir John Charles Fox's examination in *The Byron Mystery* (1924) of the incest evidence was inconclusive, and the battle continued to wage. In the recent three-volume biography, *Byron,* by Leslie A. Marchand (New York, 1957), the incest is accepted without moralistic judgment. Byron the man and the poet was a complex being, and there is no reason to discard one of his aspects because we may disapprove of another.

While the war of the biographers raged, there were many noncombatants who chose to examine the poetry rather than the poet. In our own century, *Don Juan* has been acknowledged from the start as a literary masterpiece. Paul Elmer More urged a necessary corrective to nineteenth-century views of the poem when he wrote in 1905 that it is a mistake to regard the poem as a "mere work of satire." It is more than merely satirical. "The very scope of the subject classes it with the more universal epics of literature rather than with the poems that portray only a single aspect of life." (*Shelburne Essays,* Third Series, pp. 170–71.)

Although others have recognized greatness in *Don Juan,* critics have found different ways of explaining or describing it. It has been clear to some that Byron's are "not the purest, the highest gifts of the poet." His greatness lies, according to H. J. C. Grierson, in the "force, passion, humour and wit, narrative and descriptive power, oratorical fire and conversational ease and flow" of his style. (*The Backgrounds of English Literature* [1920], New York, 1960, pp. 112–13.) T. S. Eliot was "distressed" by Byron's poetry, but he found in *Don Juan* one major virtue. Although Byron was insensitive to English words, used too many of them, and made no new discoveries in the language, as a poet should, Eliot conceded that Byron's animosity to English hypocrisy gave him his "first genuine emotion." To Eliot, the English cantos at the end of *Don Juan* are the great ones. Similarly, E. J. Lovell recognized the imperfect poetry of *Don Juan* and agreed with Eliot that Byron lacked the "delicately tuned ear . . . to the subtleties of sound combinations." Nevertheless, Lovell too found the work one of "great originality and undeniable excellence." (In *Major English Romantic Poets,* ed. C. DeW. Thorpe, et al., Carbondale, Ill., 1957, p. 129.) In respect to the English cantos, T. G. Steffan among others concurs with Eliot. These cantos "are alive with

terse and mocking comments on the vanity and folly of human
affairs, with clever verses, ingenious rhymes, odd conceits, and
brazen incongruities." (*Byron's Don Juan,* Austin, 1957, p.
258.) To still another critic, Byron "was no philosopher, no
great social wit, nor even a writer at heart." Still, Byron is
"most impressive," especially when he is most malicious, when
he creates a convincing mood of melancholy, then defies it
"with gusto." (Paul West, *Byron and the Spoiler's Art,* New
York, 1960, p. 12.)

Not everyone agrees with Eliot that Byron had a poor ear.
Ronald Bottrall took pains to explain that Byron was writing in
a colloquial tradition in which the rhythm of the speech determined the metrical pattern of the verse. In doing so, Byron
obtained an "exact relation of thought to feeling, of rhythm to
emotion." Bottrall argued that Byron's language is colloquial,
but it is great. He especially admired the English cantos, which
he regarded as "sustained pieces of social criticism only surpassed in English verse by Pope's *Satires and Moral Essays.*"
(*Criterion,* XVIII, No. 71, January 1939, pp. 216–17.)

Lately, Byron's ear has not been troubling critics. The poem's
artistic merit must be judged on other grounds, crtics now
believe as they examine the structure of his masterpiece. Byron
had confessed to his publisher John Murray in a letter of
August 12, 1819, "You ask me for the plan of Donny Jonny: I
have no plan." But in a later letter to Murray, he admitted that
he had a loose kind of story in mind. It is this intention, or plan,
or lack of it, for which critics now search. Ernest Bernbaum
wrote that the chief rule of the poem was "to avoid the regular,"
to use digressions and to change the tone whenever whim
moved the poet. "Anything he had seen or experienced might be
admitted," for the poem was to be an "outlet for his person-
ality." (*Guide Through the Romantic Movement,* New York,
1949, p. 206.) To E. J. Lovell, however, the poem has
significant unity in its ironic theme of appearance versus reality.
It also has "significant structure [which] is a considered organi-
zation of a rich variety of ironically qualified tones." Each of
the episodes, Lovell finds, is organically related to this larger
theme. (In *Major English Romantic Poets,* p. 140.) W. H.
Marshall finds the structure loose but believes the poem suc-

cessful in that it accomplishes Byron's intention. The poem's lack of consistency is "its dominant virtue in terms of what it is supposed to do and what it does." Somewhat like Lovell, he sees *Don Juan* as "an ironic image" of his earlier heroes; this hero is intentionally inconsistent. At times he is naive and frightened; at other times, worldly and indiscreet. There are other conscious inconsistencies: the tension of the serious scenes is often broken by a ludicrous remark, and the characters are often set in ludicrous opposition to one another. This is exactly what Byron wanted to do, Marshall argues, and this is what he succeeded in doing. (*The Structure of Byron's Major Works,* Philadelphia, 1962, p. 176.)

The structure of Byron's comic epic is described still another way by Andrew Rutherford, who disagrees with Lovell wholly. It is "something of a large, loose, baggy monster, full of life, but lacking the concentrated power which comes only with organic unity." Byron polished individual lines, Rutherford explains, but he did not plan the whole satire carefully. Originally, he intended "to portray the corruption of a normal youth by Society and Experience," but as he kept getting new ideas, he soon gave up hope of arranging them into a "meaningful design." (*Byron: A Critical Study,* Stanford, 1962, pp. 140–41.)

Byron's malice and immorality rarely trouble modern critics who often enjoy these vices in him. His tin ear and faulty meters, his careless planning and loose structure continue to be noticed. Yet, in the twentieth century, as in his own time, Byron rises above all his faults. Of all the Romantic poets, he is the only one who continues to hold a wide popular audience. Perhaps it is his very lack of philosophic content and artistic form which makes his comic satire of hypocrisy the most meaningful part of his entire work and the most appealing.

PERCY BYSSHE SHELLEY

Whereas Byron was earthy, cynical, and realistic, Shelley was ethereal, guileless, and idealistic. He was courageous and never hesitated to use his remarkable imaginative powers to advance his revolutionary and humanitarian ideas and convictions. The private lives of both Byron and Shelley scandalized their contemporaries. Byron's wickedness was a part of his defiant pose, and he rather enjoyed the furor he caused, though there were times when he resented the self-righteousness of his fellows. Shelley never believed that his actions were wrong. Early in life he rebelled against authority, his father, school, the government, and religion. He thought and said that Christianity was wrong and that traditional moral codes were also wrong. But he was never negative in his thinking. He believed in the possibility of a brave new world. He believed that men could throw off the shackles of the past—superstitions, outworn political doctrines, cruel prejudices—and create an ideal society. Although Shelley's ideas may seem absurd to some modern readers, no one can doubt the purity of his motives.

LIFE: The eldest son of a wealthy country squire, Shelley was born in 1792. He attended Eton, the most famous of the English public (i.e. private) schools, where he experienced the kind of bullying that went on (and to some extent still goes on) in schools of this kind. Possessed from childhood of a fierce independence of spirit, he bitterly resented this tyranny of older boys and learned at an early age to hate all forms of tyranny.

He read widely at Eton, not only poetry but also books on political theory, science, and romantic tales. It was at Eton that he first read one of the most influential radical books of the day, William Godwin's *Inquiry Concerning Political Justice*. Godwin professed himself an atheist and an anarchist. He believed that men could live according to reason, that when they were

157

rationally persuaded of the rightness of an action they would invariably perform it. The obvious consequence was that human beings needed no restraining laws and institutions. This optimistic view of the nature of man appealed to Shelley's native idealism, his readiness to believe the best of man. Following the example of the master, Shelley became an atheist.

His atheism brought about serious consequences. When he went up to University College, Oxford, in 1810 he formed a close friendship with another young man, Thomas Hogg, who shared his enthusiasm for "advanced" doctrines. Eager to save the world from what they considered its folly, they published a pamphlet called *The Necessity of Atheism* and, defiantly refusing to answer questions about this work put to them by University authorities, they were expelled. (Oxford, without endorsing Shelley's atheism but recognizing his place among the greatest English poets, made belated amends by putting a statue of Shelley in the entrance of University College.) His father, who never showed much talent for understanding his son, was angered by his son's expulsion and cut off his allowance. The poet found himself in financial difficulties. These difficulties were, characteristically, increased by his tendency to become involved in emotional relationships. Throughout his comparatively short life, Shelley had a stormy emotional history, but there is a curious innocence about this history. He married Harriet Westbrook to save her from parental tyranny, he thought. He ran off with Mary Godwin because he loved her, and he entertained friendships with other women because he loved them platonically. Byron was frankly licentious; Shelley always thought that he saw profound spiritual qualities in the ladies he loved.

After thinking himself in love with a succession of girls, stretching back to an early conviction that he loved his cousin, Harriet Grove, Shelley impulsively married sixteen-year-old Harriet Westbrook in 1811. He had, typically, met this new source of spiritual inspiration while he was courting another young lady, Elizabeth Hitchener, with whom he carried on a long, sentimental correspondence. The fact that Harriet Westbrook was a dear friend of Elizabeth made no difference to Shelley. It was not that he was callous or brutal; it was simply that Shelley, for all of his generosity and kindness, was not very good at understanding the feelings or predicting the reactions of others.

After his marriage he spent some time in the Lake Country. By this time it was almost obligatory for aspiring poets to visit that region made so important by Coleridge and Wordsworth and by Southey, a poet now regarded as minor but who then enjoyed a considerable reputation. Shelley met Southey, but found him no longer the old firebrand liberal he once was. Southey's apparent retreat from his earlier radical position saddened the young poet.

In 1812 Shelley wrote to Godwin, telling the inflammatory sage how much he appreciated his work. Then he and Harriet went to Ireland to encourage the Irish in their fight for freedom and simultaneously to persuade them to see the necessity of atheism. There is something almost amusing and not a little touching in the spectacle of the atheist Shelley supporting the cause of Catholic emancipation, the freeing of Catholics from legal disabilities long imposed upon them.

Back in London, Shelley met Godwin and completed his first significant poem, *Queen Mab*. Published in 1813, it created a sensation by its violent radicalism. In it Shelley presents most of his favorite ideas, such as that religions are wicked, kings cruel and unnecessary, and the spirit of man in need of liberation. It is written in rhymeless verse of an irregular pattern intermingled with blank verse. It is crude and oratorical, utterly lacking in subtlety or in the poetic grace that was to mark Shelley's later work. As a document that illuminates nineteenth-century radical thought, however, *Queen Mab* has great historical importance.

It was almost predictable that Shelley would fall in love with Mary Godwin, the seventeen-year-old daughter of William Godwin. In 1814 he eloped with her to France. With them went Claire Clairmont, Godwin's stepdaughter, with whom Byron had an affair, as mentioned in the preceding chapter. One of the oddest features of the elopement, from the point of view of

ordinary mortals if not from the unworldly point of view of
Shelley, is that he wrote to Harriet, his wife, assuring her of his
friendship and suggesting that she join Mary, Claire, and himself.

The death of his grandfather in 1815 brought Shelley assurance
of an annual income which should have made him financially
secure for the rest of his life. But his generosity to various people
was excessive and he soon again found himself in financial
difficulties. Nor was he secure from personal tragedy. His
sister-in-law Fanny Imlay committed suicide, and Harriet Westbrook Shelley drowned herself in 1818. Shelley then legalized
his union with Mary Godwin.

In 1818, angry at the general disapproval of his life and actions,
harassed by impossibly involved domestic problems, Shelley left
England and settled on the Continent. He formed many important friendships, published many important poems, met a number of young ladies who, naturally, became his inspiration.

The end of this strange, turbulent, but somehow admirable and
affecting life came in 1822. On July 8, 1822, his small boat
capsized while he was returning home from Leghorn with his
friend Edward Williams. The bodies were cremated on the beach,
and Shelley's remains were placed in the Protestant Cemetery in
Rome, which also held the grave of Keats, whose elegy Shelley
had written only the year before.

WORKS: Shelley wrote so voluminously that one cannot, in a
short survey, do justice to the magnitude of his achievement.
The following list of his works is designed to call attention to
his greatest achievements. *Queen Mab* (1813); *Alastor*
(1816); *The Revolt of Islam* (1817); *The Cenci* (1819);
Prometheus Unbound (1819); "Ode to the West Wind" (1819);
"The Cloud" (1820); "To a Skylark" (1820); *Epipsychidion*
(1821); *Adonais* (1821); *Hellas* (1822); *Triumph of Life*
(1822).

ALASTOR: Never in robust health, in the spring of 1815
Shelley was convinced that he was dying. The melancholy that

attended this conviction can be detected in *Alastor,* generally looked upon as the first of Shelley's really important poems.

An allegorical poem written in blank verse, *Alastor* is about an idealist who finds happiness in his own meditations on beauty. The beauty that he reflects on is not the beauty that is to be seen in this world. It is, rather, the idea of beauty that is constructed by the mind. His dreams and visions prompt him to seek the counterpart of his ideal beauty in the real world. He fails in his search, falls into despair, and dies.

The poem is important for many reasons, chief of which are these. It shows Shelley's interest in the theory of the Greek philosopher Plato, that all things in this world are imperfect imitations of perfect things that have an eternal and changeless existence apart from everything that we know with our mortal senses and intelligence. It shows Shelley's "activism." Himself a dreamer, Shelley also knew that a man could not live in isolation from his fellow-men. He knew that a man must be willing to fight for justice. The poem shows how much the sensitive, well-meaning poet has been bruised by the world. It cannot be denied that there is a certain amount of self-pity in Shelley. *Alastor* also shows a growing sense of disillusionment. Although he continued to work for human betterment, Shelley no longer expected that the world would be changed overnight.

THE REVOLT OF ISLAM: A long poem of nearly 5000 lines, divided into twelve cantos, and composed in Spenserian stanzas, *The Revolt of Islam* was written in 1817. The imaginary revolution described proves unsuccessful. The oppressors of the Islamic people retain their power and show a terribly vengeful spirit toward the rebels. The leaders of the revolution, Laon, a high-minded youth, and Cythna, a young lady who shares his ideals and who is an eloquent champion of women's rights, are burned at the stake at the instigation of priests. The poem shows that the failure of the French Revolution had not dampened Shelley's passionate interest in reform. At the same time it shows that for all his fiery idealism he was able to recognize the facts of life.

PROMETHEUS UNBOUND: Universally acknowledged the most eloquent and persuasive of Shelley's lyrical expressions of faith in human nature, *Prometheus Unbound* was begun in 1818, completed in 1819, and published in 1820. In this verse drama Shelley reworks the legend of Prometheus, long familiar to readers of the tragedy *Prometheus Bound* by Aeschylus, the earliest of the great Greek tragic dramatists. Aeschylus' *Prometheus Bound* tells of the cruel punishment endured by the heroic Prometheus, a Titan, that is, one of the earliest "children of earth," who revealed to man the secret of fire. This secret made man the rival of the gods, and Zeus, the father of the gods, took vengeance on Prometheus. The theme, involving such things as man's hopes and aspirations and the repressiveness of traditional religion, was naturally of interest to Shelley. It is likely that Aeschylus wrote a sequel to his play, but if he did it has never been found.

Shelley undertook to supply a sequel in four acts. In Act I, Prometheus is presented after three thousand years of misery, anxious to recant his curse upon Jupiter and to convert his own spirit from pride to pity. His curse is repeated by Jupiter's ghost, and although Prometheus can barely remember uttering it, he retracts it again. Jupiter's reaction to the curse is reenacted. He is anxious for revenge and sends Mercury with a group of Furies to torture Prometheus. Out of pity, Mercury tempts Prometheus with immortal life among the gods, but like Christ, Prometheus refuses to yield to the temptation; he knows evil will disappear eventually. The torture proceeds; it is mental not physical. One torture is a vision of Christ's agony on the cross. Worse than that is a vision of Christ's religion perverted and abused by the ignorance of human society. Prometheus pities humans; the Furies leave; the chorus prophesies universal Love; and Panthea's remarks close the act, as she speaks of Asia who is in far off India, a land once bleak but now fair and sweet because of Prometheus' recantation.

At the opening of Act II, Asia is awaiting the arrival of Panthea her sister nymph. (She and her sisters represent different degrees of Love: faith, hope, and charity, perhaps; or divine love, conscious love, and instinctive love; or as Douglas Bush suggests, they are merely three aspects of love represented by a wife and two sisters-in-law, a typical Shelleyan household.) Panthea has a vision of Prometheus transfigured through love, which has been learned through suffering. She reveals to Asia through the vision within her eyes the transfiguration of Prometheus. The vision contains the enigmatic message to "Follow! Follow!" Thus, Asia proceeds on her journey to Demigorgon (Necessity, Destiny), and, in their interview in scene iv, learns the answers to questions such as: "Who made the living world?" "Who made all / That it contains?" "And who made terror?" "Who is the master of the slave?" To the first two questions, Demigorgon answers God. The answer to the third question is the cryptic "He reigns." On the last question, he hedges and finally replies, "The deep truth is imageless." The "destined hour" of Jupiter's downfall is forecast. A dark chariot waits to take Demigorgon to Olympus where he will take Jupiter into darkness. Meanwhile, Asia will travel to join Prometheus in a bright chariot. The act closes with a descriptive scene in which Asia is transfigured into "love, like the atmosphere / Of the sun's fire filling the living world."

Act III opens on Olympus with Jupiter rejoicing in his hour of omnipotence, crowing over the defeat of the "fatal child" who was to depose him. When Demigorgon alights, Jupiter's "dark hour" is swift and sure. He sinks into an endless abyss. The downfall of Jupiter, although re-enacted in Act III, has actually taken place during the same time in Act I when Prometheus had recanted his curse. As a consequence of Jupiter's downfall, Prometheus is unbound by Hercules, and Prometheus and Asia reunite. The Spirit of the Hour is sent to proclaim redemption to all the universe, and Asia and Prometheus depart for a temple beyond the Indies. At the close of Act III, the Spirit of the Hour returns to report how his joyous news was received throughout the world: "The painted veil . . . / . . . is torn aside; / The loathsome mask has fallen, the man remains / Sceptreless, free, uncircumscribed." Men are free and equal, classless, tribeless, shorn of awe and worship; still full of passion but without pain and guilt. "Nor yet exempt . . . / From chance, and death, and mutability." The final suggestion is that there is no absolute certainty of the permanent expulsion of moral evil. Jupiter is imprisoned not dead.

Act IV takes place outside Prometheus' cave and contains songs of rejoicing over universal freedom, with Panthea, Ione, Hours,

Spirits, and others participating. The act ends as Demigorgon proclaims: "This is the day . . . / . . . to hope till Hope creates / From its own wreck the thing it contemplates; / . . : . / This, like thy glory, Titan, is to be / Good, great and joyous, beautiful and free; / This is alone Life, Joy, Empire, and Victory." The forces of Love, after years of patient suffering, have prevailed.

Shelley's Prometheus is a noble champion of the rights of man who remains fearless when confronted by the threats of the cruel and vengeful Jupiter. He is supported in his cause by Earth, who, in classical mythology is said to be the mother of the Titan Prometheus, and by the thought of Asia, his wife. At the end of the poem, as one might expect, Jupiter is overthrown, and Prometheus released from his bondage. Consequently, all men and all the universe are freed.

Prometheus Unbound helps us in a remarkable way to acquire a sympathetic understanding of Shelley's thoughts and feelings. Consider, for example, Shelley's Jupiter. He should not be equated with the carefully defined or described God of trained theologians. He represents, rather, that image of God that in many lands and over many centuries has been created by men to lend "religious" justification to their cruelty, intolerance, and thirst for power. It must be understood that Shelley's thought was basically affirmative rather than negative. Behind his denial of God is a passionate and noble belief in the sacred rights of the individual, in the transforming power of love, in the possibility of creating a better world than the world we know.

As a play, *Prometheus Bound* has notable weaknesses. There is practically no story. The characters have abstract not human passions. There is no element of suspense or surprise. But as an intensely lyrical, splendidly imagined expression of Shelley's most deeply felt ideas, the poem deserves the immortality it has attained.

"ODE TO THE WEST WIND":   Published with *Prometheus Unbound* was Shelley's "Ode to the West Wind," one of the most prized of the poet's shorter lyrics. In it the poet makes exquisite use of the terza rima, the verse form employed by Dante in his

Divine Comedy. The meter of the terza rima is predominantly iambic pentameter. The stanza is made up of interlinking three-line units with the rhyme scheme a b a b c b c d c, continuing thus to the end of the stanza. The nature of the interlinking of the units and the effects produced by this interlinking can be studied in the first stanza of the ode:

> O wild West Wind, thou breath of Autumn's being, (a)
> Thou, from whose unseen presence the leaves dead (b)
> Are driven, like ghosts from an enchanter fleeing, (a)
>
> Yellow, and black, and pale, and hectic red, (b)
> Pestilence-stricken multitudes: O thou, (c)
> Who chariotest to their dark wintry bed (b)
>
> The wingèd seeds, where they lie cold and low, (modified c)
> Each like a corpse within its grave, until (d)
> Thine azure sister of the spring shall blow (modified c)
>
> Her clarion o'er the dreaming earth, and fill (d)
> (Driving sweet buds like flocks to feed in air) (e)
> With living hues and odours plain and hill: (d)
>
> Wild Spirit, which art moving everywhere; (e)
> Destroyer and preserver; hear, oh, hear! (modified e)

It will be noticed that the stanza ends not with a "tercet" (the technical name of the three-line unit) but with a couplet. The ode is made up of five stanzas constructed like the first except that the rhymes of the concluding couplets of all but the first and fifth are true rhymes. Other modifications of true rhyme have been pointed out in the stanza just quoted. Deviation from true rhyme should not be thought of as a fault. When there is no observable justification for it, it is a fault. When it is en-countered in the work of an obviously conscientious craftsman like Shelley, one is obliged to conclude that the poet is introduc-ing slight irregularities in the ordered harmonies of his structure to please and surprise the reader. The interlinking units (ter-cets) of Shelley's stanza make possible a kind of intricate, expansive utterance quite at variance with ordinary prose. It lends a special solemnity and seriousness to the poem. It forces us to realize how much and how mysteriously the experience behind the poem has been transformed by the workings of the poet's imagination.

In a note to the ode, Shelley tells us that it was suggested by a particular "tempestuous wind" that he observed one day when he was in a wood by the side of the Arno, the river that flows through Florence. The details that he noticed have been carefully recorded, but this is far more than a specimen of descriptive writing. The poet's vision becomes a vision of the never-ending cycle of birth and death, of order within seeming disorder, of beauty and terror, of the pain we all must bear, and of the obligation of the poet to be more than the painter of pretty pictures, to be a seer, a prophet, a man to awaken his fellows to their responsibilities to the future.

> by the incantation of this verse
>
> Scatter, as from an unextinguished hearth
> Ashes and sparks, my words among mankind!
> Be through my lips to unawakened earth
>
> The trumpet of a prophecy! O, Wind,
> If Winter comes, can Spring be far behind?

Shelley's ode is structured in five parts or strophes. In the first, the poet invokes the West Wind of autumn, which drives the dead leaves and scatters seeds for next spring's growth. As seed-scatterer, the wind prophetically blows "a clarion" over the earth which "dreams" of new birth. The wind is both destroyer and preserver. Seen by some readers as a political allegory, the ode, particularly in this stanza, has been interpreted as a prophecy of the social reforms which Shelley hoped would be enacted in England. Other readings, however, are just as plausible, and this stanza may be read biographically, as Shelley's desire for solace in the thought of rebirth of his own physical or poetic powers. The wind as destroyer is emphasized through the

death motif suggested by the words "dead," "ghost," "pestilence-
stricken," "corpse," "grave."

The second stanza continues to address the wind, this time as a
power which moves clouds as well as decaying leaves and brings
storms. Shelley's acute observations of nature are evident in the
image of the cumulonimbus cloud "shook from the tangled
boughs of Heaven and Ocean" between sky and horizon. The
cloud is rising vertically from "the horizon to the Zenith's
height" and is forecasting storm. (The cumulonimbus are vertically shaped clouds whose bases may touch the ground and
which may rise as high as 75,000 feet. Created by updrafts, the
clouds in their most violent forms can produce tornadoes.)
Shelley's scientific interests also appear in allusions to the
process of evaporation "Of vapors, from whose solid atmosphere," etc.

The third stanza considers the effects of the wind on the ocean.
The Mediterranean Sea, sleeping in its summer calm, and
reflecting palaces and towers along its shores, is awakened by
the autumn wind. The Atlantic is stirred to the deep by the wild
power of the wind. The reflections "quivering within the wave's
intenser day" refer to the characteristic powers of magnification
which water has. The day is magnified and seems intenser under
the water. Also noteworthy is the onomatopoetic line "The sea-
blooms and the oozy woods which wear," in which the oozy
effect of the thing described is duplicated by the repeated "oo"
sound.

The fourth stanza introduces the idea of rebirth and summarizes
the preceding stanzas by associating them with the desires of the
speaker. The leaf, cloud, and waves as they are affected by the
power of the wind have the power to soar as the poet himself
wishes to do. A new idea is introduced at this point. As a boy,
the poet was affected by the power of the wind, not in a vision
as the poet now feels it, but almost as a reality: "in my
boyhood . . . / The comrade of thy wanderings over heaven, /
. . . thy skiey speed / Scarce seemed a vision." The prayer
takes on urgency as the poet pleads for power: "Oh! lift me as a
wave, a leaf, a cloud! / I fall upon the thorns of life! I bleed!"
He is weighted by "hours," by which he may mean his physical

condition as a human is enthralled by time which is philosophi-
cally associated with weight and matter; or he may mean he is
oppressed by the times, or by his own advancing age. Nevertheless, his inner, higher spirit is "like thee: tameless, and swift,
and proud."

The last stanza specifies the nature of the prayer the speaker
makes to the wind. "Make me thy lyre," a poet through whose
voice, prophecies of new birth may be heard. His "dead
thoughts" (dead because they have been uttered and have thus
been transformed from eternal idea to finite word, or because
his poems were unknown) would fly through the world, "And,
by the incantation of this verse" would scatter sparks of eternal
ideas "as from an unextinguished hearth." The inspiration
behind the "dead thoughts" can never die. Finally, the speaker
again beseeches the wind to grant him its power so that he may
become "the trumpet of a prophecy." As the first stanza had
stated, the autumn wind carries seeds for spring birth; so the
last stanza concludes "O, Wind, / If Winter comes, can Spring be
far behind?"

Although the ode provides an accurate and perfectly structured
lyrical description of the wind, there is evidently more meaning
in the poem than that. Shelley's desire to make heard his ideas
for political and social reform is usually seen as the main theme
of the poem. There is also a way to read the poem biographically, as "the personal consolation that a Romantic poet is
offering himself" because he is aging and has lost his "adolescent ecstasies." (F. W. Bateson, *English Poetry, A Critical
Introduction,* New York, 1950, p. 216.) Objections have
been raised to individual words and images within the poem,
such as F. R. Leavis' complaints that the comparison of the
clouds and leaves is inappropriate, that the "blue surface" of
the sky seems too smooth for a "surge," and that the relationship between the Maenad with streaming hair and an approaching storm is not clear. (*Revaluation* [1936], London, 1956, pp.
204–6.)

If it is understood that Shelley is probably alluding to actual
cloud formations in the "steep sky" of the altocumulus type, it

will become clear that the puffy or leaflike balls of water droplets when passing before the sun are often seen as blue, yellow, and red, and may readily be compared to a flurry of colored autumn leaves. The "blue surface of thine airy surge" must be read in connection with the preceding line, "Thine angels of rain and lightning: there are spread." The "blue surface" does not refer to a smooth sky but to the altostratus "spread" or veil of dense rain clouds, which have a blue (sometimes gray) coloration. The Maenad's "uplifted" hair may be imagined as rising from the ocean as does the cumulonimbus cloud, the familiar forecast of heavy storms. It will do well to remember R. H. Fogle's explanation of these alleged flaws. The images are unified by the idea of Power in the wind, which acts in the same way on leaf and cloud. Moreover, Leavis' search for an exact scientific reading is not the proper way to read a lyrical ode. (*The Imagery of Keats and Shelley*, Hamden, Conn., 1962, p. 265.)

"THE CLOUD":   Appreciatively described as an Old English riddle (in which the speaker, an inanimate object, describes itself), as a "creative myth, a scientific monograph and a gay picaresque tale of cloud-adventure," Shelley's ode, on the other hand, has been sorely misunderstood and condemned as nonsense. (See Oliver Elton, *The English Muse*, London, 1933, p. 337; Desmond King-Hele, *Shelley: The Man and the Poet*, New York, 1960, p. 220; and Donald Davie, in *English Romantic Poets*, ed. M. H. Abrams, New York, 1960, p. 308, respectively.) While the poem is a lyrical tribute to one of nature's most beautiful phenomena, it is also a scientifically accurate survey of the cloud's life cycle, of all types of clouds, their functions and their phases. The aspect of the cloud at dawn and twilight, at night or day, in summer or winter is seen as an actual thing and as a symbol of natural beauty, wonder, and continuity. Scientific accuracy and poetic perception are united here to achieve a poem which, "in the opinion of many critics bear[s] a purer poetical stamp than any other of his productions." The poem was written characteristically "as his mind prompted . . . , marking the cloud as it sped across the heavens, while he floated in his boat on the Thames." (Mary Shelley, Preface to Shelley's *Poetical Works*, 1839.) We are certain that Shelley watched real clouds and saw their shapes and changes as they actually occurred. It is equally certain that his imagination soared until he entered the spirit of the cloud itself and saw behind the facts of nature a moving and animated spirit of life.

The stanzas are of varied lengths, but internal rhyme is employed consistently throughout the poem, alternating with end-rhyme lines. The first stanza, in which the cloud describes its various benevolent functions, is easily understood: it brings rain for flowers, shades leaves from the sun, spreads dew on "sweet buds," carries hail to the plains, and dissolves the hail in rain.

The second stanza is more problematic. To critics who ignore scientific theory of Shelley's day, the images seem to be impossibilities. But correctly understood, the stanza is a clear and accurate poetic paraphrase of a popular theory of electricity which was then in the process of being disproved by Shelley's contemporary, the scientist Michael Faraday. In stanza two, the cloud describes its atmospheric experiences on mountain tops where it "sleeps" pillowed on the white snow. "Lightning" is to be understood as atmospheric electricity, not only as the violent electrical charges associated with storms. Shelley's "lightning," which has a "gentle motion," is described in terms of the early erroneous theory of electricity which defined it as a strange, fine, weightless fluid, which could flow or drift like the wind through the densest materials. Poetically speaking, this ethereal fluid had life-giving powers (see Mary Shelley's *Frankenstein*), could attract or "guide" clouds, and could also be seen as a "spirit" with affinities or "love" for the "genii" (spirits) of the sea. It is this electrical "fluid" which is capable of "dissolving in rains." The love of atmospheric and oceanic spirits is Shelley's poetic vision of an ultimate oneness of all things, in which love and unity are the same thing.

The cloud next describes its experience of dawn and twilight. At dawn, the cloud is a "sailing rack," a wind-driven mass of high, broken clouds. The red-plumed sun above it seems to be sitting on its back as an eagle perched on a quaking crag. At sunset, when the sky deepens into the sea, the cloud appears to rest pensively like a dove hovering over her young. The cloud at night, in stanza four, has a flattened top and appears as a "fleece-like" floor on which the moon walks with "unseen feet." The changing form of the cumulonimbus cloud tops is compared to "the broken woof of my tent's thin roof," through which can be seen the swarming stars. Then, as the puffs of clouds separate and recompose, they become "strips" through which moon and starlight reflect their beams on "calm rivers, lakes, and seas."

The clouds of the fifth stanza are apparently of the cirrostratus class. Their "burning zone" and "girdle of pearl" are the halos formed by these wind-blown clouds around the sun or the moon. The "whirl-winds" indicate the atmospheric blasts which accompany them, and the "bridge-like shape" alludes to their elongated forms, or possibly to a rainbow. Cirrostratus clouds "hang like a roof" at altitudes of twenty to twenty-five thousand feet. They hover above mountains, which may be seen below as columns supporting the cloud-roof as in a magnificent temple. Because clouds of this type are made of ice crystals ("hurricane, fire, and snow"), their halos glow luminously in a "million-coloured bow" around the orbs of the sun and the moon.

The last stanza epitomizes the entire life cycle of the cloud: evaporation, condensation, precipitation. Born of the moisture of earth, water, and sky, the cloud is amorphous but eternal: "I change but I cannot die." After a rain, when the blue sky is bare and seems to memorialize clouds which are dead and gone, new clouds are forming in the "caverns of rain" to "rise and unbuild again."

The remarkable accuracy of Shelley's observations of nature and his inventive poetic impersonation of the cloud mark his special genius for synthesizing the real and the ideal into sublime lyrical poetry. This union of scientific fact and lyric inspiration recurs frequently in Shelley's poems and may be seen in "Ode to the West Wind" and "To a Skylark" as well.

"TO A SKYLARK": In twenty-one, five-line stanzas, designed in a metrical pattern of four trimeter lines with a final alexan-

drine, Shelley again unites in poetic form, ideas of real and
spiritual things. The skylark is an actual bird, one he has seen
and heard. At the same time, the bird functions as a symbol of
"an unbodied joy," the Platonic "idea" or essence of joy. It is a
prophet of other-worldly things and an inspiration to the poet-
prophet. The lark's song is like instinctive knowledge of an ideal
life, unseen but inferred from the existence of the human aspiration for perfection: "We hardly see—we feel that it is there,"
and "what thou art we know not."

Analogies must be made between these ideal and real things to
express the apprehensions of truth which are felt but not seen or
heard, apprehensions which cannot be perceived actually and
sensually: "What is most like thee?" the poet asks. The meta-
phors expressing his vision of the ideal are synaesthetic (one
sense impression is conveyed through terms normally employed
for another sense impression, e.g., "rain of melody" not "sound
of melody"), for in the world beyond the senses, ordinary
language symbols do not apply. The spirit of the lark is like a
"Poet hidden / In the light of thought." "Thought," of course,
has neither light nor color, nor can it be perceived by any of the
five bodily senses. The poet's thought, like the lark's joy,
belongs to a "hidden," unseen realm beyond or outside the
world of actuality. Unbidden hymns of universal ideals emanate
from the poet, revealing the deep and instinctive "hopes and
fears" of mankind which men barely know they have.

In his attempt to make his vision of the ideal even more concrete and sensually perceptible, Shelley compares the joyous
spirit to actual things. Using his favorite images of love, beauty,
and good, he says the heavenly song of the lark is like a "high-
born maiden" singing "in a palace-tower," like "a glow-worm
golden / In a dell of dew," like an embowered rose, heavily
scented, like the sound of spring rain, like everything "that ever
was / Joyous, and clear, and fresh."

Addressing the lark as "Sprite or Bird," Shelley indicates his
identification of the ideal and real bird as one, or perhaps he
wishes to show the unclear distinction between the two. Yet for
all the analogies the poet can offer, the idea of the eternal bird
cannot be fully expressed. The "sweet thoughts" of the bird-

spirit are more divine than any human song in "Praise of love or wine," or "Chorus Hymeneal," or "triumphal chant." For in all these human songs, "we feel there is some hidden want," while the song of the lark is perfect and complete. Still, as in the actual songs, the divine bird must have a subject. He must tell of something. Of what unseen "fields, or waves, or mountains" does he sing? What strange unknown love and pleasure are expressed in the song of this ethereal lark? Free of human failing and human pain, the bird must sing of some perfect joy, a perfect state of pleasure, a perfect love, for unlike the human, "Thou lovest—but ne'er knew love's sad satiety."

As men we have finite minds, Shelley goes on to say. We have hindsight and foresight, and the yearnings which are natural to the human state. (For the same idea, see Burns's "To a Mouse.") Our every joy is tinged with pain; "Our sweetest songs are those that tell of saddest thought." But even if men led lives of pure pleasure, a thing to be imagined, yet the divine joy of the spirit-lark is beyond human conception. The perfect spirit of joy, which the lark conveys, is better than all knowledge the poet can hear or read. The joy of the lark, therefore, is the highest pleasure to which the poet can aspire.

Thus, as a poet, Shelley appeals for prophetic inspiration to the blithe spirit of divine song:

> Teach me half the gladness
> That thy brain must know,
> Such harmonious madness
> From my lips would flow
> The world should listen then—as I am listening now.

ADONAIS: After "Lycidas," John Milton's famous elegy composed on the occasion of the death of his friend Edward King, Shelley's tribute to Keats ranks as the greatest of English elegies. Although Shelley had met Keats and had admired some of Keats's work, the two poets had never been intimate, and it is possible that the poem was motivated not so much by the death of Keats as it was by Keats's availability as a symbol of misunderstood genius.

The classical name Shelley adopts for Keats, Adonais, is designed to suggest Adonis of Greek legend. A beautiful youth beloved by Aphrodite, goddess of love, Adonis was killed by a wild boar. Shelley found in the myth a pleasing analogy between Adonis' wild boar and the savage critics who had attacked *Endymion,* one of Keats's early poems. Adonis was restored to life by Proserpine on the condition that he spend six months of the year with her and the other six months with Aphrodite. Proserpine, it will be recalled, lived part of her life in the underworld and is thus a symbol of winter, of the death of the year. Aphrodite symbolizes birth, spring, and summer. Keats is dead but like Adonis, he will live on forever.

The elegy is an intricate and self-conscious literary exercise in the Greek elegiac tradition, represented by the ancient poets Bion and Moschus. It opens on a note of grief. The poet complains to Urania, goddess of stars, about her failure to protect Adonais from death. The traditional mourning at the youth's bier is described, as the train of mourners arrives. They are characteristically shadowy—Hours, Dreams, "Desires and Adorations, / Wingèd Persuasions and veiled Destinies." Among the mourners, however, is "one frail Form, / A phantom among men. . . . A pardlike [leopardlike] Spirit beautiful and swift."

> He came the last, neglected and apart;
> A herd abandoned deer struck by the hunter's dart.

It is clear that this is Shelley himself and that he feels that he has also been neglected and mistreated by the world.

At stanza 39, the mood of grief shifts to one of rejoicing. Adonais lives on, the poet realizes. The closing lines of the poem trumpet Shelley's mystical faith in the triumph of spirit over death. Change is only an illusion. "The One remains." Shelley expresses his faith in Platonic essences. In the two concluding lines of this noble poem he sees the "soul of

Adonais, like a star" beaconing "from the abode where the Eternal are."

CRITICISM: The early reputation of Shelley was essentially twofold. A majority of his contemporaries regarded him as a blasphemous devil, while a minority saw him as an angelic lyricist who was essentially harmless because he had no hold on reality. There was almost no critical opinion in between, for the early critics either ignored or negated the philosophic content of his work. In our time, the same opinions are held by many, but there is now also a third area for consideration, Shelley's philosophy. One group advances the idea that Shelley succeeded in uniting poetry and philosophy into one superb organic form, while another feels he had a philosophy which he failed to project coherently.

The large body of critical reviews which appeared during the years that Shelley's poems were being made public shows, on the whole, that Shelley was "known and feared." The more than two hundred items from over eighty publications during this period which have been collected in *The Unextinguished Hearth* by N. I. White (1938) reveal that Shelley was not as unknown to the public as Mary Shelley had suggested in her notes to the 1839 edition of his works. His poetry was read and often appreciated, but his ideas were as often rejected. The position against Shelley taken by the *Quarterly Review* reflects the general disapprobation in which Shelley's ideas were held: "His works exhale contiguous mischiefs" and "contain the most flagrant offenses against morality and religion." *The Londale Magazine or Provincial Repository* called his theories "destructive," and claimed that his language, which had a "melodious richness," was being used for an evil purpose. *Blackwood's* also conceded that his poetry was great, but objected that his content was nothing more than "audacious spleen." *The Dublin Magazine* insisted his talents were devoted to an evil purpose, and *The Gentleman's Magazine* called him a genius whose work was shamefully blasphemous.

Some of his reviewers simply did not understand his work, particularly *Prometheus Unbound. The Literary Gazette*'s critic threw up his hands. Hazlitt, who appreciated Shelley's greatness in part, called *Prometheus Unbound* the work of a sophist and found his philosophy nothing more than the "cobwebs of his brain." *The Monthly Review* simply dismissed the work as "nonsense," asking "what is the meaning of the metaphysical rhapsody?"

There were a few critics, however, who defended *Prometheus Unbound*. Leigh Hunt answered charges of nonsense, claiming that unsympathetic reviewers had used the most obscure passages to charge the whole with obscurity. *The Album,* to its credit, appreciated the poem as a splendid production even though some of it was obscure. A few advocates were found later in the century among poets like Robert Browning, Francis Thompson, and political liberals like Robert Owen, Karl Marx, and G. B. Shaw. But in the nineteenth century, for the most part, even those who appreciated his work as a whole found it "thin sown with profit and delight," and "too full of wild theories." (H. J. C. Grierson and J. C. Smith, *A Critical History of English Poetry,* London, 1956, p. 350.)

Shelley's thought also was damned, although unconsciously, by critics who heaped high praise on his lyrical talents. Browning, Arnold, Swinburne, Thompson, Watson, and even Mary Shelley, each assisted in developing the image of Shelley as an "ineffectual angel." Browning had addressed him as "Sun-treader" in his poem "Pauline." Arnold had written: "In poetry no less than life, he is a beautiful and ineffectual angel, beating his luminous wings in vain." (*Essays in Criticism,* Second Series, New York, 1888.) Swinburne, who praised his great lyrical power, ignored his thought. (*Essays and Studies,* 1875.) Francis Thompson called him an "eternal child" and described him as "gold-dusty with tumbling in the stars." (*Shelley,* 1888, in *Collected Works,* III, 1909, p. 46.) William Watson described him as "Shelley the Cloud-begot, who grew / Nourished on air and sun and dew, / Into that Essence whence he drew." (*Selected Poems* [1892], London, 1902.) Mary Shelley's own remarks did much to assist the legend of Shelley as an Ariel creature when she wrote in her notes that he composed one of his best odes ("The Cloud") "while he floated in his boat on the Thames," and when she stated in reference to *The Cenci* that the play was a departure from the usual Shelley who "loved to shelter himself . . . in the airiest flights of fancy, forgetting love and hate and regret and lost hope." The idea of Shelley as an ethereal lyricist was re-enforced again and again during the nineteenth century—his friend Thomas Love Peacock immortalized him as Scythrop in *Nightmare Abbey,* as a misty character whose head was always in the sky; and W. M. Rossetti claimed "the poetic ecstasy took him constantly upward; and, the higher he got, the more thoroughly did his thoughts and words become one exquisite and intense unit." (*Lives of the Famous Poets,* 1878.)

In this century, a few early critics began to see that Shelley's poetry was more than light and air. Croce and Santayana, philosophers not literary critics, offered some penetrating insights into his thought, and the poet-critic William Butler Yeats pronounced *Prometheus Unbound* a "sacred book" of philosophy. ("The Philosophy of Shelley's Poetry" [1900], in *Ideas of Good and Evil,* 1903. Yet, professional critics at the turn of the century were still determined to show Shelley's worst work to prove him an inferior poet. (Carlos Baker, ed., *Selected Prose and Poetry,* New York, 1951, p. xi.) With a few exceptions, critics were convinced that Shelley's character and thought were static (Ernest Bernbaum, *Guide Through the Romantic Movement,* p. 251), and they misjudged Shelley by seeing his early and confused radical ideas in his later works.

Meanwhile, the moral depreciation of Shelley continued into our century. Echoing his predecessors, Paul Elmer More (reviewing a favorable account of Shelley in *Shelley The Man and the Poet,* by Arthur Clutton-Brock, 1910) found Shelley's work immoral and dangerous because in his overemotionalism, Shelley disregarded reason and betrayed a "child-like credulity" in the doctrine of perfection. (*Shelburne Essays.* Seventh Series, New York, 1910, p. 7.) Leading the anti-Romantic movement of the early decades, More attacked Shelley's "weakness of overweening self-trust which exposed him to corruptions of the age." To More, Shelley's philosophy was unliterary and destructive; to Irving Babbitt, Shelley's romanticism simply meant "decadence." In four books written between the years 1908 and 1919, Babbitt, another leading anti-Romantic of his day, claimed that Shelley was morally vicious because the insidious beauty of his verse attracted students to his irrational, radical, and immoral thought. Moreover, Babbitt charged in *Rousseau and Romanticism,* Shelley was a victim of "nympholepsia."

T. S. Eliot added his support to More and Babbitt. In *The Use of Poetry and Criticism,* Eliot claimed that as Shelley's poetry matured, his ideas remained adolescent. Both the man and the poet were repellent to Eliot; he found Shelley dull, humorless, and egocentric. Subsequently the New Critics John Crowe Ransom, Allen Tate, Robert Penn Warren, and F. R. Leavis joined the camp of the anti-Romantics, who maintained that Coleridge and Keats were the only Romantics worth saving. The idea that Shelley was a confused thinker was also promulgated by A. M. D. Hughes in *The Nascent Mind of Shelley* (1947), where Hughes sarcastically stated that Shelley showed confused thinking in his poems up to the time of *Queen Mab,* and afterwards he ceased to think at all.

Shelley's emotionalism frightened humanist critics like More and Babbitt and annoyed New Critics like Eliot, Hughes, and F. R. Leavis. Leavis was convinced, moreover, that Shelley was a bad craftsman as well as a bad thinker (*Revaluation,* London, 1936). Even less partial critics like Grierson and Smith deplored the "profound self-pity" found in some of Shelley's poems, *Alastor,* for example (*A Critical History of English Poetry,* p. 356); and F. W. Bateson was "inclined to think Shelley's light verse his best poetry," for his later poems like "Ode to the West Wind" were superficial and their apparently political interests were only excuses for poetry "that is really only concerned with Shelley himself." (*English Poetry, A Critical Study,* pp. 215–16.) The position of the anti-Romantics on the whole seems to have been aptly summarized in D. G. James's statement: "Of all the great Romantic poets, Shelley most justifies the suspicion felt by a colder age for strong feelings; and in this bad sense Shelley is the most typically Romantic poet. This weakness in Shelley can be illustrated alike from *Queen Mab* and from *Prometheus.*" (*The Romantic Comedy,* New York, 1963, p. 65.)

These anti-Romantics found opposition in men like Arthur Clutton-Brock, C. H. Herford, O. W. Campbell, Herbert Read, and C. S. Lewis. Clutton-Brock had advanced one of the finest appreciations of Shelley of the period ending in 1909, and that appreciation was shared by many others, despite Paul Elmer More's attempt to undermine it. C. H. Herford, for example, defended Shelley's reputation against Babbitt's charges, accusing Babbitt of being a mystic with the temper of a Buddhist monk who won't face facts. Shelley, aside from his moral value, was a great poet, Herford asserted. (*Essays and Studies by Members of the English Association,* VIII, 1922, pp. 109–35.) The conflict was summed up by O. W. Campbell in 1924 in *Shelley and the Unromantics.* Taking Shelley's side Campbell found him both manly and effectual. Herbert Read *In Defence of Shelley* (1935) and C. S. Lewis in *Rehabilitations* (1939) also joined in Shelley's defense.

But countercharges between critics were not enough to save Shelley's reputation. New evidence in Shelley's behalf was needed if the charges of the anti-Romantics were to be answered effectively. A new approach to Shelley criticism had begun to appear simultaneously with the anti-Romantic movement. It had long been thought that Shelley was merely a lyricist, for good or for bad, and that his ideas were simply lofty sentiments couched in melodious rhetoric. Croce, Santayana, and Yeats had already suggested that there was more than met the eye in Shelley's thought. Next, John Shawcross became aware that Shelley's work revealed a process of mental groping, which he believed was an attempt to reconcile the real with the ideal. Shawcross, however, was convinced that Shelley had failed to make that reconciliation. (Introduction to *Shelley's Literary and Philosophical Remains,* 1909.) Nevertheless, attention was now turned to Shelley's philosophy, and Winstanley in 1913 reached the conclusion that it was essentially Platonic. There was now a new approach to Shelley's works. He had a recognizable philosophy which would shed light on his poems.

A. E. Powell soon discovered that Shelley's mind was a developing one. Her analysis of Shelley's works revealed that "the philosophy of Plato helped give Shelley's thought its final shape." But Shelley's Platonic thought showed itself gradually, "a few hints in *Prometheus Unbound* (1820), more in *Adonais,*" and even more in "A Defence of Poetry." With this discovery also came the conclusion that the best critical work

Shelley did was to define the relation between poetry and morality. Shelley, then, was not immoral as charged, Powell argued. (*The Romantic Theory of Poetry,* New York, 1962, p. 219.)

The case for Shelley's morality was sustained by M. T. Solve who, in 1927, pointed out that "A Defence of Poetry" showed Shelley's belief that poets are "the institutors of laws, and the founders of civil society." His conclusion: "The moral point of view for such a one is inescapable." (*Shelley: His Theory of Poetry,* New York, 1964, p. 27.) Soon other critics began to find Christian elements in Shelley's thought. Bennett Weaver and F. L. Jones, for example, believed Shelley was a Christian, and A. C. Hicks claimed Shelley was only opposed to historical Christianity not to Jesus.

Shelley's thought was now something to be reckoned with, M. A. Bald pointed out in 1928. Shelley was "a man who grew," a man whose "mind repeated itself in spirals, not circles." ("Shelley's Mental Progress," *English Association Essays and Studies,* X, p. 112.) Bald's study was followed by Floyd Stovall's in *Desire and Restraint* (1931), where it was also shown that Shelley's thought was a developing thing and not merely a set of radical ideas learned in youth and retained in maturity. Stovall pointed out that as Shelley developed he took a position between desire and restraint and that he became a true poet in *Alastor,* where he expressed his recognition of the conflict between the real and the ideal. Studies of this type were pursued by Carl H. Grabo in *The Magic Plant* (1936), where Shelley's progress from scientific thought to materialism to political radicalism to poetic mysticism was shown through a chronological examination of his works. In effect, Grabo discovered, Shelley had grown from a rebel in youth to a platonist in maturity. A similar conclusion was drawn by Ellsworth Barnard (*Shelley's Religion,* 1937), who traced Shelley's growth from his early Godwinian period to his final mysticism, a synthesis of Platonic, neoplatonic, and Christian metaphysical ideas.

Even some who disagreed with the way Shelley's mind developed were prepared to admit that it did grow. David Lee Clark, who took exception to Grabo's theory of Shelley's development, pointed out that "what is perhaps the most pronounced fact in Shelley's mental growth was the solid strength of his early ideas." His thought, although it changed, remained grounded in the scientific and historical knowledge of his day, and he held to the end "his scientific and humanitarian point of view with a clearcut emphasis on the reality of the world around us." (*Shelley's Prose: The Trumpet of Prophecy*, Albuquerque, 1954, p. 33.)

Perhaps the strongest defense of Shelley made in recent times was F. A. Pottle's "The Case of Shelley." (*PMLA*, LXVII, 1952.) Pottle assumed the burden of answering all the charges made against Shelley before 1946. He took the stand that Shelley was a manly poet not an effusive one, that only a few of his private lyrics betray self-pity, that he was a profoundly religious poet, but a misunderstood one because he was unorthodox. In a review of the major critics who favored Shelley from 1856 to 1946, Pottle believed there was nothing new to say; he also felt that critics like himself, like Bradley and Clutton-Brock, would be forgotten in the future and that the voices of the New Critics, especially F. R. Leavis, would prevail.

Pottle was perhaps too pessimistic and too tired from long years of battling the issues to predict a more hopeful future for Shelley's reputation, for since 1946 numbers of fresh criticisms have appeared on the field with many good words for Shelley's work. Kenneth Cameron has found the poet an "impassioned thinker," an opinion which Carl Grabo quoted in assent. C. M. Bowra paid Shelley high tribute when he said of *Prometheus Unbound* that in it Shelley unites poetry and philosophy and makes "the pallid abstractions of analytical thought take on the glow and the glory of visible things." (*The Romantic Imagination*, New York, 1950, p. 125.)

At least one set of critics has been able to find in poems like *Prometheus Unbound* "the recreated universe of the Promethean imagination [which] is a world which mediates between man's mortality and man's divinity." (R. G. Woodman, *The Apocalyptic Vision in the Poetry of Shelley*, Toronto, 1964, p. 149.) If opinions of this sort continue to be expressed, then the voice of F. R. Leavis will not prevail.

JOHN KEATS

No English poet has been more dedicated to his art than John Keats. His letters are full of penetrating remarks about poetry. He wanted to do nothing in life but write poetry. His career shows such rapid and steady progress that it is almost impossible not to wonder what he might have done had he lived beyond his twenty-sixth year.

LIFE: Keats was born in London in 1795. His father was the stablekeeper for John Jennings, a fairly prosperous innkeeper; his mother was Jennings' daughter. He had two younger brothers, George (born in 1797) and Thomas (born in 1799), and a younger sister, Frances (born in 1803).

As a boy he was not particularly interested in books. He preferred scuffling with his schoolmates and being a ringleader in mischief. In his last year of school, however, Charles Cowden Clarke, one of his closest friends throughout his life, awakened in him a passionate desire to read. From that point on, Keats read insatiably.

Both of Keats's parents died while he was still very young—his father, by a fall from a horse in 1804, his mother of tuberculosis in 1810. His guardians removed him from school and apprenticed him to a surgeon. While studying medicine he found time to continue his avid reading. He was particularly excited by Edmund Spenser's *The Faerie Queene*. In 1812 he wrote an imitation of Spenser in which he used the Spenserian stanza for the first time. He later adopted this stanza for one of his greatest poems, *The Eve of St. Agnes*. He continued his medical studies in London hospitals and was qualified to practice. He decided, however, that the only thing he wanted to be was a poet and he abandoned medicine completely. He met Leigh Hunt who, at the time, enjoyed a considerable reputation as a writer but who is now chiefly known through his friendships with such poets as Shelley and Keats. Hunt recognized the talents of the young man and encouraged him. When Keats published his first volume, *Poems,* in 1817, he dedicated the work to Hunt.

His first volume was favorably received by his friends but made little impression on the public. It went virtually unnoticed. Keats had no time for idle regrets. He attempted an ambitious allegorical narrative poem, *Endymion.* Published in 1818, this poem was noticed. Savage reviews appeared in some of the prominent journals and thus was born the legend, used by Shelley in *Adonais,* that the reviewers were responsible for Keats's early death.

To get some much-needed rest and also to gain the new experiences he felt his poetry needed, Keats and a friend went on a walking tour which ended abruptly when Keats was troubled by a severe sore throat and was advised by a doctor to return to London. This proved to be the first symptom of tuberculosis, which was to cause his untimely death. Keats did not realize at first how serious his illness was. He went on with his fierce determination to make himself into a great poet.

At this time Keats was sorely distracted. His brother Tom was dying of tuberculosis and his brother George was planning to emigrate to America. Keats was always very close to his brothers and sister and was deeply involved in their affairs. He lent George money and nursed Tom until his death in December 1818.

The year 1819 was a marvelously productive one for Keats. He worked on "Hyperion," which remained unfinished at his death, and he wrote *The Eve of St. Agnes,* "La Belle Dame Sans Merci," and the six magnificent odes that are universally regarded as unrivalled in our literature.

By 1820 Keats knew that he was doomed. In a last desperate effort to regain his health, he went to Italy with Joseph Severn, one of his closest friends. He died in Rome, February 23, 1821, and was buried there in the Protestant Cemetery. Engraved on his tombstone, as he had requested, is the inscription: "Here lies one whose name was writ in water."

WORKS: His letters and fragments were collected after his death, but all his great poems were published during his brief life in *Poems* (1817); *Endymion* (1818); and *Lamia, Isabella, The Eve of St. Agnes and Other Poems* (1820).

POEMS: Keats's first volume, simply entitled *Poems,* has some charming pieces but is chiefly notable for the fact that from it we can trace the astonishing development of the poet's powers. "I Stood Tiptoe" exhibits Keats's appreciation of nature. Even more important is "Sleep and Poetry," for here he explains with eloquence his sense of the high mission of the poet.

"ON FIRST LOOKING INTO CHAPMAN'S HOMER": Even more important as evidence of Keats's remarkable abilities is this sonnet, written in 1816 and published in *The Examiner,* a weekly paper edited by Leigh Hunt.

The circumstances attending the composition of the sonnet reveal the intensity with which Keats lived and read. One night his friend, Charles Cowden Clarke, his first literary mentor, showed him a translation of Homer by George Chapman, an important English Renaissance poet, a contemporary of Shakespeare. Keats's enthusiasms were rarely moderate. He and his friend stayed up all night, reading and talking about poetry. The next morning, shortly after he had left Keats, Clarke was surprised to receive from him the sonnet prompted by his delight in Chapman's work.

Keats has been criticized for an historical blunder. In his poem he has Cortez, "with eagle eyes," staring at the Pacific. As everyone knows, it was not Cortez but Balboa who was the first European to look upon the Pacific Ocean. The blunder, however, is of no importance. The poet through his mastery of form makes his readers share in the excitement of his discovery.

ENDYMION: For all his emotionalism, Keats was a disciplined poet. He read widely and carefully because literature was his passion. But he also read because he himself wanted to be a poet; he wanted, in fact, to be a great poet. He thirsted after fame not for its immediate rewards nor even for its future rewards. He had no offensive vanity in his makeup. What he did have was an understanding of the supreme importance of poetry.

In carrying out his program to make himself a poet, he decided, after printing his early work in 1817, that the time had come for him to attempt a more ambitious kind of poem. He thought that he detected a subject suitable to his powers and adaptable to his purposes in the Greek myth of Endymion. The myth is about the infatuation of the moon goddess with Endymion, a beautiful young shepherd, and her desire to preserve his beauty forever.

As Keats tells the story, it is an allegory of the poet's search for beauty. The moon goddess becomes the symbol of the essence of beauty; Endymion is the searching poet.

There are many fine passages in *Endymion*. The poem opens, for example, with the statement of one of Keats's favorite ideas:

> A thing of beauty is a joy forever:
> Its loveliness increases; it will never
> Pass into nothingness. . . .

The hymn to Pan in the first book of *Endymion* shows not only the poet's responsiveness to external nature but also his awareness of the essential mystery of nature. Keats is often at his very best when he is attempting to give poetic expression to his awareness of an interaction between the sense and the intellect. A supremely sensuous poet, Keats never thought that man was merely the recipient of physical sensations. He knew much about the dark corridors of the mind, but he was also aware of how much he did not know.

Although *Endymion* shows the growth of Keats's powers, it is not a successful poem. Keats was not so uncritical as to think his four-thousand-line poem in four books without faults. He wrote in his Preface:

> Knowing within myself the manner in which this Poem has been produced, it is not without a feeling of regret that I make it public.

> What manner I mean, will be quite clear to the reader, who must soon perceive great inexperience, immaturity, and every error denoting a feverish attempt, rather than a deed accomplished.

One of the most attractive things about Keats is his ability to make an honest assessment of himself. He forestalled his critics with the forthrightness of this Preface, and the legend that adverse comments on *Endymion* broke his heart is demonstrably absurd. *Endymion* shows poetic powers of an unusual sort; it is, nonetheless, a poem with grave defects. The allegory is obscure; the narrative is loosely constructed; the language is much too self-consciously "poetical."

THE EVE OF ST. AGNES: As Keats himself recognized, when he wrote *Endymion,* he was still immature as an artist. How rapidly he matured is shown by his wonderful narrative poem in Spenserian stanzas called *The Eve of St. Agnes*. It is set in the Middle Ages, a period dear to the Romantic imagination. It is an enchanting tale of young love, and the sureness with which the poet handles this old but perpetually interesting subject may reflect the fact that he was deeply in love with Fanny Brawne.

According to an old wives' tale, maidens could dream of their true loves on the eve of St. Agnes (January 20) provided that they obeyed certain traditional rules.

> They told her how, upon St. Agnes' Eve,
> Young virgins might have visions of delight,
> And soft adorings from their loves receive
> Upon the honey'd middle of the night,
> If ceremonies due they did aright;
> As, supperless to bed they must retire,
> And couch supine their beauties, lily white;
> Nor look behind, nor sideways, but require
> Of Heaven with upward eyes for all that they desire.

Keats's story is about the love of Madeline and Porphyro. The situation is, basically, that with which we are familiar from Shakespeare's *Romeo and Juliet*. The families of the lovers are at strife. On the eve of St. Agnes, however, Porphyro, heedless of consequences, rides across the moors and stealthily enters Madeline's castle. Assisted by a sympathetic old servant, Angela, Porphyro makes his way to Madeline's chamber and hides himself in a closet. Madeline enters, prepares for bed, and goes to sleep, hoping for the visions promised by the legend. Porphyro leaves the closet and gently awakens the sleeping Madeline. At first she thinks that she is looking at a ghost, but Porphyro assures her that he is not a phantom but her lover and he persuades her to elope.

The story is told with remarkable skill, but the story is not so important as the language. Few poets can surpass Keats in his ability to endow everyday objects with a kind of magical quality. The atmospheric effects achieved in *The Eve of St. Agnes* also show Keats's powers at their fullest.

"ODE TO PSYCHE": The first of six great odes which Keats composed during the spring and summer of his "wonderful year" 1819, "Ode to Psyche" marks Keats's abandonment of the restrictive sonnet form with which he had been experimenting until early April of 1819. It is his first attempt at writing in the freer form of the lyric ode. The lyric is composed of sixty-seven lines of four stanzas in varying lengths and rhyme schemes. "Psyche," meaning "soul" in Greek, is also the name of the secret wife of Cupid, Venus' son, who after many trials won immortality. But she was "canonized" too late to have enjoyed the adoration of the ancients. Keats proposes to make this up to her.

The poem is addressed to Psyche, with apologies that her secret should be told even to the goddess herself. The device of a dream or vision is suggested as the poet tells how he wandered thoughtlessly into a forest and found amid the lush foliage there, Cupid and Psyche in loving embrace. The second stanza is an apostrophe on the beauty of Psyche, who is lovelier than any of the older goddesses who had temples and altars in ancient times and who were worshiped by many with flowers, song, and incense. Though the time is past when all the woods, air, water, and fire were thought holy, there is still left one worshiper of the ancient faith—one inspired by his own imagination who will sing the praises of the goddess Psyche. He will build an altar in his mind and dress it "with the wreathed trellis of a working brain," with flowers bred only in the Fancy. And there shall be for Psyche in the altar of his mind, a bright torch and an open window for her lover Cupid to come in.

Of the poem which is regarded by many as one of his most serene Greek pieces, Keats wrote to his brother: "Psyche was not embodied as a goddess before the time of Apuleius the Platonist who lived after the Augustan era." Consequently she was not worshiped "with any of the ancient fervor." Keats joked that he was "more orthodox than to let a heathen Goddess be so neglected." The richness and the "peaceable and healthy spirit" which he took pains to express are indeed imparted in this poem.

"ODE TO A NIGHTINGALE":   This poem (May 1819) is Keats's first attempt at a disciplined ten-line stanza form which would resemble the sonnet yet liberate it from the restrictions of that form. The rhyme pattern of each stanza is essentially a b a b c d e c d e. The poem is said to have been inspired by a real nightingale which engaged Keats's attention for two or three hours on a fine spring morning in May. Keats's own health was poor at this time, and his brother Tom had died in December 1818. Thoughts of early death, therefore, were lingering in his mind when he composed the poem, but he also had hopes that he might compose a few more poems before his end. The rich, sensuous imagery of this ode is its special merit. It speaks of the feeling pleasures of life experienced by a poet on the verge of death.

The languorous heart-aching happiness which is reproduced rather than described in the first stanza may be attributed to these mixed feelings Keats had over life and death. The sound of the nightingale has the power to revive the poet's spirit as it sings "in full-throated ease." This image recreates the muscular tension of the songster and is often pointed out as an instance of

Keats's ability to capture the inner being of things. When the poet calls for a draught of ancient vintage that he may drink and join the nightingale in its eternal "forest dim," where he can forget his cares, he demonstrates his special skill in using synaesthetic imagery; that is, he uses the taste of wine to explain an impression made by the sound of a song. (See discussion of Shelley's "To a Skylark" above.)

The word cluster "weariness, fever, and fret" is suggestive of the fevered illness Keats knew so well and speaks for the mortal pains and cares of the entire human condition, which the world-weary poet is so willing to escape. The poet, however, would make his escape not in the leopard-drawn chariot of Bacchus, god of wine, but on the invisible wings of poetry which the nightingale symbolizes and which would lead him to a dark and perfect eternity. "Already with thee! tender is the night," while here on this mortal plain, "there is no light." Only a few glimmers of heaven appear on earth, dimly seen through the gloomy forest of life. In the darkness of this world, the poet continues, "I cannot see what flowers are at my feet." But his other senses are certainly alert. He can smell "soft incense," "embalmèd darkness," and decaying violets hidden under leaves. The "musk-rose full of dewy wine" is a scent described in terms normally used for the sense of taste, and "the murmurous haunt of flies" is a sound effect suggesting the odors of "summer eves."

The sixth stanza, one of the most famous in all of Keats's odes, expresses the poet's thoughts of death, with which his dark sensuous imaginings are associated:

> Darkling I listen; and, for many a time
> I have been half in love with easeful Death
> Called him soft names in many a musèd rhyme . . .

And, indeed, Keats had shown this interest in death more than once (see his letters of 1818, 1819). Now in this moment of blissful song, it seems a good time to die, for the highest joy in Keats calls up his saddest thoughts. Echoing the forlorn thought frequently expressed in Romantic poetry, that spirit is infinite, man is not, Keats addresses the immortal bird whose eternal song was heard in ancient times:

> Perhaps the self-same song that found a path
> Through the sad heart of Ruth, when, sick for home,
> She stood in tears amid the alien corn . . .

This stanza and the next are linked in thought and feeling to Wordsworth who listened to "the still, sad music of humanity" ("Tintern Abbey") and to Shelley who felt "our sweetest songs are those that tell of saddest thought" ("To a Skylark"). The keynote of the nightingale's immortal song of joy is melancholy. "Forlorn! the very word is like a bell"—a bell which produces a sympathetic vibration within the poet and turns his thoughts from the eternal bird to his "sole self." The vision of the bird recedes into the glades and disappears. And as in "Ode to Psyche," the poet wonders, "Do I wake or sleep?"

"ODE TO MELANCHOLY":   The shortest of the great odes, "Ode to Melancholy" (May 1819) is composed of three stanzas in the same ten-line structure used in "Ode to a Nightingale." The theme, as in "Ode to a Nightingale," is melancholy linked with joy. The ode, addressed to a friend (and to any reader), explains in some of the richest and most sensuous images of Keats's career, that melancholy is neither to be avoided (at Lethe, the river of forgetfulness), nor dulled by poison charms and cures. For "the wakeful anguish of the soul" is a sensation to be treasured in the same way other sensations of living experience are to be known.

Should sorrow fall, encourage it, nurture it by consorting with beautiful things, the poet says. "Glut thy sorrow on a morning rose / Or on the wealth of globèd peonies." (Repeat "globèd" aloud and notice the oral sensation of spherical, mouth-filling things which is intended to reproduce the sensation of something seen.) Search for beauty within unhappy things, deep in the eyes of an angry mistress, for example. For melancholy "dwells with Beauty . . . that must die." The very joy of living beauty is accompanied by the sad knowledge that it must fade. The image of joy is a youth who is forever waving goodbye. Finally, the poet writes, the highest form of joy is the deepest sense of melancholy, and he expresses this thought in a series of exquisitely concrete and sensuous taste images: "aching Pleasure nigh, / Turning to Poison while the bee-mouth sips." No one can know true melancholy who has not known great joy. Only he who "Can burst Joy's grape against his palate fine; / His soul shall taste the sadness of her might."

"ODE ON A GRECIAN URN":   This poem (May 1819) is composed of five stanzas in essentially the same ten-line rhyme scheme of the earlier odes. Inspired by the sight of the Elgin Marbles and Grecian urns at the British Museum, Keats describes a scene engraved on an urn, which he addresses as "Sylvan historian." The history unfolded on the leaf-fringed vase is not explicit. The maid and youths may be gods and goddesses or reluctant girls and eager young men, whose pipes and timbrels suggest a "wild ecstasy" played and felt. These are the imaginings of the poet gazing upon the incomplete story of the urn. "Heard melodies are sweet, but those unheard / Are sweeter," for then the imagination may play its own tune, and the musical images on the urn (like the nightingale) may suggest eternal songs. The enduring quality of art is seen also in the engraved youth who will sing forever and in the "bold lover" who will ever seek his kiss. There is nothing for these eternal figures to grieve over. "Forever wilt thou love, and she be fair!" The unfulfilled lovers of the urn will never know what Shelley called "love's sad satiety."

Although the trees and leaves are blissfully immortal—the piper and his song, the panting lovers—all are depicted with human passions that are strong and intense, leaving the human viewer deeply affected in a human way, with "a heart high-sorrowful and cloyed, / A burning forehead, and a parching tongue."

The final stanza contains perhaps the most controversial lines Keats ever wrote. The phrase, "With brede / Of marble men and maidens overwrought," has raised objections among some critics over the propriety of the diction, its archaic term and suggestive puns: "brede," meaning "design," suggests "breed" (race) and (procreate); "overwrought," meaning "engraved deeply," suggests "highly impassioned." The silent eternal art form addressed as "Cold Pastoral" has also posed a few problems. As an art form the urn is "cold," but "pastoral" suggests "warmth." The two concepts are incompatible, captious critics would have us believe. Others insist the ideas are paradoxical not contradictory and, therefore, rich in meaning. The urn is both.

It is the last lines which have provoked the greatest number of disputes:

> Thou shalt remain, in midst of other woe
> Than ours, a friend to man, to whom thou say'st
> "Beauty is truth, truth beauty,"—that is all
> Ye know on earth, and all ye need to know.

A. C. Bradley thought these lines were an intellectual statement of Keats's faith in art, that "truth transformed would have turned into beauty" (*A Miscellany,* London, 1929, pp. 189–90). Cleanth Brooks read the lines as the voice of the "Sylvan historian," speaking to the poet as it will speak to future generations, and saying "that 'formed experience,' imaginative insight embodies the basic and fundamental perception of essentials." This vision is beautiful and also true. (*The Well-Wrought Urn,* New York, 1947, p. 150.) The message of the urn, according to E. R. Wasserman, is that art is "the source of the highest form of wisdom." (*The Finer Tone,* Baltimore, 1953, p. 49.) And Kenneth Muir thinks "the urn is proclaiming that there is not merely a close relationship but an actual identity between beauty and truth." (*John Keats,* Liverpool, 1959, p. 70.)

The lines meant nothing so metaphysical to H. W. Garrod. Keats was simply saying "there is nothing real but the beautiful and nothing beautiful but the real," an interpretation shared by Douglas Bush. Bush believed that the truth Keats embraced was "the reality apprehended through the senses," an opinion also shared by C. M. Bowra who wrote that to Keats "truth" meant "reality" and that reality is the only kind of knowledge we can have. (*Keats* [1926], London, 1950, p. 33; *Mythology and the Romantic Tradition in English Poetry,* Cambridge, Mass., 1937, p. 107; and *The Romantic Imagination,* New York, 1950, p. 146, respectively.)

The last lines of the "Ode on a Grecian Urn" struck T. S. Eliot as a "serious blemish on a beautiful poem" because the statement seemed "meaningless." (*Selected Essays: 1917–32,* New York, 1950, p. 231.) This is an opinion Allen Tate held in part when he argued that the last stanza is "an illicit commentary added by the poet to a 'meaning' which was symbolically complete at the end of the preceding stanza, number four." (*On the Limits of Poetry,* New York, 1948, p. 179.) As early as 1931, Hoxie Fairchild had written that the lines had "become one of the most nauseating phrases in literature." His disgust, he said, arose from the excessive gushing over its really simple meaning which may be found in Keats's letters: "what the imagination seizes as Beauty must be truth." (*The Romantic Quest.*)

What should be most evident in all this controversy is the one thought most frequently overlooked. Keats himself created a "Cold Pastoral," a poem warm in feeling yet frozen into a permanent form of art. Its melodies, like those of the urn's musicians, are sweet, "but those unheard / Are sweeter." The meanings which are self-evident in the poem are great, but those we find in it are greater still. The reader should come to the "Ode on a Grecian Urn" as Keats went to the original treasure, with a poet's eye, ear, nose, tongue, and hand, and with a poet's imagination.

CRITICISM: Aside from a number of loyal friends like Shelley, Hunt, Reynolds, and Severn who praised his work, Keats received virtually no encouragement while he was alive. Even after his death, those who recognized his genius and appreciated his verse, besides surviving friends, were an exclusive group of Cambridge students who did not make their tastes prevail until about 1848. After that Keats's nineteenth-century reputation grew in leaps and bounds. When subjected to the scrutiny of the anti-Romantics, the New Critics, and other scholars of this century, his reputation emerged not only unscathed but greater than ever before. No other Romantic has earned the almost universal acclaim of Victorian and modern critics alike.

Keats had reason to believe that he would be forgotten, for he was a severe critic of his own work, keenly aware of imperfections which he was constantly trying to eliminate. He agreed with the harsh critics of the *Morning Chronicle* (October 3, 1818) who had called *Endymion* "slip-shod," and he did not want to publish the "smokeable" *Pot of Basil,* which he considered a "weak-sided" poem. (H. B. Forman, ed., *Letters of John Keats,* London, 1952, p. 143.) In fact, he took criticism very well. He was annoyed when he read in *Blackwood's* (August 1818) that *Endymion* was merely a vulgar product of Leigh Hunt's "cockney school" of writing. But in spirit at least, he followed *Blackwood's* advice of October 1817 to "go back to your gallipots," and abandoned his London friends to write *Endymion* in isolation. He expected criticism of his defects, but he also hoped that some appreciation would be shown for his merits. None was forthcoming. The *Quarterly Review* (September 1818) joined *Blackwood's* attack on *Endymion,* and its reviewer John Wilson Croker condemned it outright. Keats's friends tried to defend the poem, but their opinions had very limited influence. The last volume of verse, published before his death, was *Lamia, Isabella, The Eve of St. Agnes and Other Poems*. It received approval from a few contemporaries: Leigh Hunt, Charles Lamb, and Francis Jeffrey of the *Edinburgh Review,* and, to a degree, John Wilson Croker of *Blackwood's,* who claimed only *Isabella* and *Lamia* deserved praise.

In 1821, Keats was dead. His after-fame received some stimulation from the publication of Shelley's *Adonais* (1821), an eloquent tribute to Keats's genius in which Shelley blamed the *Quarterly Review* for the young poet's death. In the twenty years that followed, contempt for Keats was not universal, but it was the most publicized attitude. Most praise for Keats appeared in brief references outside the popular critical journals. Byron praised Keats in a few lines of *Don Juan;* Hazlitt defended him in an 1824 essay for the *Edinburgh Review* where he censured *Blackwood's* for its rough treatment of the poet. Thomas Hood paid silent tribute to Keats by imitating him in works such as "The Plea of the Midsummer Fairies" (1827). Browning at fourteen (1829) was captivated by the magic of

Keats's poems. William Morris called Keats "one of my masters." Tennyson and Rossetti were also loyal disciples, and Elizabeth Barrett Browning paid him tribute in *Aurora Leigh* (1857). (See Sidney Colvin, *John Keats,* New York, 1917, p. 539; and G. H. Ford, *Keats and the Victorians: 1821–95,* 1944.)

The first biography, *The Life and Letters of Keats,* 2 vols., edited by Monckton Milnes (Lord Houghton), appeared in 1848, after which enthusiasm for Keats as a man as well as a poet began to grow. Those like Jeffrey who had believed Keats's poems were "rich" but ephemeral were found to be mistaken. Late Victorian critics added immensely to Keats's reputation. Matthew Arnold called him "clear-sighted and lucid," found him "fascinating," ranked him "with Shakespeare" (*Essays in Criticism,* 1888) and edited an edition of Keats in 1883. Palgrave included him in the *Golden Treasury* of 1884; Sidney Colvin published his letters to America in 1887; and Robert Bridges studied his relationship to Wordsworth soon after. Interest in Keats even extended to his friend Joseph Severn, whose *Life* by William Sharp was published in 1892.

When the twentieth century opened, the public was fairly well sated with writings emphasizing Keats the man. A good edition of his poems, which had long been awaited, finally appeared in 1905 with excellent notes and an introduction by Ernest De Selincourt. De Selincourt found superior merit in most of Keats's poems, but "in the Ode," he wrote, Keats "has no master; and the indefinable beauty is so direct and so distinctive an effluence of his soul that he can have no disciple." (*The Poems,* London, 1954, p. lx.) Another sorely needed study, a biography which took account of Keats's works as well as his life, was presented in 1917 by Sidney Colvin. Still the best biography of Keats in our time, Colvin's book is also respected for its sympathetic and keen analyses of the poetry.

Keats has had few detractors in our time, although there are some who would charge him with alienation from his own time. But C. DeW. Thorpe has explained Keats's apparent lack of interest in the social and political movements of his day: "Keats was keenly alive . . . [to these movements], took an active interest in history and studied past events in the light of their probable effect upon the present and the future." (*PMLA*, XLVI, 1931, p. 1244.) His "remarkable psychological insight" was seen by M. R. Ridley, who also noted Keats's "imaginative conception of truth" and his "clear perception of its Beauty." (*Keats' Craftsmanship*, Oxford, 1933.) Even the skeptical T. S. Eliot wrote in 1933 "Keats seems to me . . . a great poet." (*The Use of Poetry and Criticism,* p. 100.) The idea that Keats was a great craftsman had been suggested by earlier critics and was finally demonstrated by W. J. Bate in *The Stylistic Development of Keats* (1945), where he showed that Keats developed a skill in prosody which almost reached perfection. What was also especially enjoyed was his sensuous imagery: "None of the other Romantics surpassed him" in this. (Ernest Bernbaum, *Guide Through the Romantic Movement,* p. 235.)

Of the individual poems Keats wrote, modern critics have been fairly consistent in finding them admirable, although their judgments have varied in choosing the "masterpiece." Keats's first published volume is generally regarded as the promising work of a junior, but it is never so severely condemned as it had been in its own time. *Endymion,* too, although full of faults, has received milder treatment from the moderns than it had from its first critics. Amy Lowell said of it: "With all its faults, obscurities and digressions, *Endymion* is the spirit of youth rampant. Its adolescence is irresistible; to read it is to touch the spring of life." (*John Keats* [1925], Boston, 1929, I, 455.) Dorothy Hewlett also found it youthful but "full of the enchantment of this dream world." (*A Life of John Keats* [1937], New York, 1938, p. 170.) Other Keats idolaters have tried to elevate *Endymion* to the realm of philosophy, and orthodox interpretations of the poem have made it a "hymn to Platonism" or some related idealism. N. F. Ford, however, believed that Keats was not a Platonist, that his only religion was poetry, and when he speaks in *Endymion* of things like "fellowship with essence" and "fellowship divine," he is being figurative not philosophical. (*PMLA,* LXII, 1947, pp. 1061, 1076.)

Criticism of *Isabella* has also been a mixture of appreciation and disapprobation. De Selincourt, writing in 1905, found it "uneven in execution" and faulty in taste and craft. Nevertheless, it had "vivid poetic feeling." (*The Poems,* p. liv.) Colvin, however, defended *Isabella* wholeheartedly and found its digressions were useful effects, its images beauties. To Ridley, *Isabella* was an "unequal" piece, "fumbling" and immature. Its ottava rima stanza was indecorous, its introduction was limp, its obscurities were too numerous, its epithets too feeble. But Ridley never denied the artistic merits of the poet.

The Eve of St. Agnes, on the other hand, has had an entirely different critical history. De Selincourt, who had found *Isabella* uneven, judged *The Eve of St. Agnes* nearly perfect (p. lvii). Colvin, who had admired *Isabella,* found *The Eve of St. Agnes* even better. *The Eve of St. Agnes* "throbs in every line with the life of imagination and beauty." It is the "most complete and enchanting English pure romance poem of its time," Colvin wrote (p. 399). J. M. Murry thought *The Eve of St. Agnes* superb, a poem of "opulent and triumphant love," and, using Keats's own words about Fanny Brawne, said " 'the richness, the bloom, the full form, the enchantment of love after his own heart' " was realized in this poem. (*Keats and Shakespeare* [1925], London, 1951, p. 109.) M. R. Ridley, however, reserved his highest praise for *Lamia*; he believed that *The Eve of St. Agnes* had much more "felicity" than *Isabella,* but that it was not quite perfection.

Of the romances as a whole, most modern critics would agree with Garrod who said, "Of all the world's books, [they are] upon the whole, the most marvellous. . . . not the greatest, but the most marvellous." (*Keats,* p. 62.)

There is also substantial agreement on the greatness of the odes, a lyric form in which Keats had no master. "The Odes are enough for [Keats's] . . . reputation," T. S. Eliot declared, choosing "Ode to Psyche" as perhaps the best of the group. Others like F. R. Leavis and Catherine Peace picked "Ode to a Nightingale" as the "best of Keats." (*Revaluation,* p. 245; *John Keats,* New York, 1960, p. 182, respectively.) A number of critics, Colvin for one, share G. G. Hough's opinion that " 'To Autumn' is the most perfect in form and detail of the odes," which as a whole, express "an enjoyment of such intensity and depth that it makes the moment eternal, in quality if not in duration." (*The Romantic Poets,* p. 178.)

The most interesting and most controversial of these great poems is "Ode on a Grecian Urn," especially its last two lines.

Nineteenth-century readers considered these lines profoundly philosophical. In our own century, many critics have thought the same. C. H. Herford saw the poem as "a glorious clear-eyed apprehension of the spiritual eternity which art . . . affords." (In *Cambridge History of English Literature,* ed. A. W. Ward and A. R. Waller, Cambridge, England, 1914, XII, p. 90.) To Cleanth Brooks the poem had philosophical consistency expressed throughout by paradox and irony, and the final lines, he believed, stood in logical consequence to the earlier stanzas of the poem. (*The Well-Wrought Urn,* pp. 150–51.) To critics such as these, despite variances in their interpretations, the ode as a whole, and especially its closing lines, makes a serious philosophical or ethical statement. Others disagree.

I. A. Richards and William Empson laughed at philosophical interpretations of "Ode on a Grecian Urn" and insisted that the last lines had emotional meaning only, Empson arguing that the philosophic meaning Cleanth Brooks gave the poem was the critic's not Keats's. (*The Structure of Complex Words* [1947], Norfolk, Conn., 1951, p. 368.) Sharing this opinion, R. H. Fogle wrote that the poem is an "expression of emphatic feeling and emotion" arising from the contemplation of a beautiful object until the emotion becomes an aesthetic one. (*The Imagery of Keats and Shelley,* p. 172.) The number of disputations over the "Ode on a Grecian Urn" continues to grow with no signs of letting up. In fact, criticism of all Keats's poems keeps expanding and has been extended even to the unfinished works which were once largely ignored.

The general estimate of Keats in our time is higher than that of any other major Romantic poet, all of whom were better educated, wrote much more, suffered less, and lived much longer than John Keats. D. G. James spoke for many of us when he said Keats was "no mere sensuous dreamer but a manly person who saw in misfortunes the opportunity of trying the resources of his spirit." Like James, "we may fairly see him not only as the youngest but also as the wisest poet" of the Romantic movement. (*The Romantic Comedy* [1948], London, 1963, pp. 196, 272.)

THE MINOR ROMANTIC POETS

GEORGE CRABBE

George Crabbe first attracted attention in 1780 when, through the kindness of Edmund Burke, he found a publisher for his poems. Born in 1754, he had been apprenticed, like Keats was to be later, to a surgeon. He practiced medicine for a few years but had no taste for it and abandoned it, determined to make a name for himself as a poet.

In 1783 he published one of his best poems, *The Village.* This was a relentlessly realistic account of the harsh actualities of rural life. It was designed to shock readers into an awareness of the falsehood of sentimental descriptions of happy plowmen and their carefree children. Crabbe focuses attention on dirt, drabness, poverty, and disease.

In his interest in the common people Crabbe partakes of the Romantic spirit, but he very much belongs to the neoclassical age in his literary style.

After the early success of *The Village,* he entered the Church and for twenty-two years devoted himself to Church affairs. Then in 1807, when the Romantic spirit was at full tide, he began to publish a series of notable narrative poems. Like *The Village,* they are uncompromisingly realistic and thus bear little resemblance to the great body of Romantic poetry. They were well received, however, and Crabbe enjoyed the friendship of many of the Romantic writers. He died in 1832.

ROBERT SOUTHEY

Although he was a very prolific poet and a versatile prose-writer, Southey has been almost completely neglected by posterity. Born in 1774, and educated at Westminster School (until

his expulsion for an essay against flogging), Southey attended
Balliol College, Oxford. While a student at the University he
met Coleridge and with Coleridge planned the establishment of
an ideal community on the Susquehanna River, the "Pantisocracy," mentioned in the chapter on Coleridge. In 1803, Southey
settled at Keswick, in the Lake District. He is, accordingly, one
of the so-called "Lake Poets."

Today Southey is chiefly remembered for his associations with
Coleridge and Wordsworth, for his conversion from youthful
radicalism to staid conservatism, and for the merciless satire
directed against him by Byron. In 1813, Southey was appointed
Poet Laureate. This honor is not always bestowed on the
greatest poets and the official poems composed by the Laureates
for state occasions are often pompous and dull. Southey's were
no exceptions. In 1820, George III died and Southey felt
obliged to memorialize the event by a long poem, *A Vision of
Judgement*. It is a remarkably silly poem. Byron was moved to
write a parody of it that has given it a rather unfortunate kind
of immortality.

Southey expected that through an ambitious series of epics he
would leave a name "That would not perish in the dust."
Almost the only poem by Southey that now is read is a ballad
on the futility of war called "The Battle of Blenheim." In 1704,
the English and Austrian armies fought against the French and
the Bavarians near a little village in Bavaria. The English and
Austrians were victorious. Southey in his ballad imagines that,
years later, a little boy in Blenheim finds a skull and brings it to
his grandfather, old Kaspar, who proceeds to tell the boy and
the boy's sister, Wilhelmine, about the "famous victory." There
is considerable effectiveness in the contrast between the horrors
of war and the quiet, matter-of-fact style of old Kaspar's narrative.

> "But what good came of it at last?"
>   Quoth little Peterkin.
> "Why that I cannot tell," said he,
>   "But 'twas a famous victory."

It is hard not to be a little sorry for Southey. He was intelligent, had many interests, accumulated a great library, was a good critic and historian. He died in 1832.

WALTER SAVAGE LANDOR

Born in 1775 when the neoclassical spirit was still strong and living until 1864 when Victorianism was in the ascendency, Landor, like Crabbe, does not fit easily into a history of English Romanticism. It is doubtful that even if his chronology more neatly matched that of Romantic literature he would be easy to classify.

Landor's parents were well-to-do. He had the usual classical education that privileged boys of the eighteenth century received. He went to a good school, Rugby, and to Trinity College, Oxford. He became passionately attached to the great classical authors, both Greek and Latin, and one of his most important contributions to English poetry was his constant effort to bring into English poetry the ideals that characterized classical literature: restraint, orderliness, maturity. In a sense he was doing what the neoclassical poets thought that they were doing. But Landor was re-examining the classical tradition in his own way and he succeeds in introducing new notes into our poetry.

Although a classicist, Landor was also as fierce an individualist as any of the Romantics. At Oxford he was disciplined by the authorities because he fired a gun at the shutters of a fellow-student's room to show the extent of his displeasure at something the other man had said or done. In later life he was always finding himself involved in lawsuits.

There were many attractive sides to his character, but he was very much inclined to hold himself aloof from the crowd. He wrote to please himself and any discriminating readers he might eventually find. He wrote voluminously, and even in his own day found appreciative readers. Since his day he has scarcely been a popular writer but there has always been lively interest in his work.

Best known of Landor's works to the general reader are his lovely elegy on the death of a friend, Rose Aylmer, a poem that the essayist Charles Lamb was never tired of quoting, and the magnificent "Iphigeneia" from *The Hellenics* and a few short lyrics in which he expresses his proud attitude toward life.

The Hellenics is the title chosen by Landor for a series of short tales or dialogues in verse based on Greek mythology and literature. It was frequently Landor's custom to compose first in Latin and then to translate his Latin into English verse. This accounts, of course, for the very special classical quality of Landor's English poety.

The best known of *The Hellenics* is Landor's pathetic account of the ritual sacrifice of Agamemnon's daughter. After the abduction of Helen by Paris, Prince of Troy, Helen's husband Menelaos and his brother Agamemnon assemble a Greek army to move against Troy. The ships on which the warriors sail, however, are delayed by adverse winds at Aulis. Calchas, a soothsayer, a priest, explains to Agamemnon that only the death of his daughter will satisfy the goddess responsible for the winds at Aulis. Landor in "Iphigeneia" imagines the last conversation of the hapless girl and her grief-stricken father. Agamemnon loves his daughter. He also has responsibilities toward his brother, his men, his country. Iphigeneia begins by suggesting that Calchas may not have heard distinctly what the goddess said. Landor lets us see how gradually and poignantly she comes to the brave recognition that for the public good she must die. The final scene is the awful sacrifice. The father is undergoing agony, but

> A groan that shook him shook not his resolve.
> An aged man now enter'd, and without
> One word, stept slowly on, and took the wrist
> Of the pale maiden. She lookt up, and saw
> The fillet [head-band] of the priest and calm cold eyes.
> Then turn'd she where her parent stood, and cried
> "O father! grieve no more; the ships can sail."

One of the more amusing of Landor's short poetic reflections on his relation to his fellow men is that four-line lyric beginning "I strove with none, for none was worth my strife." The haughtiness of the protest we recognize as general. The literal truth of the statement seems open to question.

There is still another delightful little effort on the part of the poet to come to an understanding of his character:

> I know not whether I am proud,
> But this I know, I hate the crowd:
> Therefore pray let me disengage
> My verses from the motley page,
> Where others far more sure to please
> Pour out their choral song with ease.
> And yet perhaps, if some should tire
> With too much froth or too much fire,
> There is an ear that may incline
> Even to words so dull as mine.

Landor's "guests" will, in all probability, always be "few and select." With the decline of the classical tradition they may, in the future, be even fewer. He is not, however, likely to fall into complete neglect. He is an important poet and has a permanent place in the history of English literature.

THOMAS MOORE

The convivial Irish poet Thomas Moore (1779–1852) came from a prosperous home and was educated at Trinity College, Dublin, the alma mater of other well-known figures in English literary history, such as Swift, Goldsmith, and Edmund Burke. In 1798, Moore moved to London for law study at Middle Temple, one of the oldest law study centers in England. Apparently a man of unusual personal charm, he was a great social success in England. As a poet he was especially talented in the writing of songs and he impressed his English friends mightily by his own sweet singing of his songs.

His work was praised by Shelley. He was a very close friend of Lord Byron. His songs still have the power to move readers and listeners. Moore's reputation, however, has largely disappeared. His achievement is conspicuously less than that of Burns, but he did much to make the English Romantics aware of Ireland. He is not one of our great poets. He is one of our most attractive minor poets.

LEIGH HUNT

Like Southey, Leigh Hunt (1784–1859) today is remembered almost entirely because of his association with greater men of letters than he was himself. His essays, however, are beginning to be read again. He was one of the first of his generation to recognize—and to encourage—the genius of Shelley and Keats.

He had a good education at Christ's Hospital, the famous charity school where both Coleridge and Lamb acquired their educations. He did not go on to a university but became a government clerk. While still a young man, however, he and his brother John founded a weekly newspaper which they called *The Examiner*. The paper figures prominently in the history of the radical movement in England but to students of literature it is especially remembered as the paper in which Keats first found a public.

Hunt was a literary critic of some perceptiveness. We do not go to him expecting to find the profound ideas of, let us say, Coleridge. But he is a good journalistic critic.

As a poet, Hunt is remembered only for some of his minor lyrics. "Abou Ben Adhem" is unquestionably the best known of these. The rondeau "Jenny Kissed Me" is familiar to most readers of English poetry, and although of no great consequence, has a certain charming quality:

> Jenny kissed me when we met,
>   Jumping from the chair she sat in;
> Time, you thief, who love to get
>   Sweets into your list, put that in;
> Say I'm weary, say I'm sad,
>   Say that health and wealth have missed me,

> Say I'm growing old, but add,
> Jenny kissed me.

On the whole, Leigh Hunt has fared somewhat better than Southey. It is nonetheless true that his place in English letters is the result of his friendships and associations and of his essays not his poetry.

JOHN CLARE

Interest in John Clare's poetry has grown considerably in the twentieth century. Clare (1793–1864) was a farm laborer. We now know that he ranks among the very best of the "poets of the people" the eighteenth century so ardently sought, but the appreciation of the importance of Clare came too late to do the poet good. He was, it seems, an exceptionally sensitive man. He loved the countryside and is one of the most faithful describers of the rural England that he knew. But Clare never had an easy life. His worries, disappointments, and periods of heartbreak ultimately drove him mad. He was put into an insane asylum in 1837 and remained there until his death. While in the asylum, during lucid intervals, Clare wrote some of his best poems. His early poems, descriptive of nature, are notable for their accuracy of detail; his later poems have an extraordinarily pathetic quality. The moving lyric "The Dying Child" shows the tenderness that marks the poetry of John Clare.

THOMAS HOOD

His life a courageous struggle against ill-health and poverty, Thomas Hood (1799–1845) earned most of his living by comic verse, which was highly regarded by his contemporaries and deserves renewed interest in our day. He is not much valued for his Romantic poems, however, although his treatment of the great love story of Hero and Leander is an astonishing triumph. One of the earliest disciples of Keats, at times Hood is not unworthy of his master. Nevertheless, he is not remembered for his Keatsian management of beautiful phrase and rich imagery. His poems of social protest are his best known. Even in his own day his most successful poem was "The Song of the Shirt," which called attention to the intolerable condition of the working classes. "The Song of the Shirt" was first printed in the popular magazine *Punch,* but it created such a sensation that it was circulated in churches.

THOMAS LOVELL BEDDOES

One conspicuous feature of the Romantic movement was a heightened interest in Elizabethan poetry. One of the strangest of the English Romantic poets, Thomas Lovell Beddoes, cannot be omitted from an account of this "Elizabethanism."

Born in 1803, he was educated at Charterhouse, a famous school then located in the environs of London. The essayists Addison and Steele and the novelist Thackeray are among the many distinguished men of letters who studied at Charterhouse. Beddoes then went to Pembroke College, Oxford, the college which Samuel Johnson had attended and which he had described as "a nest of singing birds." While still an undergraduate Beddoes wrote and published two tragedies in the Elizabethan manner. They were ignored by the public.

After Oxford Beddoes studied medicine in Germany and decided to settle in Zurich. He began work on his most important drama, *Death's Jest-Book,* in 1825, revised it frequently, and left it unpublished at his death. It is an Elizabethan tragedy concerned with revenge and madness.

Beddoes himself seems to have been more than a little mad. He was certainly obsessed by the phenomenon of death. In 1849 he took his own life. *Death's Jest-Book* was published in the following year.

Beddoes also left, to be published after his death, a half-dozen of the finest lyric poems in our language. They show the influence of Shelley but they have an individual quality of their own. "Dream-Pedlary" is usually thought to be the most striking of them all. It begins:

> If there were dreams to sell,
> What would you buy?

Some cost a passing bell;
    Some a light sigh,
That shakes from Life's fresh crown
Only a rose-leaf down.
If there were dreams to sell,
Merry and sad to tell,
And the crier rung the bell,
    What would you buy?

Beddoes apparently never found the answer.

SUMMARY: This chapter is meant to show two things: (1) that there are many different kinds of Romantic poetry, and (2) that even the lesser-known Romantic poets have made important contributions to English literature. One can readily see, for example, that when one compares the handful of first-rate lyrics left by Beddoes with the extraordinarily prolific work of a Shelley or a Keats, Beddoes is properly labeled a "minor" poet. It must not be forgotten, however, that so-called "minor" poets have left us some of our most treasured masterpieces.

That it is extremely difficult at times to make a clear-cut distinction between "major" and "minor" poets is pointed up by the career of Landor. His productivity compares favorably with that of poets who have made a more permanent and deeper impression on the reading public. And discerning readers have recognized great artistry in his work. He is "minor" almost by accident and almost by mistake. The fact remains that for every reader interested in Landor there are dozens interested in the Romantic poets who have been given chapters to themselves in this study guide.

ESSAY QUESTIONS AND ANSWERS

1. Why do we distinguish between pre-Romantic and Romantic poets?

ANSWER: When we attempt to distinguish periods of literary history, we must remember that dividing lines cannot be looked upon as having the accuracy or the authority of geographical boundaries. Most readers feel that the *prevailing tones* of the poetry written between roughly 1666 and 1780, and that written after 1780, are sufficiently different to justify our giving different labels to the two periods. The first we have agreed to call "neoclassical" or "Augustan"; the second we call "Romantic." "Pre-Romantic" identifies transitional poets, those who most notably exhibited in their writings, traits that came to be associated with Romantic poetry.

The pre-Romantic poet James Thomson, for example, in his greatest and most influential poem, *The Seasons,* anticipates Wordsworth in his precise descriptions of nature. In "Winter," Thomson records the behavior of various animals as they sense an approaching storm.

> With broadened nostrils to the sky upturned,
> The conscious heifer snuffs the stormy gale.
>
> Assiduous in his bower, the wailing owl
> Plies his sad song. The cormorant on high
> Wheels from the deep and screams along the land.

Thomson, however, shows little sense of the deep mysteriousness of nature that one finds in Wordsworth. In his highly artificial language and in his determination to draw a general moral from everything he sees, Thomson shows himself firmly rooted in the Augustan Age.

So with other pre-Romantic poets. Bishop Percy showed an admirable willingness to listen to the voices of the Middle Ages. Having heard them, however, he felt obliged to change the accents to those more suitable in "polite" society of his own era; he did not wish to retain or imitate what he regarded as the crudities of an untutored age.

When we come to a poet like Blake, on the other hand, we encounter a man who is convinced that a new day has dawned. Blake rejected the ethics, the language, and the symbols of his predecessors who had tried to school English society in Augustan manners and thought, who believed that civilization belonged exclusively to the urbane society of the court, and who were persuaded that the common man was by nature a clown. Blake released in his poetry the energies of the common man. He discarded the classical symbols of restraint and moderation and showed that even the poor were capable of excellence and nobility. He developed new forms to express new ideas, and when he reshaped old forms, they were scarcely recognizable. Blake added power to his rhetoric, personal commitment to his pronouncements. In his poetry, he turned the world upside down and asked for a new man and a new society that would resemble nothing that had ever gone before.

The Romantics who followed Blake were equally original. Coleridge's "The Rime of the Ancient Mariner" was the first extensive moral tale in ballad form which explored the relationship between man and the natural and supernatural worlds. He used a completely imaginative situation and scene, and yet did not ignore the essential reality of human and nonhuman creations. Wordsworth too eschewed classical forms, conventional poetic language, symbols, and subjects. Although earlier poets had begun to appreciate inanimate nature, Wordsworth actually gave nature an important role in the development of man. He was the first poet (aside from Blake who was barely known in his time) to formulate a system of thought which explained the interinvolvement of God, man, and his environment. Keats was also a new and Romantic spirit. He went back in his mind to the Golden Age of the Greeks, which had long preceded the Augustan Age of Rome, and recapturing the pagan awareness of life, showed the sensual connection between man and matter. He implied that intervening civilizations were merely encrustations upon the soil of pagan truth, obscuring the essential relationship between man and his environment.

2. What are some of the reasons for Burns's high reputation as a poet?

ANSWER: All great poetry has qualities that go beyond definition or description. We can, nevertheless, distinguish certain elements in the poetry of Burns that have contributed to his reputation.

a. His use of his native Scottish speech. The Northern dialect used in Burns's native Ayrshire had a vigor and homeliness that contrasted favorably with the overconventionalized language used in English poetry. Burns was born with an exceptional sensitivity to language and early learned to use his native speech to achieve wonderful comic effects. There was something about the language that made it suitable not only to comedy and satire but also to the direct expression of simple emotion. Burns is one of our great comic poets; he is also the author of some of our best love lyrics.

b. His musical sense. Related to Burns's recognition of the value of his dialect was his passionate love of all native literary traditions, notably the tradition of Scottish song. He devoted much of his life to the collection of specimens of Scottish song and much of his own poetry finds its inspiration in that tradition.

c. His awareness of the relation of literature to life. Burns had his weaknesses. It is regrettable that some readers seem to be more interested in his weaknesses than in his many virtues. His poetry shows how intensely Burns valued honesty, including honesty with one's own self. He hated hypocrisy, sanctimoniousness, holier-than-thou attitudes. He also believed in bravery and courage. He had a special talent for friendship. He was anxious to learn and quick to learn.

Some of his weaknesses are the direct outcome of his virtues. Thus his conviviality proceeds from his friendliness. His difficulties with the elders of the church reflect his determination to be completely honest. His rejection of the prevailing religion of Scotland, a conspicuously cheerless Calvinism, at least in its usual manifestations, was in part a repudiation of what he considered to be spiritual pride and in part a defiant profession of his belief in the joy of life.

d. The fertility of his imagination.　　When we say that Burns loved life we mean that he loved it in its many shapes and forms. He loved the Scottish landscape, the bustle of market towns, the coziness of taverns, flowers, pretty girls—life in its totality. He loved the strange tales told for generations by the people and especially relished the more grotesque figures of the popular imagination. Burns shows a special fondness for the popular representations of the Devil. "Tam o' Shanter" is one of the greatest narrative poems in English, probably the best comic narrative poem. It achieves its effects through the miraculous blending of the natural (Tam and his cronies oblivious of time, the long ride home through the blinding storm and the ghost-haunted countryside) and the supernatural (the wild dance of the witches, the furious flight to gain the safety of the bridge) and through Burns's own relish for the story which he communicates to the reader.

3.　　Why did Wordsworth compose a Preface to the second edition of *Lyrical Ballads*?

ANSWER:　　In 1797, Coleridge and Wordsworth lived within a few miles of one another and met almost daily. They, with Wordsworth's sensitive and talented sister Dorothy, talked for hours about poetry, its function, its relation to life. Gradually, they formulated theories of poetry very much at variance with the prevailing theories. They were anxious to test the value of their theories and thus planned *Lyrical Ballads, With a Few Other Poems*.

Although the volume opened with Coleridge's "The Rime of the Ancient Mariner" and closed with Wordsworth's "Tintern Abbey," it was not an unqualified success. Few such experimental volumes ever are. Wordsworth's contributions include some verse anecdotes about rustic life and some efforts to make psychological studies of simple, unspoiled country folk. These almost inevitably seemed more than somewhat strange to the first readers of *Lyrical Ballads*. The book, however, sold and by 1800 the authors decided to bring out a second edition.

Wordsworth's professed purpose in writing a Preface to this new edition was not to persuade readers of the merits of the poems. It was rather to explain the principles which lay behind this "new" poetry.

The first principle was this: poetry ought to concern itself with "incidents and situations from common life." Wordsworth hoped that by studying "common life" he might be able more effectively to trace "the primary laws of our nature." Logically there would seem to be much of value in the theory; in practice it led to some of Wordsworth's worst failures. It was, perhaps, too theoretical, but it arose out of a justifiable conviction that poetry was more and more cutting itself off from ordinary life.

The second principle is closely related to the first: the poet should use "language really used by men." Like the first, this makes sense until one realizes that the language used by men is often dull, repetitious, imprecise, and utterly lacking in power to arouse, stimulate, bring about intellectual and spiritual change. The problem of poetic diction is a permanent problem in literary criticism. Fashions in poetic language can become merely fashions. On the other hand, an earnest striving to reproduce the language of everyday life can be boring and ludicrous. Wordsworth at least deserves credit for emphasizing the importance of the problem, especially in an age accustomed to a highly artificial poetic diction.

In connection with this second principle, one should also notice that Wordsworth made some effort to qualify his phrase, "language really used by men." He insisted that over this language the poet should throw "a certain coloring of imagination." This is not altogether helpful, but it reveals that Wordsworth was somewhat more aware of the complexities of the problem of diction than he is sometimes given credit for being.

A third important principle enunciated in the Preface is that poetry "is the spontaneous overflow of powerful feelings." One immediately is struck by the fact that this notion of spontaneity is at variance with the usual neoclassical emphasis on the deliberateness of the creative act. In neoclassicism the mind is definitely thought of as in control. In the new Romantic theory, the emotions are given their due.

It must, however, be observed that Wordsworth does not see the poet as the victim of his spontaneous emotions. The poem arises from a spontaneous overflow of feelings, but also "from emotion recollected in tranquillity." This is not raw emotion. Some kind of controlling imaginative faculty has intervened. The theory is not altogether satisfactory, but it forced readers to re-examine their views of the relationship between mind and emotion and to speculate again on the nature of the imaginative act.

The Preface to the *Lyrical Ballads* has its loose ends. It is not, nor was it ever meant to be, an answer to all of our questions about the nature of poetry. It raised the questions, however, that made possible a radical readjustment of our thinking about poetry. More modest than a manifesto, it signaled, more than any comparable document of its time, the end of the old order, the end of neoclassicism.

4. How do you account for the early reputation of Scott as a poet?

ANSWER: Although Scott's reputation as a poet began to decline in his own day, his verse narratives still have a spirited quality that engages the emotions and the interests of the reader. One does not go to Scott for subtle poetry, for reflective poetry. He does not have the heightened sense of language that Keats possessed. He does not have intricate theories about good and evil such as we expect to find in Blake and Shelley. His exuberance invites comparison with that of Byron, but Byron's is obviously the greater and the more entertaining. There is general agreement today that Scott is one of the minor English poets, but his place in the history of Romantic literature is permanently assured.

In the first place, Scott both responded to the new awareness of the picturesqueness of the past and helped to deepen this awareness. In the second place, he sensed the growing taste for shudders and thrills. In the third place, he was able in his poems to avail himself of the appeal of the wild "Romantic" scenery of his native Scotland.

The Lay of the Last Minstrel, the first of the great original verse narratives, is deliberately nostalgic. The confused "Gothic" tale is represented as being told in traditional fashion by one of the ancient Scottish bards, the last of his kind. The very "frame" or story of the tale itself would almost insure its popularity. But added to the frame are incidents involving wizardry and disguise. The formula, predictably, worked.

Marmion, the next of the verse narratives, retold the perennially pathetic and appealing story of a lost cause. At Flodden Field the flower of Scottish chivalry went down to defeat and the cause of Scottish nationalism was doomed. The Scots took an honest and legitimate pride in the way their ancestors fought gallantly against impossible odds; the English could not but be moved by this vivid account of a crucial moment in history. There was, also, a topical significance to this poem about bygone heroism, for England and France were at the time of the publication of the poem locked in a duel to the death. All Britons found their hearts stirred by the old story of Flodden.

Marmion also appealed to the Romantic generation by virtue of the complexity of its central character. Marmion was a strange compound of virtue and villainy. His wickedness produced agreeable shudders similar to those produced by the fashionable tales of terror. His virtues made one aware of the odd mingling of good and evil in creatures of this imperfect world. The neoclassical period liked its villains and its heroes rigidly kept apart. It liked clarity. The Romantics wished to explore the darker mysteries of existence. Marmion is, in a sense, an early version of the Byronic hero, destined to become an important part of European Romantic literature.

The Lady of the Lake is notable for many things. It not only exhibits Scott's extraordinary ability to describe the wild region around Loch Katrine but it also shows how magically he can communicate his own enthusiasm for the beauty of these scenes. Episodes such as the stag hunt and the gathering of the clans are also magnificently handled and account for the favorable reception of the poem.

Although the poems after *The Lady of the Lake* were not so spectacularly successful as the first three Romantic verse narratives, they are not without interest. Rokeby, for example, the hero of the poem of that name, is another early sketch of the Byronic hero. *Rokeby* can also be examined as a kind of preparation for the great historical novels Scott was soon to write. *The Bridal of Triermain* is a most important nineteenth-century attempt to use Arthurian story. *The Lord of the Isles* tells the story of the great Scottish hero Robert Bruce.

5. What are some of the basically serious themes of "The Rime of the Ancient Mariner"?

ANSWER: The most obvious is that evil has inevitable consequences. Sorrow for one's evil-doing obviously helps to reestablish the harmony that is broken by the evil action. The Ancient Mariner, however, can never completely erase from his consciousness the enormity of his crime.

Related to this theme is that of the senselessness, the irrationality of evil. Had the poet wished, he could have recorded motives for the shooting of the albatross. The poem gains in effectiveness through Coleridge's refusal to give an easy explanation for the Mariner's action. Who knows why he shot the albatross? Perhaps the loneliness of the Polar regions, the frightening eeriness of the icebergs, the strange sounds frayed his nerves. The point is precisely that his action is, in a sense, understandable in that we can recall many of the evil things we have done under various pressures. But, in a larger sense, evil is never really understandable. The Mariner himself makes no excuses. In stark language he reports his deed as horrible.

A third theme is that of the human preference for immediate profit regardless of principle. At first the shipmates of the Mariner are angry at him for his crime; when the ship makes its way from the dreadful seas of ice and lands of snow, they are quick to persuade themselves that the Mariner was justified in shooting the bird. Their all-too-human willingness to applaud a crime because of its apparently beneficial consequences involves them in his guilt and lends a kind of poetic justice to their deaths in the Torrid Zone.

The participation of the shipmates in the guilt of the Mariner is related to still another theme: the interaction of all of the parts of the universe. After his companions have all died, the Mariner feels himself terribly alone upon the rotting sea of the merciless equator. Only a thousand, thousand slimy things have lived on. But suddenly the slimy things become creatures of incredible beauty, and this almost involuntary recognition of the sanctity of life and the beauty of life and the variety of life is the beginning of the sinner's redemption.

Prayer represents still another obvious theme. "He prayeth best, who loveth best / All things both great and small." The presence in the poem of other themes such as those we have here mentioned suggests that this should not be interpreted in a sentimental fashion. Coleridge is not saying, "Let us all be kind to one another." He is not suggesting that we refrain from being cruel to dumb animals. Rather he is saying that prayer is far too important to be a matter of mere formula. Prayer must be more than words. It must be a total commitment to an ideal of love.

Marriage can scarcely be considered a theme of "The Rime of the Ancient Mariner," but it is surely of importance to the meaning of this extraordinarily rich poem that the Mariner's story is told to a "Wedding-Guest." The wedding suggests love, hope, an understanding of the principle of unity. Significantly, the Wedding-Guest fails to attend the wedding. Symbolically, we are not ready for the ideal order the poet hopes for. But disappointment can be an effective teacher.

> . . . and now the Wedding-Guest
> Turned from the bridegroom's door.
>
> He went like one that hath been stunned,
> And is of sense forlorn:
> A sadder and a wiser man,
> He rose the morrow morn.

6. What poets are satirized in *English Bards and Scotch Reviewers*? For what reasons? Are the reasons valid?

ANSWER: Byron directed his satiric barbs at Southey, Scott, Wordsworth, and Coleridge.

Southey's epics are represented as wild and absurd. Thalaba, for example, the hero of *Thalaba the Destroyer,* is said to have overthrown "More mad magicians than the world e'er knew." Southey's technical competence as a poet is also challenged. Byron claims that his poems are unmetrical. The final charge is that Southey is long-winded and repetitious. "A bard may chant too often and too long."

Scott is also attacked for the improbability of his stories. Byron does not refrain from caustic remarks on Scott's character and accuses him of being vain and mercenary. "Let such forego the poet's sacred name, / Who rack their brains for lucre, not for fame."

Perhaps the most entertaining satire is directed at Wordsworth, "That mild apostate from poetic rule." He is said to have shown, by both precept and example, "that prose is verse, and verse is merely prose." Byron finds particularly ridiculous a poem in *Lyrical Ballads* called "The Idiot Boy." He concludes his attack on Wordsworth with a reference to this poem:

> . . . all who view "the idiot in his glory"
> Conceive the bard the hero of the story.

The charge brought against Coleridge is that he is pretentious
and obscure. Even as Wordsworth's "The Idiot Boy" suited
Byron's satiric purpose, so did an early poem of Coleridge entitled "To a Young Ass." Thus the lines on Coleridge close with
these unfair but unforgettable couplets:

> Yet none in lofty numbers can surpass
> The bard who soars to elegise an ass.
> So well the subject suits his noble mind,
> He brays the laureat of the long-ear'd kind.

In general, of course, the charges are unfair, though posterity
has pretty much agreed to abide by his judgment on Southey.
We know, too, that Byron's political beliefs affected his views
on the "English bards" he chose to ridicule. But the portraits of
the poets cannot be dismissed as merely the result of prejudice.
Although himself guilty of a certain amount of nonsense in
verse, Byron here acts as spokesman for common sense. In their
necessary, valuable, justified reaction against the neoclassical
emphasis on reason Romantic poets occasionally seemed struck
by moon-madness. It could surely do no great harm to laugh at
some of their absurdities.

7.   Why is *Prometheus Unbound* often thought to be Shelley's
masterpiece?

ANSWER: In this powerful verse drama Shelley exhibits the
richness of his moral vision. Shelley affirms his unalterable
conviction that man can shake off his chains. He persuades us
that we can make a better world. He is sufficiently a realist to
see a vast amount of evil in this world. He sees selfishness,
cruelty, greed, and a host of other evils. But in Shelley's view
good must prevail, for evil contains within itself the seeds of its
own destruction.

The poem is about justice but it is also about compassion. In
spite of his sufferings at the hands of the vengeful Jupiter,

Prometheus is too noble to hate his enemy. In Act I, he repents the curse that he hurled at Jupiter and wishes to recall it. Knowing that Jupiter's reign is coming to an end, he even finds it in his heart to pity the tyrant. At the same time he refuses to yield up a secret locked in his breast which alone can save Jupiter. Pity must not stand in the way of justice. Evil must be dethroned.

Not only the ideas behind the poem but also the glorious language in which these ideas are communicated make this one of the greatest of English poems. Shelley shows his extraordinary mastery of many metrical patterns. Act IV is a sustained hymn of liberation that dazzles the reader by the magnificence of the language.

The poem reflects the stubborn idealism of Shelley. He hated cruelty and oppression and believed that man could perfect his nature. There is nothing childish, however, about his faith, and the myth partly inherited and partly created shows his awareness of the vastness of the universe. Shelley was not the prisoner of a single idea, and one should not read *Prometheus Unbound* merely as a tract against tyranny. It should, rather, be read as a lyrically beautiful poem that has created its own world, one that helps us to understand the everyday world in which we find ourselves.

8. Explain some of Keats's views on art and life as expressed in some of the so-called "great odes."

ANSWER: The "Ode to Psyche" is an impassioned celebration of the importance of love. Since Psyche is a goddess, the "latest born" of "Olympus' faded hierarchy," the poet can develop his theme that love is not only important but also holy, and it is the privilege of the poet to be the priest of love. Keats is not merely rapturous, however. He understands that the poet must not only consult his sensations but also explore the deeper regions of his mind. And he understands, as did Blake, that our thoughts are complicated—in his own language "branched." He confronts the strange fact that sometimes pain can be pleasant.

The "Ode to a Nightingale" develops this paradox further. The song of the nightingale is, in the poem, immortal. "Thou wast not born for death, immortal Bird!" The poet, on the other hand, is "half in love with easeful Death." The contrast between the beauty of the nightingale's song, the beauty of spring, and the poet's melancholy is remarkably sharp and affecting.

Once again in the "Ode on a Grecian Urn" does Keats consider the relationship of art and immortality. The scene painted or sculpted on the vase has a kind of permanence we cannot expect in our own lives. The musician in the scene is "For ever piping songs for ever new."

The "Ode on a Grecian Urn" is famous for its condensation of Keats's belief that truth and beauty are essentially one. " 'Beauty is truth, truth beauty,'—that is all / Ye know on earth, and all ye need to know." Although it is clear from the "great odes" that Keats is aware of the fact that man is a thinking animal, it is also clear that he believes in the supreme importance of sudden discoveries. He knows about the nature of thought; he has confidence in his ability to make a kind of leap at truth, to apprehend truth through his senses.

The "great odes" show how joyously Keats responded to the sights and sounds of this world, show how sensitive he was to sunlight and shadow, to the odors of flowers, to the taste of grape. They also show that intermingled with his joyousness is a melancholy sense of the transience of this world.

Keats wrote most of his best poetry in a period of three or four years. In that time he achieved astonishing maturity.

SUGGESTED TOPICS FOR
RESEARCH PAPERS

1. Chatterton and Walpole. The most recent and by far the best edition of Walpole's correspondence is that brought out by the Yale University Press under the general editorship of Wilmarth S. Lewis. The volume containing the letters that passed between Chatterton and Walpole was the first volume published. An examination of the existing evidence proving or disproving Walpole's heartlessness should increase the student's awareness of what literary history is.

2. Thomas Gray's interest in the Middle Ages. Gray's investigations of Celtic and Norse literary traditions expanded the neoclassical universe and helped to prepare for the new Romantic world. There have been many biographies of Gray and it should not be too difficult to make a fairly systematic analysis of Gray's medieval studies. The student should notice, for example, that Gray, with his friend William Mason, planned a history of English poetry that would include medieval poetry.

3. The Ossianic poems. Even though the problem of whether or not the Ossianic poems are authentic has long since been solved, the excitement generated by Macpherson's "translations" can still be profitably studied. Such a study increases the student's awareness of changing tastes and fashions and it also brings him face to face with a story as interesting as any detective story.

4. Blake and Reynolds. Sir Joshua Reynolds was the outstanding portrait painter of the eighteenth century. As President of the Royal Academy, he delivered annual lectures on art. His ideas are thoroughly neoclassical. In many respects they parallel the ideas of his friend, the great Samuel Johnson. Blake, however, predictably, found them odious. In the edition of Reynolds' *Discourses* which he owned he scribbled marginal

notes that are valuable insofar as they help us to understand what the new generation, the Romantic generation, was rebelling against, and why.

5. The career of Robert Fergusson. Fergusson was an important predecessor of Burns. He deserves to be better known. Not every library is likely to have adequate materials for a study of his life but the industrious student can find a considerable bit about him by consulting books of Scottish poetry and by using such standard reference works as the *Dictionary of National Biography*. The worth of an individual student can, to some extent, be measured by his (or her) ability to relate Fergusson's work to that of Burns.

6. The decline of Scott's reputation as a poet. The decline began early and was recognized by Scott himself. A student electing this subject has an almost endless number of choices. If he has available a library rich in the nineteenth-century materials, he might well want to study the beginnings of the decline. If he has not, he might conceivably be interested in seeing what recent critics think of Scott's poetry. Or, in the absence of useful materials for an historical survey, he could accept the proposition that Scott's reputation as poet has declined and could speculate on what some of the reasons for this decline might be. The subject is a challenge to the student's inventiveness.

7. The Lake Region. There are any number of books that tell us about various parts of the world. We might like to make a tour of Wordsworth's "Lake Country," but if we cannot, through books we certainly can learn a great deal about the scenery that so impressively controlled his imagination.

8. Wordsworth on poetic diction. The problem of the relationship between the language of poetry and the language of everyday life is still with us. Does Wordsworth help us to understand the problem? How? See if an examination of Johnson's Preface to his Dictionary and his Preface to his edition of Shakespeare open up new avenues of thought.

9. The appeal of *Childe Harold's Pilgrimage*. There are any number of research papers here. Some will find the appeal in the

descriptions, some in the reflections, some in the topicality of the poem. The student should be warned that the subject is vast and should be rigorously delimited. Vague generalities are useless. A disciplined student can state a thesis and support it by a careful reading of his author.

10. Coleridge and Lamb. The investigation of literary friendships almost always turns up something of peculiar value for the investigator. The materials for this particular subject are usually available. One needs, for example, a copy of Lamb's *Essays* in which one finds his account of life at Christ's Hospital when he and Coleridge were schoolmates.

11. Shelley. Without discussing the possibilities of these proposed subjects, one can suggest a number of research themes related to Shelley. For example: Shelley's Education; Shelley and Godwin; Shelley's Optimism; Shelley's Friends; *Adonais* and the Poet as Myth-Maker.

12. Keats. Any number of subjects seem worthy of the student's attention. The following list is obviously arbitrary: Keats and his family; The Reception of *Endymion*; The Purpose of *Endymion*; The Medieval Trappings of *The Eve of St. Agnes*; Unity of Theme in the "Great Odes"; *Endymion* and "Hyperion": A Study in Contrasts.

BIBLIOGRAPHY AND GUIDE
TO FURTHER RESEARCH

Abrams, M. H., ed., *English Romantic Poets,* 1960. Collection of major essays on Romantics.

————, *The Mirror and the Lamp: Romantic Theory and Critical Tradition,* 1954. Reflecting recent tendencies in literary criticism, this is a brilliant, perceptive, and challenging book. The reader will find his awareness of the importance of the Romantic movement heightened.

Allen, Beverly S., *Tides in English Taste: 1619–1800,* 2 vols., 1937. This work is not directly related to English Romantic poetry but it brilliantly shows how changes in tastes and fashions reflect themselves in various ways, in gardening, in architecture, in other arts.

Babbitt, Irving, *On Being Creative,* 1932; *Rousseau and Romanticism,* 1919, 1955. Anti-Romantic point of view.

Bald, R. C., ed., *Literary Friendships in the Age of Wordsworth: An Anthology,* 1932. An interesting collection of remarks made to or about one another by important authors of the period.

Bate, Walter J., *From Classic to Romantic,* 1946. The author of this book is a recognized specialist in the history of the changes in ideas and attitudes that brought about the rise of Romantic theory and practice.

Bateson, F. W., *English Poetry, A Critical Introduction,* 1950.

Beers, Henry A., *A History of English Romanticism in the Eighteenth Century,* 1899; *A History of English Romanti-*

cism in the Nineteenth Century, 1901. These volumes, as one might expect, have an old-fashioned quality. They are, however, entertaining and the beginning student of Romanticism will find them profitable.

Bernbaum, Ernest, *Guide Through the Romantic Movement,* 1930, rev. ed., 1949. A standard reference work. Almost indispensable to the serious student of English Romanticism.

Bodkin, Maud, *Archetypal Patterns in English Poetry,* 1934, 1951. Jungian analyses.

Bowra, C. M., *The Romantic Imagination,* 1950.

Bradley, A. C., *Oxford Lectures on Poetry,* 1909, 1955.

Brooks, Cleanth, *The Well-Wrought Urn,* 1947. Brooks has become one of the most influential of recent critics. This work has essays on Gray, Wordsworth, and Keats.

Eliot, T. S., *The Use of Poetry and Criticism,* 1933. An influential work; attacks Shelley.

Elwin, Malcolm, *The First Romantics,* 1947. A dependable and lively account of the first generation of English Romantic poets.

Empson, William, *The Structure of Complex Words,* 1947, 1951.

Fairchild, H. N., *The Romantic Quest,* 1931. Fairchild's religious convictions make him an unsympathetic student of Romanticism.

Grierson, H. J. C., and Smith, J. C., *A Critical History of English Poetry,* 1944, 1956.

Hough, G. G., *The Romantic Poets,* 1964.

James, D. G., *The Romantic Comedy,* 1948, 1963.

Knight, G. W., *The Starlit Dome: Studies in the Poetry of Vision,* 1941. Knight is a thoughtful and original critic. This book enlarges our understanding of Romantic poetry.

Leavis, F. R., *Revaluation: Tradition and Development in English Poetry,* 1936.

Lovejoy, A. O., *Essays in the History of Ideas,* 1948. In one of the essays Lovejoy shows that there are several kinds of Romanticism.

More, Paul Elmer, *The Drift of Romanticism: Shelburne Essays,* 1913.

Phelps, William L., *The Beginnings of the English Romantic Movement,* 1893. Old but still stimulating and valuable. Phelps is at his best in communicating his own appreciation of poetry.

Quinlan, M. J., *Victorian Prelude: A History of English Manners, 1700–1830,* 1941. An eminently useful background book.

Thorpe, C. DeW., *et al.,* eds., *The English Romantic Poets,* 1957. Important essay collection.

SPECIAL STUDIES

BLAKE

Adams, Hazard, *William Blake: A Reading of His Shorter Poems,* 1963.

Blackstone, Bernard, *English Blake,* 1949. A useful attempt to make readers see that Blake was a man of his time.

Bronowski, J., *A Man without a Mask,* 1944. Blake's poetry in relation to his time.

Damon, S. Foster, *William Blake: His Philosophy and Symbols,* 1924, 1947. A challenging introduction to Blake's more obscure ideas.

Erdman, David V., *Blake: Prophet Against Empire,* 1954. A fresh and stimulating study of the political situation and its reflection in Blake's poems.

Frye, Northrop, *Fearful Symmetry,* 1947. Major study, especially of symbols.

Gardner, Charles, *Vision and Vesture,* 1916. Early appreciation; not too enlightening.

Gleckner, Robert F., *The Piper and the Bard,* 1959. Readings of major value.

Grant, J. E., ed., *Discussions of William Blake,* 1962. A collection of important essays on Blake by major critics.

Hagstrum, Jean H., *William Blake, Poet and Painter,* 1964. A study of Blake's composite art.

Harper, George McL., *The Neoplatonism of William Blake,* 1961. Interpretation of symbols in neoplatonic terms.

Keynes, Geoffrey, ed., *The Complete Writings of William Blake,* 1925, 1927, 1939, 1957. The best edition.

Plowman, Max, *Introduction to the Study of Blake,* 1927. A good beginning.

Todd, Ruthven, ed., *Life of William Blake,* Alexander Gilchrist, 1942. New edition of an important early life.

Wilson, Mona, *The Life of William Blake,* 1927, 1932, 1948. The standard biography.

BURNS

Carswell, Catherine, *The Life of Robert Burns,* 1930. This popular biography is an excellent book for the student beginning his study of Burns.

Crawford, Thomas, *Burns: A Study of the Poems and Songs,* 1960.

Daiches, David, *Robert Burns,* 1950. Especially valuable because it reflects the critical temper of our time and because Daiches gives good critical analyses of several of Burns's poems.

Ferguson, De Lancey, *Letters,* 2 vols., 1931. Best edition.

————, *Pride and Passion,* 1939, 1964. A biographical study designed not merely to record the facts of the poet's life but to enlarge our understanding of the facts.

Fitzhugh, R. T., *Robert Burns: His Associates and Contemporaries,* 1943. An objective biography.

Neilson, W. A., *Robert Burns: How to Know Him,* 1917. Still one of the best introductions to Burns.

Rae, E. S., *Poet's Pilgrimage: A Study of the Life and Times of Robert Burns,* 1960. Biography.

Ross, J. D., *Henley and Burns, or, The Critic Censured,* 1901. Biographical criticism.

Shairp, Principal, *Robert Burns,* n.d. Useful biography.

Snyder, F. B., *The Life of Robert Burns,* 1932. The best modern biography.

Thornton, R. D., *James Currie, the Entire Stranger, and Robert Burns,* 1963. On an early biographer of Burns.

WILLIAM WORDSWORTH

Abercrombie, Lascelles, *The Art of Wordsworth,* 1952. Abercrombie brings a poet's sensitivity to this analysis of Wordsworth's work.

Bateson, F. W., *Wordsworth—A Reinterpretation,* 1954, 1956. Appreciative.

Batho, E. C., *The Later Wordsworth,* 1933, 1963. Defends later works.

Beach, J. W., *The Concept of Nature in Nineteenth-Century English Poetry,* 1936. This has become a standard work on the subject. Chapters II–VI are especially valuable for the student of Wordsworth.

Conran, Anthony E. M., *PMLA,* LXXV (March 1960), pp. 66–74. Good article entitled "Resolution and Independence."

De Selincourt, Ernest, ed., *The Prelude,* 1926. Excellent introduction.

Garrod, H. W., *Wordsworth: Lectures and Essays,* 1923, 1954.

Griggs, E. L., ed., *Wordsworth Centenary Study,* 1951. Collection of important essays.

Havens, R. D., *The Mind of a Poet: A Study of Wordsworth's Thought with Particular Reference to* The Prelude, 1941. A very careful and sympathetic study.

Herford, C. H., *Wordsworth,* 1930. A scholarly and reliable biography and critical introduction.

Logan, J. V., *Wordsworthian Criticism,* 1947. This provides the student with a good, detailed critical bibliography of Wordsworthian studies.

Lyon, J. S., *The Excursion: A Study,* 1950. Favorable view; analysis.

Peek, Katherine M., *Wordsworth in England: Studies in the History of His Fame,* 1943. Scholarly.

Raleigh, Walter, *Wordsworth,* 1903. Appreciative criticism.

Smith, J. C., *A Study of Wordsworth,* 1944. Probably now the best general introduction to be offered the beginning student.

Stallknecht, N. P., *Strange Seas of Thought,* 1945, 1962. Studies of Wordsworth and Coleridge.

SIR WALTER SCOTT

Buchan, John, *Sir Walter Scott,* 1932. A good modern biography especially useful to the student because it contains critical estimates of both the poetry and prose.

Gwynn, Stephen, *Sir Walter Scott,* 1930. Another good biography. Brief.

Kroeber, Karl, *Romantic Narrative Art,* 1960. Includes analysis of Scott's craft.

Lockhart, J. G., *Life of Sir Walter Scott.* This is the famous biography by Scott's son-in-law. It originally appeared in 1837 but there have been many subsequent editions. A useful one-volume edition was prepared by Andrew Lang for the Everyman series in 1906. For corrections of Lockhart see H. J. C. Grierson's *Sir Walter Scott,* 1938.

Saintsbury, G. E. B., *Sir Walter Scott,* 1897. One of the most influential critics of his generation, Saintsbury brings his characteristic enthusiasm to his scrutiny of Scott's career and literary importance.

Shairp, J. C., *Aspects of English Poetry,* 1881. This book has an interesting essay on "The Homeric Spirit in Walter Scott."

SAMUEL TAYLOR COLERIDGE

Armour, R. W., and Howe, R. F., *Coleridge the Talker: A Series of Contemporary Descriptions and Comments,* 1940. Coleridge's impact on his contemporaries was through his talk even more than through his writings. This is an extremely important contribution to our understanding of Coleridge's ideas.

Beer, J. B., *Coleridge the Visionary,* 1959. Interpretation of symbols.

Brett, R. L., *Reason and Imagination,* 1960. Chapter on "The Rime of the Ancient Mariner."

Chambers, E. K., *S. T. Coleridge,* 1938. Scholarly and sensible, this is an excellent introduction to the poet.

Clayborough, Arthur, *The Grotesque in English Literature,* 1965. Chapter on Coleridge; Jungian analysis.

Hanson, Laurence, *The Life of S. T. Coleridge: The Early Years,* 1938. Hanson goes into much greater detail than Chambers but covers only the years up to 1800.

House, Humphrey, *Coleridge,* 1953. Excellent criticism of the major poems is included in this survey of Coleridge's career.

Lowes, J. L., *The Road to Xanadu,* 1927, enlarged in 1930. One of the most famous examples of literary detective work. Lowes has managed to show how Coleridge's wide and varied reading came together in a startling way in his imagination.

Muirhead, J. H., *Coleridge as Philosopher,* 1930. A critical study of his relation to new trends in philosophy.

Richards, I. A., *Coleridge on Imagination,* 1934. This is a very important study of one of the most important subjects touched upon by Coleridge.

Schneider, Elisabeth, *Coleridge, Opium, and Kubla Khan,* 1953. The title describes the subject of the book.

Schulz, M. F., *The Poetic Voices of Coleridge,* 1963. New approach; new insights.

Tate, Allen, *Reason in Madness,* 1941. Whereas most students of Coleridge consider him one of the greatest of English literary critics, Tate offers a dissenting opinion in one of the essays in this stimulating book.

Warren, Robert Penn, *Selected Essays,* 1948. Contains symbolist interpretation of "The Rime of the Ancient Mariner."

LORD BYRON

Boyd, Elizabeth F., *Byron's Don Juan,* 1945. A very valuable critical appraisal of Byron's masterpiece.

Chew, Samuel C., *Byron in England, His Fame and Afterfame,* 1924. Chew has given us a careful and scholarly account of the reputation of Byron.

Knight, G. W., *Lord Byron: Christian Virtues,* 1953. An attempt by an important modern critic to see Byron's achievement in a fresh light, to see what valuable insights have been partially concealed by Byron's various poses.

Marchand, Leslie A., *Byron,* 3 vols., 1957. Best modern biography.

Marshall, W. H., *The Structure of Byron's Major Works,* 1962.

Mayne, Ethel C., *Byron,* 2 vols., 1912, revised in 1924. This remains the best single biography for the beginning student to consult.

Quennell, Peter, *Byron: The Years of Fame,* 1935; *Byron in Italy,* 1941. Quennell is a prolific English biographer who writes in an exceptionally graceful and lucid style. These two volumes can be highly recommended.

Rutherford, Andrew, *Byron: A Critical Study,* 1962.

Steffan, T. G., and Pratt, W. W., *Byron's Don Juan, A Variorum Edition,* 4 vols., 1957.

West, Paul, *Byron and the Spoiler's Art,* 1960. Examines the nature of his satire.

PERCY BYSSHE SHELLEY

Baker, Carlos, *Shelley's Major Poetry: The Fabric of a Vision,* 1948. One of the best studies of Shelley's art.

Barnard, Ellsworth, *Shelley's Religion,* 1936. Shelley, a neo-platonist and Christian.

Brailsford, H. N., *Shelley, Godwin, and Their Circle,* 1913. Still valuable for the light it throws on the development of some of Shelley's most important ideas and for its picture of early nineteenth-century radicalism.

Cameron, Kenneth N., *The Young Shelley: Genesis of a Radical,* 1950. Another later and more comprehensive study of Shelley's radical ideas. Carefully documented.

Campbell, O. W., *Shelley and the Unromantics,* 1924. Sides with Shelley.

Clark, D. L., *Shelley's Prose: The Trumpet of Prophecy,* 1954. On his prose and politics.

Clutton-Brock, Arthur, *Shelley The Man and the Poet,* 1910, 1923. Early appreciation.

Elton, Oliver, *The English Muse,* 1933.

Fogle, R. H., *The Imagery of Keats and Shelley: A Comparative Study,* 1962. An analysis.

Grabo, C. H., *A Newton among Poets,* 1930. One of Grabo's early important studies of Shelley's poetry. This book emphasizes the importance of new scientific theories and discoveries in the shaping of Shelley's imagination. Later significant books by Grabo are: *Prometheus Unbound: An*

Interpretation, 1935; *The Magic Plant: The Growth of Shelley's Mind,* 1936, a study of the influence of Plato on Shelley; and *Shelley's Eccentricities,* 1950.

Hughes, A. M. D., *The Nascent Mind of Shelley,* 1947. A depreciation.

Ingpen, Roger, *Shelley in England,* 1917. A remarkably detailed study of his life up to his departure for the Continent in 1917.

King-Hele, Desmond, *Shelley: The Man and the Poet,* 1960.

Lewis, C. S., *Rehabilitations,* 1939. Pro-Shelley.

Notopoulos, J. A., *The Platonism of Shelley,* 1949. This study obviously invites comparison with Grabo's book on the same general subject.

Pottle, F. A., "The Case of Shelley," *PMLA,* LXVII (1952), pp. 589–608. Defense of Shelley.

Powell, A. E., *The Romantic Theory of Poetry,* 1962. Respectful.

Read, Herbert, *In Defence of Shelley,* 1935. Defensive.

Solve, M. T., *Shelley: His Theory of Poetry,* 1927. Upholds Shelley's mind and morality.

Stovall, Floyd, *Desire and Restraint in Shelley,* 1931. On Shelley's mental development.

White, N. I., *The Unextinguished Hearth: Shelley and His Contemporary Critics,* 1938. This was a kind of preparation for White's two-volume life of Shelley which has become the standard modern biography. It was published in 1940. A condensed version appeared in 1945 with the title *Portrait of Shelley.*

Woodman, R. G., *The Apocalyptic Vision in the Poetry of Shelley,* 1964. An appreciation.

Yeats, W. B., "The Philosophy of Shelley's Poetry, in *Ideas of Good and Evil,* 1903; *Essays and Introductions,* 1961. Admiring.

JOHN KEATS

Bate, W. J., *Negative Capability: The Intuitive Approach to Keats,* 1939. An interesting attempt to devise a critical strategy for the better understanding of Keats's achievement. In 1945 Bate published a second valuable book on Keats, *The Stylistic Development of Keats.* This is a most important study of a poet's rapid and exciting mastery of his craft.

Bradley, A. C., *A Miscellany,* 1929. Section on Keats.

Brooks, Cleanth, *The Well-Wrought Urn,* 1947. Chapter on "Ode on a Grecian Urn."

Caldwell, J. R., *John Keats' Fancy: The Effect on Keats of the Psychology of His Day,* 1945. The author has made a scholarly investigation of Keats's awareness of the intellectual currents eddying around him.

Colvin, Sidney, *John Keats, His Life and Poetry,* 1917, revised in 1925. The standard biography, though later biographies should be consulted.

De Selincourt, Ernest, ed., *The Poems,* 1905, 1954. Good introduction.

Fausset, H. I'A., *Keats: A Study in Development,* 1922. Old, not as good as Bate's study, but still worth consulting.

Finney, C. L., *The Evolution of Keats' Poetry,* 2 vols., 1936. An invaluable collection of source materials.

Ford, G. H., *Keats and the Victorians: A Study of His Influence and Rise to Fame, 1821–1895,* 1944. Of major importance to those interested in the place of Keats in the history of English poetry.

Forman, H. B., ed., *The Letters,* 1952.

Garrod, H. W., *Keats,* 1926, 1950.

Gittings, Robert, *John Keats: The Living Year,* 1954. The "Living Year" was that astonishing year of creativity that extended from September 1818 to September 1819.

Lowell, Amy, *John Keats,* 2 vols., 1925. Chiefly interesting because Amy Lowell was an American poet of some distinction.

MacGillivray, J. R., *Keats: A Bibliography and Reference Guide,* 1949. Useful.

Muir, Kenneth, *John Keats,* 1959.

Murry, J. M., *Keats and Shakespeare,* 1925, 1951. An enthusiastic appraisal of Keats's remarkable gifts.

Peace, Catherine, *John Keats,* 1960.

Ridley, M. R., *Keats' Craftsmanship: A Study in Poetic Development,* 1933.

Tate, Allen, *On the Limits of Poetry,* 1948.

Wasserman, E. R., *The Finer Tone: Keats' Major Poems,* 1953. Another examination of the great poems by a seasoned American scholar and critic. Highly recommended.

PRE-ROMANTICS AND THE MINOR ROMANTICS: There are any number of good histories of English literature which supply further information about the less outstanding figures discussed in this book. *A Literary History of England,* ed. A. C. Baugh and others, 1948, although not quite up-to-date, has good bibliographies. Russell Noyes in 1956 published a generous collection of specimens of *English Romantic Poetry and Prose.* This is an admirable volume of its kind.

INDEX

"Abou Ben Adhem," 204

Abrams, M. H., 103, 139, 169

Adams, Hazard, 18

"Address to the Deil," 49, 51, 53-54

Adonais, 160, 173-75, 179, 183, 194, 223

"Ae Fond Kiss," 51

Aeschylus, 162

"The Affliction of Margaret," 75

Aids to Reflection, 119

Aiken, Robert, 57

Alastor, 160-61, 178, 180

The Album, 176

"Allan-a-Maut," 49

America, 18, 37

Anne of Geierstein, 107

The Antiquary, 107

"The Argument," 39-43

Armour, Jean, 48, 65

Arnold, Matthew, 102, 176, 195

Astarte, 153

Auguries of Innocence, 19

"Auld Lang Syne," 51, 62

Aurora Leigh, 195

Aylmer, Rose, 201

Babbitt, Irving, 135-36, 137, 138, 177-78, 179

Bacon, Francis, 14

Baker, Carlos, 103, 177

Bald, M. A., 180

"Ballad of Kynd Kittock," 49

Barnard, Ellsworth, 180

Basire, James, 15

Bate, Walter J., 196

Bateson, F. W., 104, 168, 178

Batho, Edith C., 103

"The Battle of Blenheim," 200

Baugh, A. C., 114

Beddoes, Thomas Lovell, **206-7**

Beer, J. B., 139, 140

"La Belle Dame Sans Merci," 183

Beppo, 143, 147

Bernbaum, Ernest, 114, 155, 177, 196

Biographia Literaria, 118, 119, 120-21, 134-35, 137

Bion, 174

Blackwood's, 151, 152, 175, 194

Blair, Robert, 16

Blake, Robert, 16

Blake, William, 12, **13-46,** 47, 106, 209, 213, 219, 221-22

Bloom, H., 39

Bodkin, Maud, 128, 132, 136, 139-40

The Book of Los, 18

The Book of Thel, 18, 22-24, 30

Bottrall, Ronald, 155

Boucher, Christine, 16

Bowra, C. M., 100, 181, 192, 193

Bradley, A. C., 102-3, 181, 192

Brawne, Fanny, 186, 197

Brett, R. L., 138

The Bridal of Triermain, 107, 113, 215

The Bride of Abydos, 146

The Bride of Lammermoor, 107

Bridges, Robert, 195

Bronowski, J., 18, 22, 24

Brooks, Cleanth, 192, 198

Brougham, Henry, 150

Browning, Elizabeth Barrett, 195

Browning, Robert, 51, 69, 102, 176, 194

Buchan, John, 68

Burke, Edmund, 199

Burns, Robert, 12, **47-69,** 95, 106, 173, 204, 210-11, 222

"Burns Stanza," 52

Bush, Douglas, 104, 192, 193

Byron, Augusta, 141, 152, 153
Byron, Augusta Ada, 143
Byron, Lord (George Noel
    Gordon), 12, 47, 102, 110,
    113, **141-56,** 157, 158, 159,
    194, 200, 203, 214, 217-18
Byron, "Mad Jack," 141
Byronic hero, 145, 146, 151-52,
    215

Calvert, Raisley, 92
Cameron, Kenneth, 181
Campbell, Mary ("Highland
    Mary"), 63, 67
Campbell, O. W., 178, 179
Campbell, Thomas, 151
Cariyle, Thomas, 67
Carswell, Catherine, 68
Castle of Otranto, 110
The Cenci, 160, 176
Chambers, Robert, 66
Chapman, George, 184
Chatterton, Thomas, 94, 95, 221
Chaucer, Geoffrey, 49, 94
Chew, Samuel, 114
Childe Harold's Pilgrimage, 142,
    144, 147, 149, 150, 151,
    222-23
"The Chimney Sweeper," 28
"Christabel," 115, 117, 118,
    121-27, 138
Ciardi, John, 31
Clairmont, Claire, 143, 159, 160
Clare, John, 205
Clark, David Lee, 180-81
Clarke, Charles Cowden, 182,
    184
Clarke, G. H., 136
Clayborough, Arthur, 131, 132
"The Clod and the Pebble," 30
"The Cloud," 160, 169-71
Clutton-Brock, Arthur, 177,
    178-79, 181
Coleridge, Hartley, 100
Coleridge, Samuel Taylor, 12, 70,
    71, 75, 78, 89, 96, 102,
    115-40, 144, 146, 148, 150,
    159, 178, 200, 209, 211-
    13, 215-18, 223
Collected Works (Wordsworth),
    74
*Collection of Original Scottish
    Airs,* 51

Collins, William, 19
Colvin, Sidney, 195, 196-97
"Commonplace Book," 48
"Composed upon an Evening of
    Extraordinary Splendour,"
    75
Conran, Anthony E. M., 96
"Conversation Poems," 117, 118
The Corsair, 146
"The Cotter's Saturday Night,"
    51, 57-59
Cowley, Abraham, 98; Cowleyan
    ode, 98
Cowper, William, 66
Crabbe, George, 151, **199,** 201
Crawford, Thomas, 69
Creed, Harold, 138
Croce, Benedetto, 177, 179
Croker, John Wilson, 194
Cromek, R. H., 66
The Cuckoo and the Nightingale,
    94
Cunningham, Allan, 66
Currie, Dr. James, 66, 67

Daiches, David, 69
Damon, S. Foster, 45
Dante Alighieri, 165
Darbishire, Helen, 89
"Dear Brook, Farewell," 74
"The Death and Dying Words of
    Poor Maillie," 49, 51
Death's Jest-Book, 206
"A Defence of Poetry," 179, 180
"Dejection: an Ode," 118,
    132-34
Descartes, René, 31
A Descriptive Catalogue, 19
De Selincourt, Ernest, 93, 103,
    195, 196, 197
*Dictionary of National
    Biography,* 222
Discourses, 221
Divine Comedy, 165
"The Divine Image," 27
Don Juan, 143, 147-50, 152, 154,
    155, 156, 194
Douglas, Gavin, 49
"Dream-Pedlary," 206-7
Dryden, John, 11, 107, 144, 146
The Dublin Magazine, 175
Dunbar, William, 49, 53
"Duncan Gray," 41, 51

Dunlop, Mrs., 66
"The Dying Child," 205

"Earth's Answer," 30
"The Ecchoing Green," 26
Ecclesiastical Sonnets, 72
Edgcumbe, Richard, 153
The Edinburgh Magazine, 66
Edinburgh Review, 67, 102, 142, 144, 150-51, 194
"Elegaic Stanzas," 75
Eleusinian and Bacchic Mysteries, 23
Eliot, T. S., 154, 178, 193, 196, 197
Elton, Oliver, 114, 169
Empson, William, 198
Endymion, 174, 183, 184-86, 194, 196, 223
English Bards and Scotch Reviewers, 142, 143-44, 151, 217-18
Epipsychidion 160
Erdman, David V., 18, 34, 35, 37, 40, 46
An Essay on Man, 10
Essays (Lamb), 223
Europe, 18, 37-38
An Evening Walk, 74
The Everlasting Gospel, 19, 25, 44
The Eve of St. Agnes, 8, 10, 182, 183, 184, 186-87, 194, 197, 223
The Examiner, 152, 184, 204
The Excursion, 74, 89, 102, 103
"Expostulation and Reply," 74, 86, 87

The Faerie Queene, 145, 182
"Fair Elenor," 21
The Fair Maid of Perth, 107
Fairchild, Hoxie, 29, 97, 193
Faraday, Michael, 170
"Fears in Solitude," 117
Ferguson, De Lancey, 68, 69
Fergusson, Robert, 49-50, 222
The First Book of Urizen, 18
Fitzhugh, Robert T., 68
"The Fly," 30-31
Fogle, R. H., 169, 198
"For A' That, An' A' That," 48, 62, 65

Ford, G. H., 195
Ford, N. F., 196
Forman, H. B., 194
The Fortunes of Nigel, 107
Fox, Sir John Charles, 153
"Fragment of Ode to Prince Charles Edward," 65
"France: an Ode," 117, 118
Frankenstein, 170
The French Revolution, 18, 34-36
Frere, John H., 147
Fricker, Sarah, 116, 118, 132
The Friend, 118-19
"Frost at Midnight," 117
Frye, Northrop, 46
Fugitive Pieces, 142
Fuseli, Henry, 16

Galt, John, 153
"The Garden of Love," 26-27
Gardner, Charles, 45
Garrod, H. W., 93, 192, 193, 197
Gentleman's Magazine, 175
The Ghost of Abel, 19
Gilchrist, Alexander, 16, 45
Gilman, Dr., 126
Gleckner, Robert F., 23, 25
Godwin, Mary (Mary Shelley), 143, 158, 159, 160, 169, 170, 175, 176
Godwin, William, 143, 157-58, 159
Goethe, Johann, 146, 152
The Golden Treasury, 195
"Goody Blake and Harry Gill," 74, 80, 81
Gordon, Catherine, 141
Gose, E. B., Jr., 137-38
Grabo, Carl H., 180, 181
Grant, J. E., 37, 39
The Grave, 16-17
Gray, Thomas, 57-58, 221
"Green Grow the Rashes, O," 48, 51, 62, 63
Grierson, H. J. C., 154, 176, 178
Griggs, E. L., 104
Grove, Harriet, 158
Guiccioli, Teresa, 143, 153

Hagstrum, Jean H., 18
Hamilton, Gavin, 48

Harding, D. W., 136-37
Harold the Dauntless, 107, 113
Harper, George McL., 23
Havens, R. D., 90, 93
Hayley, William, 16
Hazlitt, William, 86, 102, 152, 175-76, 194
Hebrew Melodies, 143
Hellas, 160
The Hellenics, 202
Henderson, T. F., 67
Henley, W. E., 67-68, 69
Henryson, Robert, 49
"Her Eyes Are Wild," 74
Herford, C. H., 178-79, 198
Heron, Robert, 65-66
Hewlett, Dorothy, 196
Hicks, A. C., 180
"Highland Mary," 51, 63-64
Hitchener, Elizabeth, 158
Hobhouse, J. C., 142, 143
Hogg, Thomas, 158
"The Holy Fair," 48, 50, 51, 55-56
"Holy Thursday," 28-29
"Holy Willie's Prayer," 48, 51-52
Hood, Thomas, 194, **205-6**
Hough, G. G., 197
Houghton, Lord (Monckton Milnes), 195
Hours of Idleness, 142, 144, 150-51
House, Humphrey, 132, 137, 140
"How Sweet I Roamed," 19-20, 30
Hughes, A. M. D., 178
"The Human Abstract," 27
Hunt, John, 152, 204
Hunt, Leigh, 152, 153, 176, 182-83, 184, 193, 194, **204-5**
Hutchinson, Mary, 71, 87, 117, 132
Hutchinson, Sarah, 117, 118, 132, 133
"Hyperion," 183, 223

"The Idiot Boy," 104, 217-18
The Iliad, 114
Imaginary Conversations, 152
"Infant Joy," 28
"Infant Sorrow," 28
Inquiry Concerning Political Justice, 157
"Iphigeneia," 202
Irregular (Cowleyan) ode, 98
Isabella, 184, 194, 196-97
The Island, 143
An Island in the Moon, 18
"I Stood Tiptoe," 184
"It Is a Beauteous Evening," 75
"It Was A' for Our Rightfu' King," 65
Ivanhoe, 8, 107
"I Wandered Lonely as a Cloud," 75

James, D. G., 178, 198
Jeffrey, Francis, 66-67, 102, 151, 194, 195
Jennings, John, 182
"Jenny Kissed Me," 204-5
Jerusalem, 19, 44
"The Jolly Beggars," 48, 51, 67
The Jolly Beggars: A Cantata, 69
"John Anderson My Jo," 48, 51, 63
"John Barleycorn," 49, 51
Johnson, James, 50
Johnson, Joseph, 16, 18, 34
Johnson, Samuel, 11, 206, 221
Jones, F. L., 180
Jones, Robert, 91

Kant, Immanuel, 97
Keats, Frances, 182, 183
Keats, George, 182, 183
Keats, John, 12, 47, 160, 173-74, 178, **182-98,** 204, 205, 207, 209-10, 213, 219-20, 223
Keats, Thomas, 182, 183, 188
Kenilworth, 107
Keynes, Geoffrey, 18, 34, 37
Kilmarnock poems, 51, 65, 66, 69
King, Edward, 173
"King Edward the Third," 22
King-Hele, Desmond, 169
King Lear, 20
Kipling, Rudyard, 130
Kiralis, Karl, 46
Kroeber, Karl, 113
"Kubla Khan; or, A Vision in a Dream," 115, 117, 127-32, 138-40

The Lady of the Lake, 107, 111-13, 114, 215
"The Lamb," 26, 31
Lamb, Charles, 44-45, 115-16, 118, 194, 202, 223
Lamia, Isabella, The Eve of St. Agnes and Other Poems, 184, 194, 197
Landor, Walter Savage, 152, **201-3,** 207
Lara, 146
The Lay of the Last Minstrel, 107, 108-9, 111, 114, 214
Leavis, F. R., 103, 168, 169, 178, 181, 197
Letters on Demonology and Witchcraft, 107
Lewis, C. S., 179
Lewis, Wilmarth S., 221
"Lichtounis Dreme," 49
Life of Napoleon, 107
"Lines," 74
"Lines Written in Early Spring," 74, 81
The Literary Gazette, 175
"The Little Black Boy," 29
"A Little Girl Lost," 25-26
"The Little Girl Lost" and "The Little Girl Found," 25
Lives of the Novelists, 107
Locke, John, 14
Lockhart, John, 66, 67
The Londale Magazine or Provincial Repository, 175
"London, 1802," 75
The London Morning Post, 132
The Lord of the Isles, 107, 113, 215
Lounger, 66
"Love," 118
Lovelace, Ralph, Earl of, 153
Lovell, E. J., 154, 155, 156
Lowell, Amy, 196
Lowes, J. L., 119, 128, 136, 137, 139, 140
Lucas, E. V., 45
"Lucy Gray," 75
The "Lucy Poems," 74, 87-89
"Lycidas," 173
Lyon, J. S., 103
Lyrical Ballads, with a Few Other Poems, 7, 70, 71, 74, 75-76, 81, 85, 86, 87, 89,

102, 104, 117, 120-21, 211-13, 217-18

MacKenzie, Henry, 66
MacKenzie, M. L., 68
Macpherson, James, 221
Major, John, 49
Manfred, 143, 146-47
Marchand, Leslie A., 154
Marlowe, Christopher, 146
Marmion, 107, 110-11, 114, 214-15
The Marriage of Heaven and Hell, 18, 38-44
Marshall, W. H., 155-56
Marx, Karl, 176
"Mary Morison," 51, 63
Mason, William, 221
"Matthew," 74-75
Matthew, Rev. Henry, 16
Mazeppa, 143
Medwin, Thomas, 153
"A Memorable Fancy," 39, 40, 41-43
The Mental Traveller, 19
"Michael," 75
Milbanke, Anne Isabella, 142-43, 149, 152, 153
Milnes, Monckton (Lord Houghton), 195
Milton, 19, 44
Milton, John, 40, 53, 78, 90, 173
Minstrelsy of the Scottish Border, 7, 107
The Monthly Review, 176
Moore, Thomas, 153, **203-4**
More, Paul Elmer, 45, 102, 154, 177, 178, 179
Morning Chronicle, 194
Morris, William, 195
Morton, Richard, 68
Moschus, 174
Möser, George Michael, 15
Muir, Kenneth, 192
Murray, John, 152, 153, 155
Murry, John Middleton, 197
"My Heart Leaps Up," 74, 75, 94, 101
"My Heart's in the Highlands," 48
"My Silks and Fine Array," 20

The Necessity of Atheism, 158

Newton, Isaac, 14
"The Nightingale," 117
Nightmare Abbey, 177
Night Thoughts on Life, Death and Immortality, 16
"Nuns Fret Not," 75
Nurmi, Martin K., 39
"Nutting," 74

"Ode to Duty," 75, 97
"Ode on a Grecian Urn," 191-93, 197-98, 220
"Ode: Intimations of Immortality from Recollections of Early Childhood," 75, 98-102
"Ode to Melancholy," 190
"Ode to a Nightingale," 188-90, 197, 219-20
"Ode to Psyche," 187, 190, 197, 219
"Ode to the West Wind," 160, 164-68, 171, 178
Old Mortality, 107
"On First Looking Into Chapman's Homer," 184
"On Shakespeare and Milton," 129
Ossianic poems, 221
Owen, Robert, 176
"O, Wert Thou in the Cauld Blast," 51, 62

Paine, Tom, 16, 34
Palgrave, Francis Turner, 195
"Pantisocracy," 116, 200
Paradise Lost, 40, 53
Paton, Elizabeth, 48
Paul, Hamilton, 67
"Pauline," 176
Peace, Catherine, 197
Peacock, Thomas Love, 177
Percy, Thomas, 105, 209
Peterkin, Alexander, 67
"Piping Down the Valleys Wild," 24-25, 30
The Pirate, 107
Plato, Platonism, 99, 161, 179, 196
"The Plea of the Midsummer Fairies," 194
Plowman, Max, 17, 39, 46
Poems (Keats), 183, 184
Poems, 1807 (Wordsworth), 74, 94-102
Poems, Chiefly in the Scottish Dialect, 48, 50, 52-59, 65-66
Poems in Two Volumes (Wordsworth), 71, 101
Poems on Various Occasions, 142
"A Poet!—He Hath Put His Heart to School," 75
Poetical Sketches, 7, 18, 19-22
Pope, Alexander, 11, 143, 146, 155
Pot of Basil, 194
Pottle, F. A., 181
Powell, A. E., 179-80
Praz, Mario, 152-53
The Prelude, or, Growth of a Poet's Mind, 74, 86, 89-93, 98, 103
Proclamation against Divers Wicked and Seditious Writings, 34
Prometheus Bound, 162, 164
Prometheus Unbound, 160, 161-64, 175-76, 177, 178, 179, 181, 218-19
Prophetic Books, 16, 36-37, 44
"Proverbs of Hell," 39, 41
Punch, 206
Purchas His Pilgrimage, 128

Quarterly Review, 67, 151, 175, 194
Queen Mab, 159, 178
Quentin Durward, 107

Rae, E. S., 69
Raleigh, Walter, 102
Ramsay, Allan, 49, 53
Ransom, John Crowe, 104, 178
"The Rantin' Dog, the Daddie o't," 51
Read, Herbert, 178-79
The Recluse, a fragment, 74, 89
Redgauntlet, 107
"A Red, Red Rose," 48, 62-63
Reliques of Ancient English Poetry, 105
Reliques of Robert Burns, 66
"Resolution and Independence," 75, 94-97, 132
"The Reverie of Poor Susan," 74

The Revolt of Islam, 160, 161
Reynolds, Sir Joshua, 102, 193, 221-22
Rhyme Royal, 94
Richards, I. A., 198
Ridley, M. R., 196, 197
The Rights of Man, 34
The Rights of Women, 37
"The Rime of the Ancient Mariner," 75, 115, 117, 118, 119-21, 135-36, 137, 138, 209, 211, 215-17
The River Duddon, 74
The Road to Xanadu, 119, 128, 136, 137, 139, 140
Rob Roy, 107
Rokeby, 107, 113, 215
Romeo and Juliet, 187
Ross, J. D., 68
Rossetti, Dante Gabriel, 45
Rossetti, William M., 45, 177
Rousseau, Jean Jacques, 73, 90-91
Royal Academy, 15, 221
Rutherford, Andrew, 156

Saintsbury, George E. B., 113-14
Santayana, George, 177, 179
Satires and Moral Essays, 155
Schneider, Elisabeth, 139
Schulz, M. F., 133, 138, 140
"Scotch Drink," 51, 52-53
Scots Musical Museum, 50
"Scots Wha Hae," 48, 51, 65
Scott, Sir Walter, 12, 67, 69, **105-14,** 144, 146, 151, 213-15, 217, 222
The Seasons, 208
Severn, Joseph, 193, 195
Shairp, Principal, 66
Shakespeare, William, 22, 146, 195
Sharp, William, 195
Shaw, George Bernard, 176
Shawcross, John, 179
Shelley, Mary—*see* Godwin
Shelley, Percy Bysshe, 12, 47, 102, 143, 150, 152, **157-81,** 183, 190, 193, 194, 203, 204, 206, 207, 213, 218-19, 223
"She Was a Phantom of Delight," 75

"Simon Lee," 74, 80-81
"Sir Patrick Spens," 133
Sir Tristrem, 108
"Sleep and Poetry," 184
Snyder, F. B., 68
"The Solitary Reaper," 75, 131
Solve, M. T., 180
"The Song of the Shirt," 205-6
Songs of Experience, 17, 18, 24-34
Songs of Innocence, 17, 18, 22, 24-34
Southey, Robert, 102, 107, 115, 116, 125, 148, 159, **199-201,** 204, 205, 217-18
Spenser, Edmund, 145, 182
Spenserian stanza, 145, 147, 182, 186
The Spirit of the Age, 152
Stallknecht, N. P., 97
Steffan, T. G., 154-55
Steward, Dugald, 66
Stoll, E. E., 137
Stovall, Floyd, 180
Stowe, Harriet Beecher, 153
Swedenborg, Emanuel, 38, 40, 42, 43
"Sweet Afton," 51, 64
Swift, Jonathan, 107
Swinburne, Algernon, 45, 176

"The Tables Turned," 87
The Talisman, 107
"Tam o' Shanter," 49, 51, 59-62, 68, 211
Tate, Allen, 178, 193
Taylor, Thomas, 23
Tea-Table Miscellany, 49
Tennyson, Alfred, 195
Thalaba the Destroyer, 217
There Is No Natural Religion, 18
"This Limetree Bower," 117
Thompson, Francis, 176
Thomson, George, 51
Thomson, James, 19, 208-9
"The Thorn," 74, 79-80, 81
Thornton, R. D., 69
Thorpe, C. DeW., 154, 195-96
"Tintern Abbey," 74, 75, 81-85, 86, 98, 190, 211-12
Tiriel, 18, 22, 24
"To Autumn," 197

"To the Evening Star," 21

"To a Louse," 51, 53, 56-57

"To a Mouse," 51, 53, 56, 173

"To the Muses," 21

"To My Sister," 74, 85-86

"To a Skylark" (Shelley), 160, 171-73, 189, 190

"To a Skylark" (Wordsworth), 75

"To a Small Celandine," 94

"To Spring," 19

"To Toussaint L'Ouverture," 75

"To a Young Ass," 218

Trilling, Lionel, 104

Triumph of Life, 160

Troilus and Criseyde, 94

Troilus Stanza, 94

Turkish Tales, 143, 145-46, 149, 151

"The Twa Dogs," 48, 51, 54

"The Tyger," 17-18, 26, 31-33, 44-45

Vala, or The Four Zoas, 18, 44

Vallon, Annette, 71, 82, 91

The Village, 199

"A Vision of Judgement," 200

The Vision of Judgment, 143

The Visions of the Daughters of Albion, 18, 36-37

"The Voice of the Devil," 39, 40

Walpole, Hugh, 110, 221

Warren, Robert Penn, 137, 178

Wasserman, E. R., 192

Watson, William, 176

Waverley, 106, 107, 113

"We Are Seven," 74, 78-79, 90, 104

Weaver, Bennett, 180

West, Paul, 155

Westbrook, Harriet, 143, 158, 159, 160

"Westminster Bridge," 75

Weston, J. C., 69

Whalley, George, 137

White, N. I., 175

Wicksteed, Joseph, 18

Williams, Edward, 160

Wilson, John, 151

Wilson, Mona, 16

Winstanley, Lilian, 179

"Winter," 208

Wollstonecraft, Mary, 16, 37

Woodman, R. G., 181

Woodstock, 107

Wordsworth, Christopher, 97

Wordsworth, Dorothy, 70, 71, 75, 82, 85, 86, 87, 92, 93, 117, 120, 121

Wordsworth, John, 97

Wordsworth, William, 12, 47, **70-104**, 106, 113, 115, 116, 117, 118, 120, 121, 131, 132-33, 134, 135, 144, 146, 148, 150, 159, 190, 195, 200, 208, 209, 211-13, 217-18, 222

"The World Is Too Much with Us," 75

"Wowing of Jock and Jenny," 49

"Written in Very Early Youth," 74, 75

Yarrow Revisited and Other Poems, 74

Yeats, William Butler, 177

"Ye Flowery Banks," 64

Young, Edward, 16

NOTES

NOTES

NOTES

NOTES

NOTES

NOTES

NOTES

NOTES

***MONARCH*®**
NOTES *AND STUDY GUIDES*

ARE AVAILABLE AT RETAIL STORES EVERYWHERE

In the event your local bookseller
cannot provide you with other
Monarch titles you want—

ORDER ON THE FORM BELOW:

Complete order form appears
on inside front & back covers for
your convenience.

Simply send retail price, local
sales tax, if any, plus 25¢ to
cover mailing & handling.

IBM #	AUTHOR & TITLE (exactly as shown on title listing)	PRICE
	PLUS ADD'L FOR POSTAGE	25¢
	GRAND TOTAL	

MONARCH® **PRESS,** a division of Simon & Schuster, Inc.
Mail Service Department, 1 West 39th Street, New York, N.Y. 10018

I enclose........................dollars to cover retail price, local sales tax,
plus mailing and handling.

Name_____
(Please print)
Address_____

City_____ State_____ Zip_____

Please send check or money order. We cannot be responsible for cash.